Not Paved for Us

SERIES | **RACE** AND **EDUCATION**

Series edited by H. Richard Milner IV

OTHER BOOKS IN THIS SERIES

Not Paved for Us

Black Educators and Public School Reform in
Philadelphia

Camika Royal

HARVARD EDUCATION PRESS
CAMBRIDGE, MA

Second Printing, 2022

Copyright © 2022 by the President and Fellows of Harvard College

All rights reserved. No part of this publication may be reproduced or transmitted in any form or by any means, electronic or mechanical, including photocopy, recording, or any information storage and retrieval systems, without permission in writing from the publisher.

Paperback ISBN 978-1-68253-735-0

Library of Congress Cataloging-in-Publication Data is on file.

Published by Harvard Education Press,
an imprint of the Harvard Education Publishing Group
Harvard Education Press
8 Story Street
Cambridge, MA 02138

Cover Design: Wilcox Design
Cover Image: ©Sahar Coston-Hardy

The typefaces in this book are Adobe Garamond Pro and Helvetica Neue.

for my great cloud of witnesses

my friends—
Maya Buseman-Williams
Tonya Northington

my elders—
Frances Leysath
Carter Missouri
Irene Alexander
Barbara Royal
L. Jean Teagle
Peter Murrell
LeRoi Simmons
Doris Shirley

On Working White Liberals

I don't ask the Foreign Legion
Or anyone to win my freedom
Or to fight my battle better than I can,

Though there's one thing that I cry for
I believe enough to die for
That is every man's responsibility to man.

I'm afraid they'll have to prove first
That they'll watch the Black man move first
Then follow him with faith to kingdom come.
This rocky road is not paved for us,
So, I'll believe in the Liberals' aid for us
When I see a white man load a Black man's gun.

—Maya Angelou, *The Complete Collected Poems of Maya Angelou* (New York: Random House, 1994), 47

Contents

Series Foreword

Not Paved for Us: Black Educators
and Public School Reform in Philadelphia
H. Richard Milner IV,
Vanderbilt University

Grounded in scholarship and substantiated by empirical data, this book advances the Race and Education Series in truly significant ways. As Camika Royal explains: "Black educators lend their intellectual insight as sources of theory building and analysis, not just data." Royal examines complex intersections of education policy, people, race, and place in ways that are deep and broad. Although the content of this book is stimulating, forward-thinking, scholarly, and bold, the writing itself is breathtaking. Royal has a unique ability to capture reality through compelling prose and position. Readers across disciplines will be captivated by the book. Practitioners and policymakers committed to knowing more in their journey toward transformation will refer this book to their colleagues across the country. *Not Paved for Us: Black Educators and Public School Reform in Philadelphia* "deepens and widens the intellectual discourse around school reform; it goes beyond liberalism as panacea and tacit notions of overt racist acts to name, dissect, and challenge the[m]." This is the book our field needs.

Not Paved for Us will surely advance theory, research, policy, and practice in ways similar to other important books on the topics of race, place (especially Philadelphia), and educational justice, such as Eve Ewing's *Ghosts in the Schoolyard: Racism and School Closings on Chicago's South Side*, Vincent P. Franklin's *The Education of Black Philadelphia: The Social and Educational History of a Minority Community, 1900–1950*, and Elizabeth Todd-Breland's

A Political Education: Black Politics and Education Reform in Chicago Since the 1960s. Royal astutely analyzes her own experiences and history, tracing family roots from North Carolina to Philadelphia. She weaves together a complex history of educational reform in Philadelphia that has done very little to cumulatively create just and equitable classrooms, schools, and districts.

Although the book is focused on educators in Philadelphia, it has important implications for educators and education in other cities. As the second-oldest public school system in the United States and one with a long history of racist policies and politics for students and Black teachers, Royal explains how Philadelphia is a particularly rich context for understanding why reform efforts have been too disconnected from the worlds and needs of those most vulnerable to inequity. Building on the city of Philadelphia as a site of inquiry for transformation, this book strikes a delicate and important balance of knowledge construction of race and place: the book represents truth-telling, powerfully grounded and substantiated, at its best.

Royal examines the interplay of policy and Black educators. For example, she studies the Black press, the Philadelphia Board of Education, and Black communities. *Not Paved for Us* uses the stories of real people to point out historical and contemporary challenges that must be understood to chart an agenda forward for those most grossly underserved in schools. Indeed, too often, Black educators' views and voices have been treated as inconsequential to school reform. To the contrary, Royal demonstrates how effective reform cannot be realized, particularly for Black students and communities, without deliberate centering of Black educator voices. Although reforms were misguided from 1967 to 2017, Royal's analysis found that Black educators continued to educate their students at high levels in spite of policies that did little impact the lives of minoritized students and families.

Indeed, this book honors and demonstrates a powerful layer of respect for (and on behalf of) "Black Philly educators inside the system and on the margins, ancestors, elders, and contemporaries who fought and fight for public schooling to meet Black children at their highest aspirations." This is the book we need—at a time when our world needs it.

Foreword

I confess. I do not come to this foreword with any pretense of objectivity or neutrality. I am a third-generation Philadelphian on both sides of my family. My surviving grandparents came to Philadelphia as a part of the Great Migration in the 1920s.[1] My mother lived eighty-five of her ninety years there, and my father lived seventy-one of his eighty-five years there. Although they reminisced fondly about South Carolina, they were Philadelphians, and it never occurred to them to live anywhere else. My brother and I grew up in West Philadelphia in the 1950s and 1960s. We attended public schools there, graduated, and went on to college. Although I went out of state for college, I returned after graduation to begin my career as a teacher in the same school district in which I was educated.

I returned to teach in Philadelphia in 1968, one year into the time frame of this volume. The year 1967 marked a major Black student protest in the city. Black students across the school district walked out of their high schools and converged on the School District of Philadelphia's stately art deco building at 21st Street and the Benjamin Franklin Parkway. For those unfamiliar with the Parkway, it is the promenade that is lined with major cultural institutions—the main branch of the Free Library of Philadelphia, the Museum of Natural History, the Cathedral Basilica of Saints Peter and Paul, the Rodin Museum, the Horwitz-Wasserman Holocaust Memorial Plaza, the Franklin Institute and Fels Planetarium, and the Moore College of Art & Design—and that culminates at the iconic Philadelphia Museum of Art, where Sylvester Stallone's character, Rocky, ran the stairs and pumped triumph fists at the end of his workout.

On November 17, 1967, the Philadelphia Police Department estimated that some 3,500 students—Black and white and from public schools, Catholic schools, middle schools, and high schools—converged on the school district building to demand an end to tracking that regularly prevented Black students from entering college, improvements in the facilities in schools serving Black and poor students, and the inclusion of Black history and culture in the curriculum. By the time I entered the school district the following fall, changes had already begun to happen. The people who had been working on Black history curriculum were moved out of the social studies office into the new office of African American studies. William Green and Gwendolyn Brightful led that office for many years and produced curricula that spanned social studies, literature, art, and music. It may have been one of the only standalone offices of African American studies in a public school district.

When I was hired, the school district was led by two "progressives"[2]— Superintendent Mark Shedd and the very well regarded (by liberals) Ricardson Dilworth as president of the Board of Education. Dilworth had previously served as mayor of the city. They inherited a school district embroiled in scandal and locked in a struggle with the federal government over its maintenance of racial segregation. The district was about 70 percent Black and other students of color, and its teachers were about 70 percent white. It was a large district serving 280,000 students in about 280 schools. (Today the district has about 119,492 students enrolled in its schools with another 80,000 students enrolled in charter and cyber charter schools.) The 1968 district reflected the reality of the 1968 neighborhoods. They were deeply segregated by race, and many communities actively resisted school busing. In an attempt to alleviate segregation among the teaching staffs, the school district restricted the placement of new hires. Despite growing up in West Philadelphia, I could not be assigned to any vacancies in West Philadelphia. Thus, my first teaching assignment was in South Philadelphia in a white, ethnic, working-class community. My students proudly identified as Italian, Irish, and Polish Americans. A few Black students were bused to my school, but they were never really accepted as a part of the school community. As tough as my first year was in my attempt to negotiate the racial climate at my school (yes, I was called the "n-word" by a number of parents), I recall a variety of professional development opportunities that Superintendent Shedd required for all new teachers. Once a month, all new teachers were required to attend professional development sessions. Those early professional development experiences taught me that even a big, bureaucratic organization could strive to meet the specific needs of individual members. Unfortunately, the most draconian, almost neofascist candidate in the city's history, Frank L. Rizzo, decided to run for mayor on a platform vowing to get rid of both the superintendent and the Board of Education president.

His win signaled the move away from progressive reform ideas in the schools to what was known as the "back to basics" movement.

I spent ten years as a teacher in the School District of Philadelphia. During that time, I had various roles—classroom teacher, reading specialist, and social studies consultant. I also had an opportunity to watch the various political moves and scandals that emerged in the district. After the firing of Mark Shedd came the appointment of Matthew Costanzo (who incidentally was my brother's eighth-grade math teacher) as superintendent, the firing of Costanzo as he lay flat on his back in the hospital, the hiring of Michael Marcase (who was an industrial arts teacher at my high school), and the issue of his having received a doctoral degree via what was then a correspondence school. Later, Marcase came under federal investigation for having district maintenance personnel work on his New Jersey shore vacation home.

While the superintendency seemed in turmoil, *Philadelphia Magazine* wrote an exposeé on the Board of Education sometime in the early 1970s. Unlike most municipalities, Philadelphia has an appointed school board of nine members. The appointments are made by the mayor, and historically major political donors and interest groups have lobbied for specific appointments. The magazine article revealed that the board, at that time comprise primarily of white men, had at least one member who did not even live in the city. He operated a dental practice in Philadelphia but lived in New Jersey.

Although the board members do not receive a salary, there were many perks. For the nine board members, the school district purchased eleven Chrysler New Yorkers and hired nine chauffeurs at a salary greater than that of a beginning teacher. When asked why eleven cars for nine people, the board president insisted that there must be an available car in case one or two were out of commission. An audit revealed that a frequent destination for the cars was Atlantic City, where board members had "meetings" since apparently there was no place to meet in the City of Philadelphia. Each board member was given an American Express corporate card, and the audit of those bills also showed extravagant dinners and entertainment expenses at the New Jersey shore. A climate of corruption is something that Philadelphians have grown accustomed to, and it was so entrenched that it is difficult to see how schools could ever improve.

The work of this volume is to describe what has transpired in Philly schools since 1967, through the 1980s when a Black woman, Constance Clayton, took the reins, followed by a series of "reformers." Although I knew Dr. Clayton (she was the head of early childhood education when I was a social studies consultant), I was no longer living in Philadelphia when she became superintendent. I worked in Philadelphia through two teachers' strikes and the clash of the mayor and the teachers' union representatives. I witnessed the district struggle with white flight and a shrinking tax base. I watched from the other side of the country as the district bounced from one scandal to the next. As a graduate student, I began to look at big school districts from another vantage point. I could see that San Francisco, Oakland, Los Angeles, Houston, and Chicago shared some unfortunate similarities with Philadelphia.

Big urban districts all seem to be drowning in bureaucracy, and as a consequence they are rarely nimble. Each of them grapples with rapidly changing demographics—becoming more Black and Brown not just because of birth rates but also because white families began seeking nonpublic options. In San Francisco, for example, the overall city population is about 45 percent white, but the public school population in the city is only 15 percent white. The white community is deserting the urban public schools both physically and in terms of economic support. The moves toward charter schools and choice also represent an attempt to appease white families, but often the largest users of these options are Black and Brown families. White families choose to leave cities altogether and find what they want in suburban districts.

For me, the saddest part of deteriorating support for public schools is the loss of the vision of the schools as democratizing and equalizing agencies that had the possibility of fostering social mobility. My generation, the baby boomers, may have been the last that realized the full benefits of public schooling in big cities. When we graduated from high school, we entered a robust economy bolstered by Lyndon Johnson's Great Society. We became the generation that was able to take advantage of the work of civil rights struggles and a nation that showed some level of remorse for horrific way it had treated its citizens of color, especially those who were Black, Latinx, and Indigenous. I had high school friends who decided not to attend college but were able to get good jobs that would eventually support families and allow them to purchase homes and cars. In short, their high school diplomas meant a ticket to the American dream. My earning a bachelor's degree almost assuredly guaranteed me financial stability and social advancement.

Today, we look at students graduating from schools in districts like Philadelphia and worry that their diplomas are not worth the paper on which they are written. Are the students prepared to enter postsecondary education or the world of productive work? Have they been well served by the public system that their parents and community have paid into? Does the constant churning of school leadership, fiscal mismanagement, and cheating scandals mean we should give up on public schooling? Surprisingly, I maintain just enough hope to believe the catastrophe of the COVID-19 pandemic may be just the crisis that can force us to utterly redo our schools so that we might be more responsive to this next generation of young people.

Watching our youth take to the streets in the summer of 2020 with protests sparked by the brutal murders of George Floyd, Ahmaud Arbury, and Breonna Taylor convinces me that our young people are among the world's best and brightest. I believe they are hungry to learn important knowledge and skills that can reshape our society and save our planet. I believe adults owe them a real opportunity to become the citizens we need them to be.

Gloria Ladson-Billings
University of Wisconsin–Madison
May 2021

Homebase

The Introduction

Black[1] public school educators in Philadelphia have grown weary, for good reason. *Not Paved for Us: Black Educators and Public School Reform in Philadelphia* examines the racial and cultural politics of school reform implemented on the backs of Black people in a "disguised southern city," as Sonia Sanchez called it, engaged in constant clashes over who schools benefit. Racism and racial capitalism have obstructed public school reform in Philadelphia. So have liberal ideals and neoliberal practices, austerity tactics, insider-outsider tensions, and politics at the local, state, and federal levels. From the Common School Movement of the nineteenth century through the Every Student Succeeds Act of 2015, school reform has been a platform for politicians and a rallying cry of community members. In the twenty-first century, despite political demands and policy shifts, universal public school improvement remains elusive, especially for large urban school districts.

Education reforms have not revolutionized schooling processes, academic outcomes, or career opportunities for the masses. Large urban districts with high levels of poverty and majority Black students still struggle to fully implement reforms with fidelity and in ways that advance Black students academically and wholistically. While the current moment presents challenges for all schools, urban schools are especially vulnerable given their conditions and extreme needs. And in the context of the COVID-19 pandemic, the "reimagining" schooling narrative became empty and limp, merely reifying the inequities that existed prepandemic. Schools that struggled with asbestos removal since the 1980s and 1990s and even as recently as 2021, schools where safe drinking water was an anomaly and there was rarely soap in the restrooms, let alone hot water and paper towels, were terribly ill-equipped to

1

provide an in-person learning experience during the COVID-19 pandemic and crisis. Historically and contemporarily, the weight of school reform has been borne by urban educators striving to meet the extensive needs of their students, families, and communities despite having the fewest material, financial, and people resources. In cities like Boston, Chicago, Milwaukee, Washington, DC, New York, and Philadelphia, the disparate impacts of school reforms have been stratified by race.[2] No segment of educators has experienced the intersection of policy pressures, economic issues, and racialized problems like Black educators. This book focuses on Black educators and school reform in my hometown, Philadelphia, Pennsylvania.

For me, this research is neither scientific nor neutral. I am biased, personally and professionally. At the time of this writing, I am a forty-three-year-old Black woman educator born at Chestnut Hill Hospital, reared in the Penrose section of southwest Philly. My parents both arrived in Philadelphia in the early 1960s: my dad from Person County, North Carolina, and my mom from Bronx, New York, where her Sumter, South Carolina, parents met. My parents were married at Enon Tabernacle Baptist Church on Coulter Street in 1968 and are still together. I graduated from one of the oldest public high schools in the nation, Central High, a special-admission, college preparatory magnet school, and was privileged to attend that school as part of Philadelphia's stratified schooling system. I arrived there from Pepper Middle School, my neighborhood public school, which was closed with Philly's mass school closings in 2013.

I was a student in the School District of Philadelphia (SDP) from 1989, when I began the seventh grade, until I graduated from high school in 1995, which spans the years of Constance Clayton and David Hornbeck as superintendents. To Black public school children in Philly in the eighties and nineties, Constance Clayton was legendary. She was a household name. We spoke of her like some beloved, taskmaster auntie, especially when it snowed. Our school conversations went something like, "Do you think we gonna have school tomorrow?" And the response was always some version of, "Y'all know Constance Clayton is gonna make us go to school tomorrow!" I met her while I was dissertating, and she cheered for me when I told her I had been a student in the district under her tutelage.

I didn't begin my education in Philly's public schools, though. My mother had had enough. She graduated from the now-closed Germantown High

School in 1965, and there, her counselors put her in the commercial track of classes and told her she was not college material. She sent my older sister, Genyne (who is now the other Dr. Royal), to Penrose, our neighborhood public elementary school, for first grade. But when my mom questioned Genyne's teacher about why her reading skills were only slowly progressing, the principal questioned my mother's lack of education credentials, suggesting she was not qualified to inquire about how well her child was or was not reading. So my mother switched Genyne to private school. Thus, my early formal education (1984–1989) tracks back to a conservative, white Christian school located in suburban Brookhaven, Pennsylvania. My experiences with racist/racialized practices at that school—like having a white male second-grade classmate tell me to "get to the back of the line where all the niggers belong"—made me a critical race theorist before I knew what that was. I also began to notice the racial differences at the school—that in its academically tracked classes, Black students were overly present in the "slow" class, few were in the advanced class, and not a single Black adult was employed anywhere in the building, not teaching, not answering the phones, not serving food, and not changing light bulbs. These experiences are the foundation on which my views of race and racism have been built and have shaped how I have approached my personal life, education, and career.

Technically, I am in the first generation of my family, on both sides, to graduate from college. On my father's side, though, my Uncle John's wife—Aunt Barbara—joined the School District of Philadelphia as a paraprofessional in 1967, the year this volume begins with. Eventually, she earned a bachelor's degree and became a teacher. Aunt Barbara was proud that I became a teacher when I graduated from North Carolina Central University, a historically Black institution, in 1999. I joined what I soon perceived to be an overwhelmingly white nonprofit alternative teaching organization, Teach For America (TFA). At that time, TFA was small and had only thirteen sites throughout the nation with one training institute in Houston, Texas. I wanted to teach in Philly, but TFA would not make its way there until 2003. I began teaching in a public middle school in Baltimore, a district whose student population at the time was 89 percent Black. I, however, was assigned to teach in a poor white neighborhood, where I taught seventh-grade language arts for three years to a population that was 40 percent white students from the neighborhood and 60 percent Black students bused in from East North Avenue area. Issues of race resurfaced for me again there: white parents who made racialized comments to me and some who questioned why I allowed students to read about the execution of Amadou Diallo and torture of Abner Louima, both at the hands of police; Black students who noticed opportunity and access differences between them and some of their white peers.

I was a third-year teacher when the No Child Left Behind Act of 2001 (NCLB) became the national policy governing public schools. But in Baltimore City, we were already under an accountability plan that required all Baltimore City teachers—and no teachers elsewhere in the state—to submit a "Demonstrated Student Achievement Portfolio" at the end of the school year and that labeled schools as "Reconstitution Eligible" if its scores on the Maryland School Performance Assessment Program (MSPAP) dropped. I taught at Robert Poole Middle School (now closed), and our school's scores showed a slight decline in December 2001, so we became a Reconstitution Eligible school for the 2002–03 school year. It didn't matter that MSPAP was ending to make way for the NCLB-compliant Maryland State Assessment. The intervention prescribed for us was that all Robert Poole Middle School educators had to reapply for our jobs. At twenty-four-years-old, with a new masters of arts in teaching degree in hand and some unwarranted arrogance, I declined to reapply. Instead, I joined TFA's staff in Baltimore as an instructional coach for new TFA teachers. Race was an ever-present factor when I worked for TFA, especially as I navigated relationships with school principals, many of whom were Black, and the TFA teachers I coached, most of whom were white. I noticed then that Black educators tended to share information with me that they hesitated to share with white TFA colleagues. The openness, comfort, and familiarity I realized with them played a significant role as I approached this research years later.

Black educator chronicles are essential to school-reform discourse, but our voices have traditionally been muted. Too often, Black educators themselves have been treated as passive or tangential objects, rather than agentive subjects, of school reform. *Not Paved for Us* takes the position that race narratives matter in education, particularly the experiential knowledge of Black educators and community members. These narratives are central to understanding the sociopolitical context of urban school systems.[3] For this book, I interviewed Black educators whose work in The School District of Philadelphia spanned at least two superintendents or chief executive officers between 1967 and 2018. To protect their identities, I refer to them in this text with a single-name pseudonym. I center Black perspectives in this book, challenging extant anglonormative discourse and neoliberal school reform. Anglonormative school-reform discourse centers whiteness in all discussion of school progress and school reform. It pedestals wealthy whiteness, all its trappings, benefits, and privileges, and measures everyone and every group that is not wealthy and/or white according the distance from the pedestal and the center. Anglonormative school-reform discourse is rooted in whiteness as the standard-bearer. It discusses the idea of the so-called achievement gap instead of the education debt.[4] It values test scores as valid measures of student and school success, which is why I was moved to the "high performers" seventh-grade class at Pepper Middle School after my mother fought for me to take the citywide tests. But anglonormative school-reform discourse never acknowledges the ways standardized tests are used as weapons against Black people to sift, to sort, to stratify, to decide who is more or less worthy. It views Black people's high academic achievement as exceptional, not normal. Rooted in a deficit, dangerous view of anyone or any group that is not wealthy and white, anglonormative school-reform discourse seeks to glorify white educators brave enough to work in underresourced communities while blaming veteran Black educators for public schools' shortcomings. Neoliberal school reform has led to the shrinking of learning standards into what can be measured on high-stakes standardized tests; the decrease of traditional public schools, and increase of charter management organizations. While neoliberal school reformers claim charter schools are public schools, they gloss over the idea that public dollars should fund public schools that are accountable to the public. When public dollars fund charter schools with boards that are not accountable to the people, this creates more levels of bureaucracy and stifles public accountability, merely replicating problems that often plague traditional public schools.

When I try to think back to some of the stories I overheard Aunt Barbara telling about being a Philly teacher, all I can recall is fight in her eyes and fire coming from her mouth. I have wished many times I could sit at her feet since I began this research. Aunt Barbara passed away in 2005, before I ever began the doctoral studies that led to this inquiry. In *Not Paved for Us*, Black educators lend their intellectual insight as sources of theory building and analysis, not just data. This text locates Black educators as active participants in school reform who provide narratives as well as theoretical considerations and implications for school reform over time. This approach represents an epistemological shift that builds on critical race theory's use of counternarratives to offer a thicker description of the complications of race and history in general and the intersections of education policy, race, and market-based school reforms, specifically. *Not Paved for Us* deepens and widens the intellectual discourse around school reform; it goes beyond liberalism as a panacea and tacit notions of overt racist acts to name, dissect, and challenge racism in school-reform policies and practices, even when perpetuated by Black leadership. This book also critiques false notions of meritocracy, even when its purveyors are Black educators. White supremacy and structural racism have fueled education policies and practices that impede collective Black progress. Until white supremacy and its various political, social, economic, and gendered entanglements are subdued and dismantled and until liberalism and meritocracy are complicated as mythical and farcical, school reform will continue to change its clothes without ever taking a bath.

In 1937, more than a hundred years after the School District of Philadelphia was established, the Board of Education ended its racist hiring practice by merging its race-based lists of eligible teachers into a single list.[5] Despite this policy reform, the district maintained this racist practice via preferential positions for white educators.[6] Since then, professional obstacles and clashes between the district and Black educators remain, while pressure and stresses have increased for all urban public school districts.[7] Philadelphia's public schools bear the legacy, hallmarks, and consequences of being at the intersection of school reform and racism. This can be seen in the people who were appointed to leadership positions in the district, the types of reforms these leaders attempted to implement, the ways Black educators fought for themselves and their communities, and the political controversies that plagued public schools during each superintendent's era. By examining school reform in Philadelphia from 1967 through 2017, *Not Paved for Us* examines how Black educators and community members viewed, created, and coped with school reform while advocating for their students, themselves, and their communities.

In the 1960s and 1970s, racial and ethnic politics controlled access to professional opportunities in Philly. White liberals who attempted to give opportunities to Black people were upended by white supremacist politics masked as equality. In the 1980s the first Black woman school superintendent instituted a type of meritocracy that included race-based equity efforts. But in the 1990s, quests for power determined the public schools' sociopolitical landscape. In the new millennium, this landscape was proliferated with reforms such as the state takeover of the city's public schools in 2001, the No Child Left Behind Act and its concomitant money and consequences, as well as corporate systems and structures. These reforms correlated with constant tension, flux, and uncertainty for Black educators, students, families, and communities across the city, especially those who needed strong schools the most. While all underresourced schools struggle with these conditions, primarily poor Black neighborhoods experience school closures and the exodus of resources most severely, demonstrating that America is far from the postracial narrative employed when President Barack Obama was elected. The years of state control did not yield less political wrangling or better fiscal management for the school district or bring about collective academic improvements for Black Philadelphians, and in 2017, Philadelphia's state-controlled School Reform Commission voted to dissolve itself so the city could regain control of its own schools from the state.

Chapter 1 of this book details how Superintendent Mark Shedd attempted to advocate for Black students and incorporate Black professionals into the School District of Philadelphia. However, he undermined his own efforts by clinging to white liberalism. Chapter 2 explains how Mayor Frank Rizzo, the Black Board of Education president he controlled, and his superintendent appointees oversaw racial turmoil in Philadelphia's schools. School desegregation by busing was attempted in policy but thwarted by practice. Teacher strikes and lockouts occurred almost every other year, elucidating the racial politics of strikers and alliances of strikebreakers. Chapter 3 examines the Herculean task of Philadelphia's first Black and first woman superintendent of its public schools, Constance Clayton. This chapter points to the stability she brought to the district, as well as the racism that became evident itself when a slim budget revealed Clayton's racial allegiance and class priorities.

Chapter 4 recounts how Superintendent David Hornbeck upset white powerbrokers who thought he would advocate for white Philadelphians instead of Black children across the city. Hornbeck fashioned himself a champion of the downtrodden, instituting Philadelphia Freedom Schools and his signature policy, Children Achieving.[8] But his refusal to acquiesce to political gaming led to his ouster and the state takeover of Philadelphia's public schools by the Commonwealth of Pennsylvania. Chapter 5 shows how, after his alleged success in Chicago, Paul Vallas was the perfect candidate to be Philadelphia's first public schools' CEO. With the district newly taken over by the state, as No Child Left Behind urged greater high-stakes testing, market-based reforms became the *modus operendi*. But more money led to more accounting problems, which ultimately led to Vallas's abrupt resignation. And Chapter 6 explores the tenures of Superintendents Arlene Ackerman and William Hite, the next two Black educators who led the school district through state control and back into mayoral control and navigated the tensions of being outsider leaders for a majority-Black school system that continues to subtract resources from Black schools and communities. All chapters in this book are named in honor of prophetic, prolific hip-hop albums from the soundtrack of my youth.

While I never worked in a Philly school or for the School District of Philadelphia, I did work around the district when I returned to Philadelphia, first to teach at Lincoln University and then to pursue a doctorate in urban education. I was a doctoral student at Temple University when Arlene Ackerman became superintendent of schools in 2008, and when I met her, she was warm and welcoming and invited me to shadow her at work for a day, which I did on November 18, 2008. As a doctoral student, I worked in the Institute for Schools and Society (which was called the Urban Education Collaborative when I was first hired as a graduate research assistant there), which was involved in school-reform work in Philadelphia in several ways. I was a graduate research assistant on an evaluation team that examined several the relationships between professional development, merit pay, and students' test scores in several Philadelphia charter schools. While I worked there from the fall of 2008 through the spring semester of 2011, as well as when I taught for the Governor's School in Urban Education in the summer of 2008, Heidi Ramirez, a Philly School Reform Commission member, led the Urban Education Collaborative. I also worked for Research for Action as a graduate student summer intern in 2009. As Research for Action's graduate intern, I spent time meeting with people from various entities concerned about education from across the city, including the Philadelphia Education Fund, the Philadelphia Student Union, the William Penn Foundation, and the Philadelphia School Partnership. I coauthored the report on teacher appraisal for the Education First Compact's platform, "Effective Teaching for All Children: What It Will Take." Around the time Bill Hite was becoming Philadelphia's superintendent of schools in 2012, I facilitated groups at the church that helped to raise me regarding the Boston Consulting Group's recommendation to close sixty schools. And when Hite was making his community rounds, I was his escort for a day at the church where I was a member. Though I moved out of Philadelphia in 2014 to be the assistant professor of urban education at Loyola University Maryland, I continued my research on schooling in my home city, as well as my advocacy for Black educators. I testified before City Council in November 2016 on the significance of Black educators for the School District of Philadelphia and why the district needed to make significant strides in retaining them, not just recruiting them.

Not Paved for Us explores the politics of school reform, but those politics are not limited to American political parties. Republicans have pushed defunding public schools in favor of vouchers and other forms of privatizing schooling for decades. Democrats have been no better. They have controlled Philly since the 1960s, and that control has meant little to no collective progress for anyone who is not white. Throughout the nation, Democrats have fostered and fueled corporate, neoliberal school reform while defunding and disrupting public schooling as a democratic function of American society, at the expense of Black and Brown students, families, and communities. With Democrats like these, who needs Republicans? By *politics*, I mean how people compete for, manage, and respond to scarce resources.[9] Like Issa Rae, this book roots for *almost* everybody Black and still critiques Black leaders when their work positions individual achievement at the expense of collective Black progress. To make it plain, the analysis I aim to lend in this text aligns more with Reverend Jeremiah Wright than President Barack Obama. This book arises out of a left-of-the-Democratic Party stance that seeks to complicate questions and ideas regarding for whom school exists and to what extent state-controlled schooling can be positively transformative for Black people in large cities, especially those relegated to underresourced schools in districts controlled by market-driven, neoliberal ideologies, policies, and practices. This book believes in traditional public schools but is not anticharter schools. Indeed, charter schools have offered Black students, families, and educators opportunities for small amounts of autonomy and sanctity at a time when traditional public schools have been places of violence inflicted by faculty, staff, and curriculum. However, this book questions the effectiveness of charter school chains equipped with marketing strategies that obscure the harm they sometimes cause and the destabilization they often bring with them as they are planted in various cities across the nation with few insights about local context and without mass buy-in. This book examines who benefited from the school reforms implemented over fifty years and what the politics of these reforms cost Black educators and Black communities in Philadelphia. This book seeks to challenge how school reforms advance and/or transform Black educators and Black communities. School reforms happen in the context of racial politics. Cultural and political contexts—who tells the stories, who controls the narratives of reform, and what people believe about those at the helm of reforms and behind them—matter. This book is decidedly not objective. I seek to offer critiques of school reform without demonizing or lionizing the Black educators who dealt with and, at times, implemented these reforms. I hope readers are informed and intrigued by this examination of school reform over time, and I hope readers leave with more questions about what types of schooling—and politics of school governance and leadership—will yield students, educators, communities, and society that are more just, more free, and more committed to collective improvement, not just advancement for a few. I hope this book honors Black Philly educators inside the system and on the margins, ancestors, elders, and contemporaries who fought and fight for public schooling to meet Black children at their highest aspirations, who worked and are working to disrupt and dismantle white supremacy perpetuated throughout school systems and in classrooms, who dream of the kind of schooling that centers Black strength, joy, and possibility, and then who work to create just that.

1

Fear of a Black Planet

Racial School Reform, 1967–1971

*Does the superintendent and this board condone
educational colonialism?*

—Dr. Samuel Woodard,
director of program implementation,
School District of Philadelphia[1]

*Get those fucking Black kids back to school. This is my
town. No softie from the outside is going to come in and
screw it up. If you don't keep those kids in school,
I'm going to run your ass out of Philadelphia
if it's the last thing I do.*

—Frank Rizzo, commissioner,
Philadelphia Police Department[2]

The School District of Philadelphia (SDP) brought in a white liberal
reformer, Mark Shedd, to lead its underfunded school district through
racial reforms at the end of the civil rights movement.[3] Liberal reforms had
produced significant benefits for Philadelphia's Black population in the
1950s, but those benefits faded by the end of that decade.[4] Many Black

Philadelphians were already skeptical about the district's unkept promises by the time Mark Shedd appeared locally. Liberal ideals of access and opportunity for Black people were hailed as the way out of America's racism, but Shedd's leadership of Philly's schools would test the limitations of white liberalism and white liberals, given the perception that advances for Black people meant disadvantages for white people. Race-neutral color evasiveness is a fallacy that often precludes the dismantling of white supremacy.[5] As superintendent, Shedd clung to liberalism, and he adopted the color evasiveness demanded of him. Though he initially said he would disrupt the district's racism, ultimately, Shedd's tenure demonstrated that race neutrality was farcical. In his attempt to promote equality, he shielded the district from racial school reform and preserved Philadelphia's longstanding color line.

Shedd arrived to lead Philadelphia's schools just as the nonviolent rhetoric of the civil rights movement was giving way to its Black Power ideology. This shift represented the ever-present tension between Black radicals, Black liberals, and the white people who claimed alignment with civil rights quests while clinging to white supremacy. In keeping pace with the lukewarmth of white liberal politicians who sought the appearance of opportunity, equality, and justice for Black Americans while maintaining the systems that upheld white supremacy, the public schooling landscape changed in 1965. President Lyndon Johnson's War on Poverty and Elementary and Secondary Education Act of 1965 (ESEA) brought federal funds to school districts throughout the nation.[6] Locally, voters adopted the "five percent rule," which was intended to get more Black people and women into leadership positions.[7] Philadelphia's Board of Education (BOE) had a reputation for paralysis and reneging on promises of substantial racial advancement. It consistently overpromised—but less than what was needed for full Black citizenship and opportunity through Philadelphia's public schools—and then would woefully underdeliver. Racial integration of its public schools became its new attempt at liberalism.[8]

Like other school districts around the nation at that time, Philadelphia designed a busing program to integrate students and a school transfer policy to integrate teachers.[9] The Philadelphia Federation of Teachers (PFT) became the sole collective bargaining unit for district teachers in 1965, and it advocated a voluntary teacher-transfer plan to "improve racial balance," though many Black public school advocates desired a *forced* teacher-transfer plan.[10] The board's lack of commitment to racial integration was still evident early in 1967 when it negotiated a new contract with the PFT that did not mandate teacher transfers for faculty integration.[11] The PFT threatened to strike over forced transfers, and the *Philadelphia Tribune* positioned the board as placating those supporting white supremacy over the needs of Black children in public schools.[12] This is one of the ways liberalism obscures racism—by negotiating with the racist desires of a prejudiced teachers' union under the guise of democracy and compromise.[13]

Busing also failed, deliberately sabotaged in Philadelphia.[14] No white students were bused to Black schools in Philadelphia for racial integration.[15] Black Philadelphians had been the victims of the school district's racism and bore the brunt of remedying its racism through busing. Discriminatory testing was used to determine which students would be bused.[16] Bused-in Black students were more likely to be taught by a substitute teacher.[17] Schools kept "bus kids," bused-in Black students, separated from the white school population, perpetuating segregation.[18] Racists taunted Black bused children, who were met with discrimination and prejudicial treatment at the schools to which they were bused.[19] White educators attacked Black students with racist stereotypes, while white administrators denied the comments or the underlying vitriol in the comments.

From the Outside, In

As Board of Education president, former mayor Richardson Dilworth wanted to reform Philly's public schools, but the white power structure's wooden nickels had not satiated the majority of Black Philadelphia.[20] The district's sociopolitical climate was tense, and Mark Shedd was received in a lukewarm fashion.[21] He was met with factious racial politics and lagging student achievement issues. White ethnics resisted school reform, believing any advancement for Black people would represent a loss for their children.[22] Majority-Black schools had as much as 82 percent of their faculties filled with substitutes, while white schools had half that number.[23] Many Black Philadelphians were skeptical of this newcomer and Philadelphia outsider, who was brought in by the board president to "clean up this educational pattern of De Facto Segregation and policies of subtle racism."[24] Shedd had relocated from New England by way of New Jersey and was a white Anglo-Saxon Protestant. At only forty-one years old, he had ascended to the district's helm.[25]

For 150 years, Black educators had been kept out of positions of power within the School District of Philadelphia, making them professional and political outsiders, despite the district's high Black student population.[26] Though approximately 60 percent of the district's 278,000 students were Black, only 30 percent of its twelve thousand teachers were Black.[27] There were thirty Black principals in the district in March 1967 and three Black regional superintendents out of eight local regions throughout the city. There were two Black men working in the superintendent's office as deputy superintendent and administrative assistant for staff.[28] Deputy Superintendent Robert Poindexter, who had been a teacher and a junior high school counselor before he moved into district administration, became acting superintendent in the time between Whittier's fade from the forefront and Shedd's arrival.[29] At that time, Poindexter was the highest-ranking Black man in public education in the nation, but he wasn't promoted to superintendent.[30]

Given the imbalances represented in the Black population in the school district in the 1960s, combined with the longstanding experiences of Black people in this city and nation, Black skepticism about how impactful Shedd's leadership would be was warranted.[31] Schools' Superintendent Allen Wetter (1955–1964) was a Philadelphia native, an educator, and an associate superintendent in the district before he assumed the number one spot.[32] Shedd's immediate predecessor, Superintendent C. Taylor Whittier (1965–1967), was a Philadelphia outsider. Black Philadelphians were still trying to understand his departure, since he was brought in to "straighten out Philadelphia's massive educational problems" but retired after having been superintendent for only two years. Even Black Board of Education member Henry Nichols said the board made a mistake by allowing Whittier to leave.[33] There were also Philadelphians who believed Marcus Foster, the highly respected and revered principal of Gratz High School who would briefly become one of Shedd's associate superintendents, should have been the first Black superintendent of schools in Philadelphia. Instead, Foster left Philadelphia and became the superintendent of schools in Oakland, California, where he was murdered by the Symbionese Liberation Army in 1973.[34]

Shedd approached the district intending to disrupt some of its longstanding, tangled professional issues, but he underestimated the constant threat of white supremacy in this zero-sum landscape. In his first address to principals and administrative staff, Shedd said he had been meeting with people from all walks of life in Philadelphia since he was appointed as superintendent in order to get multiple perspectives on the local landscape. He said he wanted to make the district "more responsive and more relevant" and that the district and its schools should be "more responsive to the needs of pupils, communities, teachers and individual schools and more relevant to the lives of students, their environment and future, as well as relevant to the needs of teachers and the community."[35] He believed flexibility, spontaneity, and individual instruction would make the district successful.[36] To these ends, Shedd began his tenure by ordering an independent agency to research pay raises for principals in an effort to avoid nepotism and long-held and entrenched old boys' network rules.[37] He also praised a Dobbins High School teacher for taking chances and getting students involved in school and reinstated him after he had been fired by his principal for refusing to confiscate a magazine students created that included stories about sex, drugs, and homosexuality.[38] The Education Equality League and the Urban League both supported Shedd's decision, advocating creative teaching and efforts in getting Black students interested in school.[39]

Still, the embeddedness of racialized practices and racial tensions were far more complicated than Shedd estimated. While he did initially garner cautiously optimistic support from Black people throughout the city, the cost for that support was constant opposition from white ethnics and the white power structure. Over time, Shedd moved from cautious Black optimism to an ever-increasing Black speculation.[40] Additionally, Shedd's own liberal ideals led him to practice a form of color-evasive racism that actually secured the hold whites had on power in the district.[41] The existing white power structure in Philadelphia was neither willing nor ready to embrace the birth pains required for change in the School District of Philadelphia. Shedd inherited a system that had been historically problematic, and he found himself constantly in the middle of conflicts over the fundamental question: *For whom do schools exist?* Despite claims of schools as the great equalizer, urban public schooling was never intended to provide a transition for the marginalized populations they served beyond their racialized social and economic standing. Urban schools were sites for the social reproduction of the white, wealthy power structure and not for the social mobility of the Black masses.[42]

Thus, when Shedd began making sweeping changes that were perceived as largely benefitting Black students, white people fought him on every front.[43] White Philadelphia political leaders attempted to assuage Black communities with new school buildings and position appointments, but Black activists saw these as shallow attempts at smokescreens that allowed white people to maintain the stronghold they had on the public school system in Philadelphia.[44]

Black Educators and Mark Shedd

Shedd attempted to distinguish himself from previous district superintendents and Philadelphia's history of racist practices.[45] He allowed academic programs that incorporated the significance of African history and African Americans in American history, society, and culture.[46] Black educators saw Shedd as more receptive to change than his predecessors and many of his contemporaries on the Board of Education.[47] He also brought Black educators into positions of influence within the district. Bernard Watson, Shedd's associate superintendent for innovative programs, was one of the Black men afforded an opportunity in education leadership in Philadelphia under the Shedd administration.[48] Robert Poindexter, the Black man who had been interim superintendent after Whittier's departure and before Shedd's arrival, became Shedd's second in command, and Shedd created a new position, director of integration and intergroup education, that also was staffed by a Black man.[49] Frederick Holliday was promoted to be Shedd's administrative assistant.[50] Midway into Shedd's first year as superintendent, there were four Black principals in the district's eighteen high schools.[51] This was no small feat, given the slow speed with which Black people had previously received promotions within the district, especially appointments to senior high schools. There were also three Black high school department heads.

Still, Black education activists sought more Black representation on the district's nine-member Board of Education.[52] Floyd Logan urged the mayor to maintain three Black members on the board, given that almost 60 percent of the Philadelphia student population was Black.[53] Both the *Tribune* and Georgie Woods, a Black Republican candidate for Philadelphia's City Council, also advocated for a Black woman's appointment to the board.[54] However, Mayor Tate never appointed additional Black people. Though Shedd appeared agreeable to promoting Black access to positions within the district, that sentiment was not shared throughout the city. There was also controversy surrounding the professional status of many Black teachers with the official title of "long-term substitute." Initially, it was believed that a thousand of these long-term substitutes would lose their jobs in order for the district to raise its "intellectual base." Those scheduled to be terminated had not passed the National Teacher Exam (NTE) and therefore could not be offered full-time employment. As long-term substitutes, they were paid per diem and had no additional benefits. The district would offer summer classes to help them pass the NTE, but if they did not pass, they would be replaced by recent college graduates who would be hired on a provisional basis.[55] These provisional teachers would keep their positions if they passed the NTE at the end of their first year of teaching. Advocates for the long-term substitutes argued that these Black educators were more qualified than the recent college graduates, though they had not been able to pass the NTE. The NTE was not a reliable predictor of classroom success, yet SDP was willing to replace experienced Black educators with inexperienced recent graduates who also had not yet passed the NTE.[56] Nationwide, many Black teachers were fired with the implementation of the NTE, which some states began using to lawfully remove Black educators from their teaching roles and to sidestep desegregation edicts from the federal government.[57] Ironically, one of the teachers slated to be fired was the same Dobbins High School teacher whose job Shedd saved because of his ability to engage his students in school.[58] Many Black educators were dissatisfied with their reclassification as "auxiliary teachers," viewing this new title as a demotion and relegation to serving in schools as "glorified flunkies" to classroom teachers.[59] This teacher classification policy is especially interesting when juxtaposed to the voluntary teacher transfer for integration policy. The teacher-transfer policy was supposed to address racially imbalanced faculties and other issues of understaffing at schools in mostly poor (and Black) neighborhoods. But the district was willing to lose Black educators, even though the schools were understaffed. The board would not require its certified educators to teach in schools where they were deemed most needed, but they would release experienced educators for not passing a test that could not determine how successful they would be in their classrooms.

Though Shedd seemed amenable to Black advancement, Black educators' struggles extended beyond position appointments. Contradictions always abound for Black public school educators. They are agents of the state and are workers who need to perform their jobs with a high degree of professionalism in order to earn their paychecks.[60] As Black people, they often experience conflicts regarding racial and cultural needs and desires that may not be in accord with the demands of the state. At some point, all educators have to decide if they will perform the will of the state, be a buffer for their students, or relent against the state's oppression. This was the tightrope Black Philadelphia educators were forced to walk. Nichols, one of the Black board members, became enraged when two administrators of North Philly schools "allegedly made immoral advances to Negro female teachers" and the board did not handle this situation to Nichols's liking. He thought it was moving too slowly and that the consequences were not severe enough. He challenged Shedd and Dilworth about how they would handle the situation, and he threatened to resign from the board. Dilworth gave the administrators a letter telling them that their actions had been in "poor judgment," but Nichols remained dissatisfied.[61] In addition, a Black woman elementary school teacher was beaten in her classroom by her white student and his father for implementing the school policy that a student bring a note from a parent to excuse his absence from school. Though police were called to the school, they refused to arrest the parent.[62]

Shedd's Reforms

When the 1967–1968 school year began, the federal government issued a report stating that the School District of Philadelphia was engaged in "the most dramatic revolution in a city school system in the post-war period." It credited the district with "leading the nation in school reform," and Shedd ushered in "the most far-reaching program of change in the recent history of the Board of Education."[63] Shedd demonstrated an extraordinary willingness to spend money on innovation and projects and efforts undertaken at the classroom level.[64] Under his leadership, the district implemented a standardized testing program and innovative learning programs that became national models, increased free and reduced lunch programs, added library books and personnel, developed a more relevant high school curriculum, and added a Student Bill of Rights and Responsibilities.[65] The district added school counselors, improved college guidance programs, and increased the percentage of its college-bound graduates. Business and vocational programs received updated technological equipment. The district gave scholarships to four hundred of its high school graduates who agreed to come back to teach in the district. There were also new educational and health programs for pregnant students in order to decrease student dropout rates. Adult education and evening high schools became more prevalent throughout the city.[66]

Under Shedd, the district gave money directly to teachers for self-designed instructional programs aimed at improving students' academic performance.[67] New teachers received support from teacher supervisors.[68] New programs encouraged Philadelphians to enroll in local colleges and work in the district while earning their undergraduate degrees.[69] District administrators were encouraged to earn advanced degrees.[70] Alternate-route teacher programs brought recent college graduates to teach in Philadelphia's understaffed schools.[71] Using federal money, the district began a program for students from high poverty areas open to public and non-public school students to equip them with vocational skills for post–high school employment. Sites for this program were strategically chosen to foster integration of various social and racial groups.[72] Summer employment was available for almost four thousand district students.[73] Shedd also funded projects in three majority-Black schools for projects centered on Black history and culture.[74] Under Shedd's leadership, the district was "moving to develop a more effective program in African history and the inclusion of Negroes and the part they played in American history."[75] He asserted that "Progress is being made in the Philadelphia School System, but we need to stop thinking in terms of stereotypes in judging the capacities of the Negro child. We need to raise the educational exceptances [sic] of all children."[76]

Shedd attempted to disrupt the School District of Philadelphia's racism with his liberal reforms, but innovations were expensive, yielded insufficient results, and often preserved racist desires and structures. His work in Philly was an example of superintendents' efforts at improvements as mere symbolic political moves that yield little change in school systems and even less school-level and classroom-level success.[77] He had good ideas that were poorly implemented, hindered by the caustic political climate of the district. His innovations were also thwarted by constant underfunding.[78] Mary, a Black educator who began her teaching career under Shedd, commented, "Shedd was the new guy with all these new-fangled ideas. There was that kind of in-sular Philly thing about *Who is this guy? Why did he spend up all the money?*"[79] Long-time Black Philly activist LeRoi Simmons commented, "He was not a bureaucrat. He didn't know how to run a system."[80] Perhaps Shedd knew how to run a different type of school system. He had relocated to Philadelphia from running a system in New Jersey, but he characterized the district as "too large to manage successfully."[81] Moreover, Shedd was criticized for the lack-luster results of other new district programs on which he had ordered millions of dollars spent.[82] Some Black Philadelphians were discontented with the ex-perimentation associated with new programs in their schools.[83]

Shedd had two major racialized school reform failures, one that would de-centralize the control of schools in North Philadelphia. In his Model School District plan, local residents would choose their own regional superinten-dent. Some Black educators and community members saw this as an effort to further segregate Black children.[84] Other Black education advocates argued that Black people should control everything that happened in predominately Black North Philly, including schooling.[85] One *Tribune* writer commented that responsibility for the schools had been given to the Board of Education when schools, as institutions, should be the responsibility of the people:

> I, personally, have no fears of all black schools. This has been my experience up to graduate schools and there is some evidence to indicate that my educa-tion prepared me as well as most whites and better than many Negroes who went to mixed schools. Let's give the proposal a try. Let's opt for maximum participation by black, or whatever shade of the Negro citizens in North Phil-adelphia. But most of all, let us take advantage of the opportunity to show our talents.[86]

While many white concerned citizens groups had been requesting more say in the leadership and management of the district's schools and policies, they actively protested community leadership for Black Philadelphians in North Philly's schools.[87] Shedd's efforts at decentralizing North Philly schools were fought and defeated by the American Civil Liberties Union, the Educational Equality League, and the Philadelphia Federation of Teachers.[88] Shedd's other notable failed racial school reform was the Paxson Parkway School, which was supposed to be innovative but actually ended up being racist. It had been established for the benefit of white students who had been attending mixed-race schools in Germantown. Black children had been removed from the school building so that these white children could attend this specially formed school. The Paxson Parkway School's opaque student selection process somehow yielded only white students.[89]

Shedd's administration could not create a desegregation plan to satisfy the Pennsylvania Human Relations Commission, which stated that the School District of Philadelphia was becoming a "dual school system" and that an inability to create a plan threatened funding since federal money could not be used in segregated school systems.[90] Dilworth and the Board of Education had proposed educational parks to foster integration, as well as regional school districts instead of those bound by city and county lines. Educational parks and regional school districts may have begun to redress systemic racism embedded in Philly's public schools, but they never materialized because of the resistance of state lawmakers, especially those in the suburbs surrounding Philadelphia whose public schools were enjoined in these reforms. To them, the cost of racial progress was too high if it meant blurring city and suburban boundaries, inviting in the urban problems they escaped when they went to the suburbs. White leadership would not participate in dismantling their intentional white enclaves.[91] The necessary will for such radical change simply did not exist within the existing power structure.[92] Left to solve school desegregation on their own, Dilworth argued that the district could not afford it, especially with a $34 million shortfall looming.[93] Busing students for desegregation had not achieved its goals, and it was expensive and dangerous. Black bused students were constantly under attack from dangerous white people who threw rocks and bottles at school buses while students were on board. One student was even stabbed in the back.[94]

Early in Shedd's tenure, the Human Relations Commission (HRC) had urged the district's board to implement mass teacher transfers in order to achieve racial balance in school faculties. A group of Black teachers who called themselves "Teachers Concerned" agreed with them, but the teachers' union asserted that these forced transfers would not yield the intended results since there were only seven schools with no Black teachers and no schools without white teachers.[95] The HRC conducted a three-part investigation and ordered all districts in the state to develop local desegregation plans immediately.[96] The district's plan contained "reversed busing," which would have some white children bused to Black schools to make white students between 20 percent to 30 percent of the total student enrollment in all schools. When the board revised that plan in 1969, its two Black members, George Hutt and Henry Nichols, voted against it.[97] Dilworth, the board's president, said the board's target was that 90 percent of schools would have racially balanced faculties, achieved through the new Black teachers they had recruited to the system. This meant new Black teachers would have decreased options of schools to consider because they would be placed only where the district said they needed racial balance. The responsibility of racial balance was on Black teachers.[98] It was clear that the voluntary transfer plan had not accomplished the desegregation of school faculties on the basis of race and teaching experience. By 1971, public schools in Philadelphia were more segregated than schools were across the state of Mississippi.[99]

Protests, Pushbacks, and Strikes

Conflicts abounded on all fronts for Shedd throughout his tenure.[100] One notable clash happened early in the Shedd years on November 17, 1967. On that day, approximately 3,500 students converged on the district's headquarters to protest for better Black schools with Black principals, more Black teachers, community control of schools, Black history and culture courses, the removal of police and nonteaching assistants from schools, permission not to salute the American flag, permission to wear African clothes, and permission to form Black clubs.[101] Shedd met with protest leaders and was open to their demands. Henry Nichols was on the scene with the protestors. But the swelling crowd alarmed those charged with keeping order. Philadelphia Police Commissioner Frank Rizzo dispatched more than a hundred newly promoted police sergeants to the scene of the protest with the instruction, "Get their Black asses."[102] Most Black community members said they didn't witness Black student protestors being violent. Instead, they saw the police, including Rizzo, beating Black students. Frederick Holliday, a Black district administrator, was beaten by police while trying to calm the situation. After the protest and the police response, some lamented that both caused more friction and racial harm than good.[103] In the days and months that followed, the Philadelphia Federation of Teachers sided with Rizzo, condemned Black students who protested, and blamed Black educators for the protest.[104]

In response, some Black members of the teachers' union collectively moved to join the Greater Union of the Black Community as a result of the PFT's failure to support students' protest.[105] Fearful of future Black student revolts, the Board of Education instituted its "Policy on Disruption of Activities," which forbade students from attending rallies and protests, aimed to prevent "outside influences" on students during the school day, advocated "solid discipline," and leaned on police to prevent "unauthorized persons from entering schools."[106]

Following that showdown at district headquarters, when the 1968–69 school year began, the mayor and one of the board members were livid with what they considered a "lack of control" within the district. Black students had been having sit-ins and demonstrations at Ben Franklin High and Olney High, demanding more Black administrators, more Black history instruction, and better facilities. Students also wanted the name of Ben Franklin High changed to Malcolm X High. When Shedd agreed to meet some of their demands, students agreed to stop making prejudicial remarks and mistreating white teachers.[107] The record is mute as to whether Shedd investigated what teacher behaviors and school policies may have mitigated Black students' alleged mistreatment. More than seven thousand students dropped out of Philadelphia public schools during Shedd's tenure, and absenteeism was the highest it had ever been. Violence in the schools was an ongoing concern.[108] One student killed a teacher at Leeds Junior High School.[109] Some teachers were afraid to teach in predominately Black schools.[110] Board member Henry Nichols highlighted this irony: "Teachers are reportedly afraid to teach in the North Philadelphia schools, but it's amazing how fast they lose their fears when they are promoted to principal."[111]

White educators steeped in white supremacist logic via color evasiveness were a major hindrance to racial reforms in the School District of Philadelphia in the 1960s, and the Board of Education and the Philadelphia Federation of Teachers were complicit in this obstruction.[112] Black administrators also fought the Principals Association as the sole collective bargaining entity, which was mostly white and didn't represent the concerns of Black students or families. Educators Round Table, a group of eighty-eight Black principals and other administrators within the district, suggested that principals wanted to unionize because they feared proposals for community-controlled schools.[113]

White educators believed in community control as long as it meant control for them through unions, not control for Black citizens.

The PFT is why forced teacher transfers never succeeded during Shedd's tenure. These power struggles centered on the mandatory transfers for teachers to ensure that schools with a majority Black student population had a balance of experienced and inexperienced teachers and that school faculties were integrated. The teachers' union blamed the board for not integrating faculties since 1966. Shedd blamed the union.[114] Black educators were constantly caught in the controversy between the district and the union.[115] Among Black educators, there were competing narratives regarding the contract's transfer clause and subsequent teacher strikes. Board member Nichols was engaged in a bitter battle with Black members of the union who were on the team that negotiated the contract with the no-forced-teacher-transfer clause. He and other Black Philadelphians deemed them "sellouts" who supported the union over Black children. The assumption was that teachers' preferences were benign and that when white teachers arrived at Black schools to which they had been forcibly relocated, they would be amicable to the Black students they never wanted to teach despite anecdotal evidence and pervasive narratives of white educators' low expectations, dislike, disgust, disregard, and disrespect for Black students, families, and communities.[116] This perspective was rooted in an integrationist ideology that held schools with faculties balanced racially and by teaching experience would yield greater results for Black students. The underlying assumption was that white educators would bring the same energy, interest, and vigor to their teaching assignments, even if they were teaching children they feared where they did not choose to teach. This ideology aligned with the prevailing American belief that separate Black education was inherently inferior and that "inferior schools meant inferior teachers."[117] But Black union negotiators took the opposite stance—that compulsory transfers could harm Black students if white teachers were unwillingly transferred to schools where they did not want to teach.[118] In Philadelphia, the PFT's ever-present threat to strike in resistance to forced integration placed the teachers' union in control of the district and fortified a political culture whereby there would always be winners and losers.[119]

Shedd, Dilworth, and the Board of Education were unable to garner the funding they needed from the Pennsylvania State Legislature to adequately fund the city's schools. Throughout Shedd's tenure, the board would announce budget shortfalls, cuts to positions, financial belt-tightening, and layoffs, and then the union would announce its promise to strike.[120] Striking workers were commonplace across the United States at this time.[121] There were at least four periods when teachers did not work when Shedd was superintendent—January 1968, September 1968, September 1970, and October 1970.[122] During the 1970 strikes, many Black educators resisted. Hundreds of Black teachers, principals, and other community members agreed to break the September and October strikes and to teach without pay, going against the union.[123] During the October 1970 strike, Dilworth ordered schools to remain open.[124] By the end of October, that strike had ended, but questions remained. Students at West Philadelphia High were baffled by their teachers' behavior during this strike. The year before, when students walked out to protest one of their teachers, they were court-ordered to stop their demonstrations, and they did. However, their teachers defied an injunction and went on strike. When the strike was over, students questioned their teachers about why that was the case. Shedd stated that after the strike, he hoped for "a totally new and more aggressive start" to educators making differences for their students. The *Tribune* weighed in on the strike conversation: "The result of the teacher strike is that we will have better-paid teachers, to which no intelligent person objects, but they will be doing the same kind of poor work and each year dumping on the city hundreds of functional illiterates and unemployables."[125]

Shedd's Liberalism Fails

Although Shedd's leadership had brought new efforts to empowering individual Black people within the School District of Philadelphia, several challenges remained for Shedd, Black educators, Black students, and the schools. Many schools were still overcrowded and unsafe. Improved instruction was needed in basic skills. Teachers and administrators were still challenged by their urban context. And many students remained in segregated schools.[126] The ways Shedd tried to navigate this terrain typify the limits of liberalism in saving urban America from the conflicts public schooling. Over time, many Black Philadelphians questioned why Shedd's care for Black people yielded so little power for Black people.[127] Already turned off by the longstanding white power structure that ran Philadelphia's politics and its schools, there emerged a mistrust for Shedd parallel to the already existing mistrust for white leadership. Activist LeRoi Simmons shared this criticism of Shedd:

> I saw him as being the last of the good old boys' club. … Mark Shedd wasn't somebody that you could impact with information from the bottom. … Folks like Dave Richardson couldn't get his ear. Folks like us who were trying to organize for poor Black children couldn't get substantial input with him. … 'Cause he was there when Rizzo was acting the plumb idiot. They were rumbling back and forth. And I don't think there was a whole lot of difference, although it looked like it in the press, I don't think there was a whole lot of difference in mentality. … A lot of things were happening around him. There was a Black Power movement coming up and there was a white oppressive movement coming down. And he was, like, in the middle. And he had to figure out where he was gonna sleep at night. And he knew he had to be with the white community and they were kind of following, rallying around Rizzo because they were afraid of these children.[128]

There were multiple interpretations of Shedd, and those interpretations impacted how Black educators viewed the district. They saw Frederick Holliday, Marcus Foster, Bernard Watson, and Samuel Woodard all resign abruptly from their district leadership posts.[129] According to James "Torch" Lytle, a retired white educator who began his work in the district under Shedd, the School District of Philadelphia was a training ground for excellent Black education administrators.[130] But why didn't the district value their excellence enough to retain them? Foster and Watson announced their resignations on the anniversary of the assassination of Martin Luther King Jr.[131] Board of Education member Nichols predicted a battle over Foster's replacement. Foster had been promoted from being principal of Gratz High School to Shedd's associate superintendent for community planning. Nichols believed that leaders from three influential Black groups and a group of Italian educators would engage in an ethnic battle for Foster's post.[132] After Foster's and Watson's unanticipated resignations from highly visible school district positions, Shedd would not guarantee they would be replaced by other Black educators.[133] Concerned with perceptions of his leadership due to Rizzo's constant criticism and riling up of angry white ethnics, Shedd articulated a color-evasive stance, saying that he would look for the best qualified for the positions and race would not be a consideration.[134] But in a system with so few Black educators, even fewer

Black administrators, and a history of such egregious racialized practices for its education professionals, ideas such as objectivity, neutrality, color-evasiveness, and merit are used to maintain longstanding white control.[135] If merit mattered, why had there been such a long and arduous fight for Black people to get promoted within the district?[136] Why was there one Black board member when the district's Black student population was 17 percent, and why were there just two Black board members when the district's Black student population increased to 60 percent?[137] One concession Shedd made during his superintendence was making appointments in groups of three so that Italians/Irish, Jews, and Black people were balanced in their positions of power.[138] In Shedd's attempt to appease white ethnics, he surrendered neutrality and further demonstrated that meritocracy was a sham for Black educators. Thus, the little hope Black people wanted to have in Shedd diminished over time.[139] Black educators questioned the implications of their colleagues rising to and yet not maintaining positions of power within the district. If someone as talented and beloved as Marcus Foster could not remain in Philadelphia, what might be possible for other Black educators? Black educators became disillusioned with the change they hoped Shedd's leadership would produce.

Sam Woodard's account is compelling. In 1970, he was the district's director of program implementation, and he announced that he was leaving due to the lack of credit he received for the proposals he drafted. Instead, his work was presented by white administrators who were given credit and accolades for his work. Further, Woodard complained that Black educators had sought advanced degrees but could not get positions within the district to match their education or credentials. At the same time, white people with less training were given positions higher than their Black counterparts who were more educated.[140] Woodard asserted "the Board had a horrifying amount of dehumanization and a very low trust level." He pushed Shedd on these questions:

1. Do you condone Blacks doing the work for a project or activity and Whites getting the credit?
2. Does the Superintendent and this Board condone Educational Colonialism?
3. Will the Superintendent accept my proposal to appoint the following people in policymaking positions?

a. A Black Deputy Superintendent of Instruction to serve with the present head of that Division possessing equal power to formulate policy.
He felt the curriculum is not serving the needs of our children.

b. Black Co-Directors in the following areas:
Pupil Personnel and Counseling
Division of Vocational and Industrial Education.[141]

Woodard's inquiry is jarring and significant. His questions were rooted in his understanding of a relationship between the pushback against coloni-alism that was taking place around the world during that time, which ran concurrent to the pushback Black educators and community members were unleashing on the School District of Philadelphia. Woodard's second ques-tion was informed by the ideology and rhetoric of Black liberation typi-fied and articulated by Stokely Carmichael (later known as Kwame Ture) and Charles V. Hamilton in their 1967 book, *Black Power: The Politics of Liberation*. In articulating his question around "educational colonialism," Woodard demonstrated the interconnectedness between Black struggles for education in Philadelphia's public schools and the national and internation-al politics of that time. His questions show that Black educators' concerns superseded schools in Philadelphia; they were also pushing America to live up to its democratic ideals. They were fighting for full citizenship and hu-manity in this nation and around the world; their battleground was public schools. Woodard deduced that he and other high-ranking Black educators could not be successful in the district because of its racism, and therefore, he was leaving.[142] Shedd's reforms were symbolic, not substantive. And the racist policies and practices he attempted to disrupt were merely preserved through his tenure.

A month later after Woodard's public inquiry, he openly pressed Shedd for answers to his questions. Shedd's responses articulated evasiveness of racial oppression by using the phrase "whatever his color." Shedd added, "I person-ally understand that many vestiges of colonial attitudes still exists [sic] in the minds of many who work within the School System. I feel that there is an honest and sincere attempt to recognize when and where this exists."[143] Shedd offered recognition of racism, but he also reduced colonialism to attitudes, not intentional systems of oppression perpetuated through the structure of the district. Shedd's response to Woodard showed that, without recognizing systemic, structural oppression at play in the School District of Philadelphia, there could be no disrupting it. Anything less than disruption upheld white supremacy—or as Woodard called it, "educational colonialism" under the guise of equality.

2

Thug Life

Frank Rizzo's Law and (Dis)Order, 1971–1982

It is a question of law and order and terror under Rizzo.

—Rev. Leon Sullivan,[1] founder,
Opportunities Industrialization Centers

Philadelphia has sunk so low that we must squabble over
what is the minimum for our children rather than decide
what should be the maximum for our children. ...
If the Mayor doesn't have enough sense to know that you
can't have a viable city without an excellent public school
system them [sic] you ought to have that sense. ... You
refused to ask City Council for taxes and our schools were
closed for weeks. ... The issue really is whether this Board
is going to crucify those children on the course of Mayor
Rizzo's political ambition.

—Charles Bowser,[2]
executive director, Philadelphia Coalition

Frank Rizzo (1920–1991) is legendary, iconic, and famous for his brashness, bravado, and combativeness. This chapter examines how Mayor Rizzo—through the Board of Education that he controlled and the public school superintendents he appointed—facilitated race-based turmoil, deliberate underfunding of Philly's public schools, obstruction of school desegregation, and other dysfunctions. Under his leadership, the district's central administration was a hierarchical old boys' network, and people were promoted in lock-step to avoid disrupting the culture or structure.[3] There was a lazy work culture and a lack of concern for and investment in education.[4] Teacher absenteeism was high.[5] White resistance to and resentment of racial progress was constant. Repeated obstructions, objections, and deliberate sabotage occurred and sometimes were permitted by the Black school district leaders that Black Philadelphians had begged for. The Rizzo era in Philadelphia's public school history calls into question racial representation in politics. One of the takeaways from the civil rights movement and the National Black Political Convention of 1972 was the elevation of Black people to positions of power. But what is the purpose of Black faces in high places when their positions maintain oppression? To what extent can Black people rely on individual Black advancement when collective improvement remains elusive? Though public schools should exist for the public good, to what extent can public schools be trusted when policies placate whites' interests and practices favor whites' preferences?

The 1970s and early 1980s would prove to be a complex era for Black Philadelphians in local politics and public schooling. The Democratic Party controlled the city but provided few advances for the masses of Black people. The city's Black Political Forum was comprised of Black activists and others frustrated by the established Democratic Party. They sought to help elect Black politicians who would work toward Black community advancement and empowerment.[6] Their mobilization launched the election of Black candidates who separated themselves from the Democratic machine, such as Hardy Williams to the state legislature in 1970; Ethel Allen to Philadelphia's City Council in 1971; David P. Richardson, the activist who led the student uprising at school district headquarters on November 17, 1967, to the state legislature in the 1972; Lucien Blackwell to City Council in 1975; Rev. Bill Gray to United States Congress in 1978; John Street to City Council in 1981 (he would become mayor of Philadelphia in 2000); and W. Wilson Goode to mayor in 1984.[7] Black Philadelphia's biggest fights of this era would involve Frank Rizzo, who died in 1991 and was immortalized in a statue placed in front of the city's Municipal Services building in 1999. Hailed as a monument to racial oppression and police brutality, the Rizzo statue was removed in 2020 during the nationwide Black uprising ignited by the police murder of George Floyd in Minneapolis.

Rizzo was notorious in Philadelphia for years before he was elected mayor in November of 1971 and for the decades since he passed away in 1991 during his fifth campaign to run the city. He was appointed police commissioner in 1967.[8] An Italian American who was born and reared in South Philly, Rizzo dropped out of formal schooling in high school and rose through the ranks of the Philly police force.[9] He was revered and reviled. Seen as racist by many, Rizzo was known for wearing a baton inside the cummerbund of a tuxedo and for infamously forcing young Black men affiliated with the Black Panthers to strip on a North Philadelphia street after a police officer was shot and killed.[10] Local Black activist Cecil B. Moore called Rizzo "a bigger fascist than Adolf Hitler."[11] During the 1967 campaign season, Moore unsuccessfully ran for mayor as an independent candidate. With Superintendent Mark Shedd's permission, Moore held campaign rallies in Black Philly high schools, organizing young Black people around sociopolitical consciousness and their rights as citizens, which made the police commissioner see them as adversaries rather than engaged citizens.[12] He argued that Rizzo was a foe to democracy, evidenced by Rizzo's demand that Mayor Tate abolish the city's police oversight board in 1969.[13] Rizzo held questioners, rabble-rousers, dissenters, and activists in low regard. He did not distinguish between young Black people pushing back against a government that was opposed to them and gang members, the latter of whom were a big concern throughout this era.[14] When school administrators called for police to resolve school-based conflicts, Rizzo showed up each time.[15]

Despite his omnipresence and reputation, Philadelphia still saw a significant rise in crime and gangs while Rizzo was police commissioner. It was also rumored that he covered for organized crime in the city.[16] His violent response to the Black Philly student uprising in November 1967 further solidified accusations of his racism. Not wanting to be cast in this light, Rizzo thereafter made a point of criticizing white activists as well as Black activists and claimed to be an equal opportunity brute.[17] He was a proponent of color-evasive racism, though it worked better for Rizzo than it did for Shedd.

Rizzo saw Shedd as too light on student activism, and he positioned education as oppositional to order and policing. Rizzo had a fan in President Richard Nixon.[18] As the "law and order" candidate, Police Commissioner Frank Rizzo ran for mayor of the city of Philadelphia in 1971.

Their admiration was mutual. Rizzo modeled his mayoral campaign after Nixon's 1968 presidential campaign.[19] Rizzo positioned the quest for Black power as moving toward anarchy, which required policing and punishment.[20] He used a racist syllogism to advance his campaign: since he was against criminals and his rivals were against him, his rivals must be for criminals.[21] Three Democrats opposed Rizzo in the mayoral primary, one Black and two white: Pennsylvania State Representative Hardy Williams; City Councilman David Cohen; and US Congressman Bill Green Sr. Rizzo's opponents were seen as similar in their anti-Rizzo stance. Ultimately, Green and Williams split the anti-Rizzo vote, while the rest of the party seemed unified around Rizzo. Once he had the Democratic Party's nomination to be mayor of Philadelphia, one of Rizzo's campaign slogans for the general election was "Firm but fair." Thacher Longstreth, his Republican opponent, called out Rizzo's reputation as a racist, saying Rizzo was "firm to the blacks, fair to the whites."[22] Rizzo chided his political enemies with, "Just wait after November, you'll have a front row seat because I'm going to make Attila the Hun look like a faggot."[23] As mayor, he promised not to raise taxes and to hire two thousand more policemen. But his most important campaign promise boasted, "I used to say that Shedd wouldn't last eight minutes after I'm elected. Now I say he won't last eight seconds."[24]

Rizzo did not campaign in any Black neighborhoods. Noteworthy Black Philly activists endorsed Longstreth in the general election, as did most Black Philly voters.[25] Philadelphia has, historically, been a city of Democrats. Rizzo took the votes of white Republicans in Roxborough, Manayunk, South Philly, and the Northeast, earning more Republican votes than Longstreth. Philly's white ethnics (Italians, Irish, and Polish of Jewish and Catholic faiths) were increasingly abandoning the Democratic Party, yet they threw their support behind Rizzo, believing he would defend their interests. White resistance to school reform served as major fuel for the success of Frank Rizzo's mayoral campaign.[26] Rizzo was a polarizing and controversial political figure who often drew strong support along racial lines, with white ethnics heavily favoring him.[27] It was primarily white Philadelphians who gave Rizzo two tumultuous terms as mayor of Philadelphia, from 1972 to 1980. His adherence to ethnic patronage remains legendary.[28]

The Rizzo Board of Education

The Board of Education was comprised of nine people who were chosen by the mayor for a six-year term. Around the time of Rizzo's election to mayor, there were several exits from the board. Dilworth resigned in the summer of 1971.[29] Henry Nichols, acting board president once Dilworth left, left in November 1971.[30] George Hutt was the only remaining Black board member, and there were calls for there to be more than two Black members in a school district that had almost 70 percent Black students. Hutt was the only remaining Black board member in 1972 until Rizzo appointed two Black men: Adolphus Baxter was a city planner and community activist, and Arthur Thomas was director of community affairs for SEPTA, Philadelphia's public transportation system, and secretary for the Board of Trustees of Philadelphia Prisons and would become president of the Council of the Great City Schools.[31] Though Black people had rallied for years for more Black representation on the Board of Education, especially as the school district was solidly two-thirds Black, Rizzo was the first mayor to have three Black men on his board. One of his Black appointees, Arthur Thomas, was elected board president, the first Black person in this role.[32] This countermove to redress those accusations of Rizzo's racism challenged just how liberal Democratic mayors had been, especially Dilworth. If Dilworth was so liberal, why had he not prioritized the Black presence on Philly's Board of Education? Why didn't he make the Black contingency of the board more representative of the almost two-thirds majority Black population enrolled in Philly's public schools? Still, increased Black presence on the board was not enough to substantially shift how or for whose benefit the district worked. The board still approached Black students and families as "culturally deprived," and while there were individual Black people whose careers advanced with three Black men on the board, a less racist educational experience and increased opportunities for the masses were slow to come.[33] There were mostly modest improvements—such as the addition of more academic programs through magnet schools—and symbolic gestures, such as monuments for notable Black men after their deaths.[34]

As mayor, Rizzo appointed middle-class people to the Board of Education instead of millionaires.[35] Rizzo's board was always riddled with questions about their integrity and accountability, including a public spectacle over Black board members' uses of district-funded chauffeured cars, a perk available to all board members.[36] An argument can be made for providing transportation for public servants of modest means who shoulder enormous responsibility without compensation. But in a perpetually cash-strapped school district, offering chauffeured cars paid for with school district funds reeks of exorbitance and possible corruption.[37] Mistrust and dysfunction were typical attributes of the School District of Philadelphia under Rizzo and his Board of Education.[38] Though they commended themselves for unified decision making, they were obstructionist, feckless, and self-aggrandizing. They were in constant conflicts with the teachers' union and the principals' union on the budget and working conditions and on distinctions in roles and responsibilities.[39] Though board members created a Parents Bill of Rights and Responsibilities, they were repressive and opaque regarding their discussions, meetings, and decision making.[40] Community members continuously asked for access to board meetings whether in person or by public access television.[41] Black and Brown community members and activists from across the city expressed their displeasure with Rizzo's board and requested members to resign.[42] But Rizzo's board members were not only adversarial with other entities. They also were contentious among themselves and prone to infighting.[43]

William Ross, former president of the board, was closely aligned with Rizzo when Shedd was superintendent, but their relationship had withered by the end of 1973.[44] Ross objected to Arthur Thomas being board president given Thomas's alliance with Rizzo.[45] Ross maintained conflicts with Black board members Thomas and Hutt, as well with Delores Oberholtzer, a Rizzo appointee and one of the board's few white women. Ross accused them of deliberately sabotaging the work of getting the resources the district needed to meet its obligations to children and their families.[46] Thomas was president of the board for eight years, the majority of Rizzo's tenure. Critics of Thomas abounded, and at times it was difficult to know if the criticism was rooted in his being Black while leading a major Philly institution, in the fiscally conservative agenda he permitted, or in the roughshod ways he seemed to ram issues through board meetings.[47] When Thomas was elected to a second year as president of the board, he urged, "we must give our children an adequate education."[48] But how is "adequate" defined for a system that historically disenfranchised Black students, Black families, and Black employees? In the cacophony of detractors, Thomas's only constant source of support was board member Baxter, who said other board members did not think a Black man should be in that role, so they caused constant disruption and upheaval by not following proper procedures in meetings.[49] Thomas was concerned about the pressures put on urban school boards during the 1970s, and he pushed back on the disapproval with, "We have some difficult times ahead. You can rest assured that, despite some prophets of doom, we will be in there fighting for the children of the School District."[50]

While it is debatable whether Thomas was fighting for the district's children, he certainly championed Black professionals in the district.[51] He proudly used board meeting time to acknowledge two Black women educators who had received their doctorates from the University of Pennsylvania, one who would later become the first Black woman superintendent of schools for Philadelphia.[52] Delores Oberholtzer was vice president of Philly's Board of Education for eight years, the same duration Thomas was at the helm. Having the first Black man as president of the board while having a white woman vice president was symbolic of increasing opportunities for Black men and white women, but neither of them advanced radical, progressive, or even liberal ideas for Black people or women connected to the district. Oberholtzer voted against the board's resolution on Title IX.[53] In the early days of their leadership, they appeared to move together in decision making. Over time, though, Oberholtzer began questioning if Thomas was capable of leading the board through the district's school desegregation conflicts, its constant budget deficits, the decreasing enrollment in schools, and a school system that was graduating students that she called "functional illiterates."[54] One of the biggest critiques Thomas received surrounded how the board handled the yearly budget, replete with the board's insistence every year that the schools were in crisis due to underfunding. And his biggest difficulties were with Rizzo's first choice as school superintendent, Matthew Costanzo.

Costanzo Versus Thomas

In 1972, half of those in the pool of qualified candidates for superintendent were Black educators, but the Rizzo-appointed Board of Education chose Rizzo's ethnic brethren.[55] Matthew Costanzo had been the district's associate superintendent of field operations under Shedd. He boasted of "20 years of service in the Black community," promised to have an open-door policy at the school district's headquarters for parents and community groups that wanted to share their education concerns, said he would work with Black education leaders, and urged "direct educational services" to children.[56] Costanzo was a Philadelphian who had served the school district under Mark Shedd, thus satisfying local desires for an insider to lead the district.[57] Costanzo had risen through the ranks of the district, and he was seen as a good guy in spite of the highly political context in which he worked.[58] As Mary shared, "I think [Costanzo] really wanted to do the right thing. I just think that Frank Rizzo had that incredible power to do what he wanted."[59] Costanzo's tenure began with mounting tensions with the Philadelphia Federation of Teachers over contract negotiations.[60] These tensions worsened with the district's looming budget problems, which led to teacher strikes in 1972 and 1973. For the three years Costanzo was superintendent, he constantly tangled with the Board of Education and was frustrated that the district did not have the money to run the school system in ways he was comfortable with or to provide the education students deserved. At one board meeting in May 1972, he declared the following:

> I think if you present a budget that is less than what we presented to you for the next time around we delude the public into thinking that they are send-ing their children to school for a [*sic*] education. They will be sending their children to school for babysitting if we approve anything less than what we presented for the next year.[61]

Rizzo issued cuts in city services that most directly hurt Black people who relied on the city's social services more than other racial groups, and he was intent on keeping his campaign promise of not raising city taxes, a major funding source for the city's public schools.[62]

One of the biggest budget showdowns between Costanzo and the Board of Education took place in the spring of 1974.[63] It was customary for the president of the board to send the district's expected expenditures for the upcoming school year to City Council, elucidating gaps in funding to appeal to the city's legislative body for additional funding. Because the school district could not levy taxes, it had to tell City Council what additional funds it needed so that the council could either shift funds from elsewhere in the city's coffers or raise taxes. Costanzo and Thomas had different versions of the district budget for the 1974–75 school year. Thomas's balanced budget would require no additional revenue. But the district was already underfunded, having lingering budget shortfalls from previous years. Families were fleeing Philly's public schools as the district had already shortened its school year from the state's required 180 days and eliminated services.[64] In Costanzo's budget, additional funding would be required to meet needs that did not exist in Thomas's version of the budget. Thomas claimed it was better to send a balanced budget to City Council, even if it was short of what was needed.[65] Thomas's approach seemed like he was either hiding the school district's needs, was being dishonest about them, did not believe the needs were real, or believed they were real but not the responsibility of the district. As president of the Board of Education, Thomas refused to send to City Council Costanzo's version of the budget. For the district to seek additional funds from the city would look bad for Rizzo, who had promised no new taxes. Costanzo circumvented Thomas and sent to City Council the budget he wanted to be funded, and board member Ross contacted the governor to get additional funds for the district, both which angered Thomas.[66] These white men had disrespected the first Black board president's authority.

The white gaze—the expectation of white people that their ideas, lives, and preferences are central to all aspects of American life—has often been a confounding variable for Black leaders. Black members of Philly's Board of Education did not have the benefit of removing themselves from the white gaze, as seen in the politics of this budget showdown. The white gaze proved problematic, whether it came from the conservative Rizzo or liberal board member Davidoff. Thomas pushed Rizzo's agenda, and Rizzo was adversarial to the needs of Black Philadelphia while providing an opportunity for individual elevation of Black board members. Rizzo's expectations of Thomas represented the white gaze. Black activists and community members—some of whom had been elated at the election of the board's first Black president—rallied at the last board meeting of March 1974 in support of Costanzo's version of the budget.[67] Black board members, ever aware of the white gaze, seemed conflicted in their allegiance to Rizzo versus their allegiance to Black Philadelphia and to this Black board president. A white liberal board member, Davidoff, also represented the white gaze as he questioned how the three Black board members publicly suggested that *the other* board members were not working in the interests of Philly's kids while these same Black board members were considering not supporting a budget that asked for more money to meet the needs of Philly's public schools. Baxter retorted that for Davidoff to bring up his race in this context was problematic and that his budget vote should be about his humanness, not his Blackness. Thomas accused Davidoff of subtle racism by suggesting that their racial identities should influence how they vote on the board. While it is deplorable that any board member would participate in the underfunding of the school district they have been entrusted to shepherd, it is unacceptable for a white person—who benefits from global white supremacy and all its concomitant power arrangements— to become the race police, telling Black people how they should live in and live out their Blackness. As liberal, progressive, or radical as they may be, white people can never be authorities on Blackness. It is not up to white people to police Black people through a lens of Blackness that white people can only observe but never embody. Baxter did vote for Costanzo's budget. The other Black board members, Hutt and Thomas, did not.[68] Rizzo's required allegiance from Thomas and Davidoff's demands of political and ontological choices from the Black board members both represented the white gaze, both perspectives racist.

When the majority vote on the board yielded support for Costanzo's version of the budget, the school district's general counsel came to the next board meeting, insisting the vote that members had taken at the March 28 meeting was illegal and needed to be redone. Community members, activists, and local politicians called out board members and the school district's attorney for their political posturing. A local attorney and community activist, Charles Bowser, said his legal position was that the general counsel's opinion on this matter was "as phony as a three dollar bill" and that the board's vote met the letter and the spirit of the city charter. Bowser continued:

> There is no question in anyone's mind, that that vote which you took on Thursday upset the Mayor and he got on the phone and you needed an excuse for a new meeting to change your decision and Mr. Soken gave it to you

now. ... I think you ought to individually and personally think about wheth-er you want to risk your reputation in this town, which will transcend your membership on this Board, which will transcend Rizzo's term in office.[69]

Several other lawmakers joined Bowser in advocating for more funding for the school district, including State Representative Hardy Williams, former Rizzo rival Longstreth, and City Council member Ethel Allen.[70] It was clear that Costanzo and his budget had far-reaching support.[71] At the end of the meeting, Thomas said the resolution they passed at the March 28 meeting in support of Costanzo's version of the budget would stand.[72] City Council provided additional funds in the budget they submitted to Rizzo, who vetoed City Council's budget and was overridden by City Council.[73] Shortly thereafter, when Rizzo was running for reelection, Costanzo took a $10,000 pay cut to become superintendent of schools in Haddonfield, New Jersey.[74] After refusing to be Rizzo's yes man, Costanzo was replaced with Michael Marcase, who would be investigated for fiscal and ethical improprieties and would become known as the most inept superintendent the district had ever had.[75]

From Bad to Worse

There was very little public discussion of who would succeed Costanzo. The same day Costanzo's resignation was effective, the Board of Education held an undemocratic, potentially illegal special meeting to immediately appoint Michael Marcase as superintendent of the district. Thomas said that since ten large school districts around the nation were also looking for a superinten-dent at this time and since the city had a budget crisis, it made the most sense to go with Marcase, also a Philadelphia insider.[76] In his appointment accept-ance speech, Marcase said he would use all his energy to continue Costanzo's work.[77] Before Marcase attended his second board meeting as superinten-dent, issues were raised about his professional credentials.[78] His doctorate was deemed by some as "mail-order caliber" from the unaccredited University of Sarasota.[79] Since he had not earned enough academic credits to meet the state's education requirements for superintendents, Marcase was made su-perintendent on a provisional basis with a letter from the Commonwealth of Pennsylvania's secretary of education.[80] No other superintendent require-ments for Pennsylvania school districts were changed. State Representative

David P. Richardson charged that this adjustment by the state legislature was a purely political move to put Marcase in place.[81]

Many Black educators and community activists saw Marcase as a disreputable figurehead.[82] Labeled "conservative" by the press, Marcase approached the superintendence with a commitment to "ferret every wasted nickel and dime I can find anywhere."[83] This penny pinching further steeped the district in the neoliberalism that began with Costanzo.[84] Not spending public money on school district programs meant that money needed to come from private sources, which usually meant relying on philanthropy.[85] Marcase called students "clients" and promoted "operating efficiency," harkening to the early days of mass public schooling and the factory model of education.[86] His approach further solidified the district as a "demoralized, chaotic system" in which there were constant financial problems, including a more than $230 million deficit, teacher furloughs, the rescinding of salary raises, and a district headquarters that was described as "a fortress under siege."[87] Throughout his seven-year tenure, Marcase was investigated several times for abusing his office: for using district employees to install a sundeck on his house at the New Jersey shore during work hours, for having district personnel provide security for his home in the East Falls section of Philadelphia, and for violating board policy on vacation. Each time, Marcase was exonerated.[88]

Black, Still, in the Years of Chaos

Being a Black educator in Philly's public schools during the Rizzo era came with constant confounding circumstances.[89] The ways Black educators who were hired and handled as professionals during the Rizzo era were highly problematic.[90] Black educators and community activists were concerned about the routine neglect of due process for Black employees "while highly paid and proven incompetent whites are retained and protected."[91] Many new Black teachers were hired as substitutes because the district was not making permanent appointments at the time. After principals had observed their work for the first few months of employment, they would either be hired on a permanent basis or would remain as per diem instructors. Some remained long-term substitutes for up to eight years of employment with the school district. Some were not hired to start in the district until October of each school year, and then they would be transferred to other schools quickly and without notice or explanation.[92]

Furthermore, teacher strikes and lockouts occurred almost every other year, elucidating racial fissures. Rizzo's Board of Education, Costanzo, and the Philadelphia Federation of Teachers were aligned regarding how Black students were regarded in schools and how forced teacher transfers should not be implemented for desegregation. The board and Costanzo were aligned on compensation against the teachers' union.[93] To suspend the four-weeks-long fall 1972 strike, teachers returned to work based on a memorandum of understanding agreement reached by district and union negotiators.[94] But the union ordered its teachers to strike again in January 1973.[95] The district was already in such financial distress that even if schools reopened from the strike, they would still shut down in April because a budget shortfall precluded the district from being able to pay its bills until the end of the school year. Moreover, because of the days lost in the fall to the teachers' strike and the strike that started in January 1973, high school seniors' graduation was in limbo, and the district ran the risk of losing state and federal money due to lost instructional time, which had to reach 180 days total by June 30.[96] Fighting with the union in the press, Rizzo declared, "Ryan don't run this town," to which John Ryan, chief negotiator for the Philadelphia Federation of Teachers, responded, "Ryan do, too!"[97] Their public beef made for good political theater, Black community members were amused and incensed.[98] The 1973 strike lasted for eight weeks in January and February; and during this strike, union leaders were arrested and jailed for being in contempt of court by not directing their members to return to work. Still, many schools in Black areas of the city were open, and it was estimated that more than three thousand of the district's thirteen thousand teachers went in to work anyhow.[99] Black educators and community activists organized and staffed community schools so children would have somewhere to go if their schools were closed and so high school seniors could graduate. During Marcase's tenure, there were strikes and threats of strikes by multiple unions. There was a short strike in the fall of 1980 while the board continued contract negotiations with the union.[100] But the worst strike was in 1981, when school did not start until November.[101] Though there was still no signed contract between the board and the union, people were going to work because the strike had lasted for almost three months and they could no longer afford to be out of work.[102]

Racial issues were exacerbated by the district's series of teacher strikes.[103] There was even dissent from within the union from its Black caucus. Even though there was a Black presence in the union, during the strikes, Black educators witnessed their white striking colleagues taunting strikebreakers with racist epithets, such as "uppity niggers" and "handkerchief heads."[104] Black educators who taught during strikes had to be strategic and deliberate about their travel routes to school and their arrival times because strike lines— including people from other city unions—were formed to prevent them from entering the buildings.[105] Retired Black educator Theresa recalled racial and class solidarity, but she also saw the potential for racialized and gendered violence during strikes.[106] Union strikers depended on stereotypes of Black men as brooding and scary as they attempted use the bodies of Black male teachers to intimidate would-be strike breakers from entering school buildings.[107] In addition to strike lines and name calling, Black educators who chose not to strike had home phone lines cut off, cars and homes egged, sugar poured into car gas tanks, tires slashed, paint splashed on cars; some were physically harmed, and many were harassed.[108] A Black woman nonteaching assistant was beaten badly during a strike.[109] Some Black educators did not want to antagonize colleagues by going into district schools, so they stayed away from picketing altogether, while others taught in one of the community-based alternate education sites.[110] Whatever choices they made, there were consequences when the strikes ended. When educators returned to work, the ill feelings aroused during the strikes lingered for decades.[111] Collegial interactions between Black educators and white colleagues who struck were forever marred in some cases.[112]

School desegregation was also complicated for Black Philadelphia during the Rizzo era.[113] The school district implemented a "racial balance" policy for faculty, which resulted in a federal lawsuit over whether the district could desegregate its faculties using a "quota system."[114] Federal desegregation funds were withheld from the district because officials believed it illegally segregated its teachers.[115] Additionally, having been sued by the Pennsylvania Human Rights Commission for failing to adequately desegregate its schools in 1971, there were ongoing tensions in the district regarding school desegregation throughout this time.[116] In 1972, 230 of the district's 280 schools were considered racially segregated. There was no way to feasibly physically desegregate students such that white students would not be the minority, which policymakers prioritized. Rizzo's board rejected a possible desegregation plan in 1973 because of the financial implications, as well as fear about community pushback.[117] Both Costanzo and Marcase urged desegregation through the creation of magnet schools for specialized academic programs, changing school boundaries and feeder patterns, and closing schools.[118] Regardless of method, school desegregation in Philly aimed to satisfy the court, and it marketed integrated schools in Black neighborhoods to white families who clung to anglonormative, anti-Black ideologies.[119] White people did not want their children to be the racial minority in any school, so the voluntary desegregation plan seemed mostly moot. This was most evident in the Edison High School debacle of 1979.

Edison High School had long been a contentious space.[120] Further complicating matters, as school boundary lines were changed to foster desegregation, white students from nearby Frankford High School were newly slated to attend Edison, where the students were majority Black and Spanish-speaking.[121] In August 1979, the Board of Education considered rescinding the new boundary lines because eighty white students now assigned to Edison threatened to drop out rather than become minorities in school. While the resolution to rescind the desegregation plan by changing boundary lines did not pass, the board allowed these students to formally request enrollment at another school.[122] One month later, the board held a special meeting, again, "to discuss the Frankford, Kensington and Edison boundary lines." With five votes needed, the plan stood.[123] There were serious flaws in the district's voluntary desegregation plan and logic. White board members (liberal) Boonin and (conservative) Oberholtzer worried that white students were being minoritized. But there was little evidence that school district officials ever worried about Black or Brown students being minoritized. The board prioritized fears of white flight and white anger, which demonstrated that Philly's school desegregation effort prioritized white preferences and white comfort and was a tool of white supremacy.[124]

From Rizzo to Green

While Black students were deprioritized and Black educators destabilized, Marcase's contract was continuously extended despite the turmoil surrounding his job performance.[125] By 1980, Philadelphia's new mayor was former

Rizzo rival Bill Green Sr. Just as Rizzo had campaigned on ridding the school district of Shedd, Green campaigned with the promise to remove Marcase from office.[126] When Mayor Green realized the Rizzo-appointed Board of Education would not remove Marcase from the district's helm, Green began supporting state legislation to dissolve Philadelphia's board, something that would actually materialize twenty years later.[127] Marcase had not been swift in negotiating teachers' contracts, he did not have the confidence of City Council members and community members, and his association with former Mayor Rizzo made many people uncomfortable.[128] Frustration over all these issues led to widespread and ongoing calls for Marcase's resignation, which came at the end of the school year in 1982.[129]

3

Black Reign

The Constance Clayton Era, 1982–1993

She was like Booker T of the movement. Connie Clayton was trying to reconstruct. That's what she was trying to do.

—Nina, Black educator, formerly with the School District of Philadelphia[1]

Black women have always gotten in trouble for telling the truth, and I feel as though she got in trouble for telling the truth.

—Linda, Black educator, retired from the School District of Philadelphia[2]

Before the fictitious Clair Huxtable and the real Oprah Winfrey, Constance Clayton was one of the most visible representations of Black woman excellence in Philadelphia. Many Black Philadelphians believed Clayton could fix what Superintendent Michael Marcase had wrecked. She graduated from the Philadelphia High School for Girls in 1951, Temple University, and the University of Pennsylvania.[3] She became so renowned that the University of Pennsylvania named an endowed chair in her honor in 1993.[4] Clayton was the best of Philadelphia's Black leadership. This was no small feat for a Black population that had struggled to access positions of power and then struggled *with* Black people in those positions of power.[5] Many of these intraracial struggles were along class lines and ideology around what it meant to be a Black leader.[6] For the most part, though, Black educators and families supported Clayton's leadership. For some who did not share Clayton's racial identity, their support proved temporary. As the first Black woman in the role of superintendent of the School District of Philadelphia, the pressures Clayton faced were uniquely tied to her racial identity, the ways she operationalized this identity as a professional, and her racial allegiance.[7] These pressures were rooted in the district's chronic underfunding, its racial and political climate, and its legacies of patronage and rampant fraud; in Clayton's own tensions between racial allegiance and shifting race-based priorities; and in a multiplicity of interpretations regarding what it meant to fight for Black people.[8] A cultural politics of race interrogates "how the 'problem' speaks back" to educational policy that informs and, in some ways, attempts to contain Black lives.[9] This chapter examines how Clayton was problematized, how she spoke back, and how Black educators navigated her tenure as superintendent. Would liberalism's avowed social mobility be possible for underresourced students, most of whom were Black, in a school district led by a Black woman for the first time? Could a Black woman leading the public schools prevent the legacy of racism in the schools? The Constance Clayton era in Philadelphia would examine this query.

Welcome to the Terrordome

When Clayton became "the head teacher of Philadelphia" in 1982, the city was heavy laden with poverty and a lack of resources, which expanded through the years into an ever-growing drug culture, the AIDS crisis, the crack cocaine epidemic, the War on Drugs, neighborhood shootings, community policing, and mandatory minimum drug sentences.[10] The eleven years of Clayton's tenure as superintendent spanned the United States presidencies of Ronald Reagan, George H. W. Bush, and Bill Clinton. As such, Clayton and Philly's public schools were subjected to three different presidents' approaches to governance, civil rights, and the administration of the United States Department of Education. The federal funds that once trickled into cities during the 1970s dried up significantly under Reagan, with Bush continuing in the same vein.[11] The economic downturn of the 1970s, which extended into the 1980s, was felt by the Philadelphia schools. With both unemployment and inflation high, the City of Philadelphia and its public schools were faced with a population that was becoming Blacker, more Spanish-speaking, and more Asian and that needed more resources for which the federal government decreased its support.[12] City governments needed to do more with less. Reagan's neoliberal governmental practices influenced Clayton's methods of leadership and management.[13] Further, Reagan's National Commission on Excellence in Education released the 1983 report, *A Nation at Risk: The Imperative for Educational Reform.* This report bemoaned the omnipresence of grossly underperforming public school students and teachers, substituting public school systems and their educators for poverty as the new national concern of political pundits, education policymakers, school stakeholders, and taxpayers alike.[14]

Following the financial and morale decline in Philly's public schools during the 1970s and beginning of the 1980s, school district stakeholders were looking for a superintendent who would have everyone's respect and could bring pride and life back to Philadelphia's public schools.[15] The new superintendent would need to solve recurring labor problems, restore public confidence in the public schools, and reroute the dysfunctional work culture left by Marcase and the remaining members of Rizzo's Board of Education.[16] By 1982, Black Philadelphians had grown tired of waiting for access to top posts in the city. The Black Political Forum had led to the election of several Black candidates who separated themselves from the Democratic machine.[17] The highest-ranked African Americans were Mayor Bill Green's managing director W. Wilson Goode and Donald Garvatt, a deputy commissioner of the Philadelphia Police Department.[18] Previous quests of Black contenders for the school district's top position had been fruitless.[19] Mayor Green's board sought a financial wizard and brilliant educator. They began a national search that they expected to last six months to a year.[20] A cacophony of Black Philadelphians urged that the new superintendent be Black.[21]

The pressure was mounting for Mayor Green, and he was embattled on several fronts.[22] His ability to be reelected was questionable, and his relationship with Black Philadelphians was in danger.[23] Green was perceived as blocking Black opportunity and progress in Philadelphia.[24] He was mayor during the most brutal of Philadelphia's teacher strikes in 1981, when schools did not open until November. He was in a battle of appearances with Wilson Goode, who had negotiated an agreement with the teachers' union that Green reneged on.[25] The mayor did not select the superintendent of schools; the Board of Education selected the superintendent. But the mayor did appoint board members, and they needed to choose a Black superintendent if Green had any hopes of winning back Black voters, who could assure him victory in his next campaign if he ran again for mayor. He also needed to assuage the Philadelphia Federation of Teachers. Green and influential Black political leaders in Philadelphia, including Goode, supported Clayton for superintendent.[26] The *Philadelphia Tribune* declared Clayton was the "best prepared, best organized, the most determined, and more importantly, the right person in the right place at the right time."[27] As associate superintendent of early childhood for the district, Clayton had a track record of excellence, and union members acknowledged Clayton's competence.[28] Her career with the school district began in 1955, when she student-taught at Paul Lawrence Dunbar Junior High School, which she had also attended as a student. She rose steadily up the district's ranks, holding several central office positions of increasing responsibility and status. Through all her positions, she had established herself as a "no nonsense educator dedicated to the welfare of children," a committed administrator with high expectations and a record of good results.[29] On October 4, 1982, the board appointed Clayton as superintendent of Philly's public schools.[30] A *Philadelphia Tribune* editorial rejoiced with, "The future of our children is now in good hands."[31]

Ten years later, many Philadelphians were frustrated and impatient with Mayor Goode.[32] His eight years in office had been beleaguered by his deadly mishandling of the police bombing of the MOVE organization's house on May 13, 1985.[33] And despite being a Wharton graduate, Goode maintained budget deficits for most of his tenure as mayor.[34] Goode's tenure did no favors for Clayton as she led Philly's public schools, especially when trying to secure much-needed revenue for the city's schools from the city and the state.[35] City Council rarely acquiesced. With Goode's successor, Ed Rendell, a new political landscape became apparent, which led to Clayton's unexpected retirement in the summer of 1993.[36]

Connie's Girls

Clayton's selection to lead the School District of Philadelphia was racially symbolic because it disrupted the hold whites and men had had on the superintendence since the district's inception.[37] Black educators and community members saw life coming to the district again when Clayton took the lead.[38] Many credited her with opening doors and giving opportunities to those who had previously been denied access.[39] They also indicated that the district flourished during the Clayton era, attributed to the nexus of her understanding Philadelphia personally, professionally, and racially, whereas other superintendents, specifically those who came after her, did not. As such, Clayton conveyed stability for a system that had been in flux for years.[40] Some even distinguish her superintendence by deliberately referring to it as a "reign," citing her eleven-year-long leadership as evidence for her preeminence.[41] Clayton emphasized the equality of resource distribution across the district, dismissing the notion that the best resources belonged "up the Boulevard" in the Northeast (and mostly white) neighborhoods of Philadelphia.[42] She was well aware of and determined to resist the racially entrenched politics within the school district. She insisted that the district focus on the needs of students, not the financial needs of adults.[43] Clayton established trust by valuing merit and building partnerships with businesses and foundations.[44] She inspired widespread confidence.[45]

Still, Clayton's leadership style gave some people pause. Her administration was hierarchical and opaque, there were policy implementation issues, she put undue pressure on school principals, and there was little interoffice collaboration.[46] Politically, Clayton also made people somewhat uncomfortable. In a system where political favors had historically been bought and sold and superintendents were beholden to various political factions and entities, Clayton demanded otherwise. The *Philadelphia Tribune* described her as tough and stubborn.[47] As Torch Lytle recalled:

> But when Connie was named superintendent ... a succession of influentials came to see her to tell her how things would operate. Among them was Bob O'Donnell, who was the Speaker of the House in Pennsylvania. ... And they all came to tell her how we do business here in Pennsylvania and Philadelphia. And to each one of them she said, *I am sorry, but that ain't how it gonna be.* And the idea that she will sort of put a thumb on each of these people just sort of blew people away.[48]

Clayton insisted on meritocracy while advocating Black excellence, Black upward mobility, and Black access to opportunity.[49] She brought nationally recognized Black scholars, such as Asa Hilliard and Linda Darling-Hammond, to Philadelphia to provide professional development and training for its educators.[50] Locally, she was decidedly not neutral in prioritizing Black women in professional appointments.[51] There was even a group of Black women educators who modeled themselves after her leadership and proudly referred to themselves as "Connie's girls."[52] Black educators saw some conflicts between how Clayton viewed and advanced Black men and women in the district.[53] As Joe shared:

> Black people did get power under Constance Clayton. ... And as a result of that, many Black people got promotions, got in some good positions to do some things. The thing I believe is that many Black people also were not ready to take certain positions because they didn't go to [get] their credentials, especially Black men. Because at one time the School District was controlled mostly by Black women. So Black men were not in a position to do a lot of things. I think it was a credential issue, some of it. And it might have been also a gender issue, especially under Dr. Clayton. Yeah. That's what I think.[54]

Jim explained:

> Under Dr. Clayton's regime, a lot of the people who were there were African-American females. They were on top, but they were good. If it hadn't been for them, I probably wouldn't be in a position today. Okay? Because they would come to you and say, *Look, this is what we have to do. This is how it has to be done.*[55]

While there was the perception that competent Black women were promoted with preference under Clayton's leadership, according to activist LeRoi Simmons, even when Clayton tried to include Black men in the promotions, there was extensive opposition from white people in power.[56]

The State of the School District

Educators across racial lines to trusted Clayton to be fair and balanced.[57] She insisted that school administrators not be isolated at district headquarters or alienated from school buildings.[58] She wanted even her financial and facilities staffs to remain in touch with the business of educating children because she viewed them as her most important stakeholders. Depending on how success is measured, Clayton was, arguably, the most successful superintendent of this modern era. She established new graduation requirements (last updated in 1947) and an improved bond rating, and no strikes occurred.[59] One of the most noted achievements of Clayton's superintendence was the development and implementation of the locally created standardized citywide curriculum and testing program in 1986, a shift from previous administrations use of the Iowa Test of Basic Skills and the California Achievement Test.[60] Prior to this instructional reform, there was inconsistency in what students in the same grades and same subjects were learning in various schools across the city.[61] Until her leadership, it seemed as though it was not possible to think about education quality in Philly schools.[62] Though not everyone agreed with the standardization or the pacing schedule, Black educators and community members recalled this important instructional innovation and described her as being ahead of her time with the curriculum and assessment efforts.[63] As opposed to the more punitive measures that educators felt resulted from the No Child Left Behind Act of 2001, which came sixteen years after Clayton's instructional reforms, Clayton's standardized curriculum and citywide testing program were geared toward consistent instruction and testing for instruction improvement, not testing for teacher and school accountability.[64] John, a Black Philly educator who graduated from the district in 2000, recalled being a student during the Clayton era:

> I remember being celebrated for academic achievements. I think the awards used to be called the Academics Plus Award or something like that, where we got a little plaque, went to Temple, to McGonigle Hall [and were] celebrated. ... I remember taking the citywide tests or something like that, but I don't remember our teachers stressing over it AT ALL.[65]

Nina described this new curriculum effort this way:

> Math levels and reading levels and you needed to show proficiency before graduating. It's very interesting that some of that stuff has come back around and yet when Connie Clayton was doing it, the focus seemed to me to be on providing structure and support for us to do what we needed to do for our children. ... We weren't under the kind of pressure that it was about *If you need to cheat, cheat.* That *it's the scores that are most important, not if the children are actually learning.* It really was *Okay, if these children don't get it, this is what you need to do in order to be able to get them to the next level.* So you get chance after chance after chance in order to teach these children this particular information or this content.[66]

There was concern over the development and implementation of these curricula—that perhaps Clayton was not transparent enough with test scores and did not focus enough on principal and school-based buy-in to the new instructional efforts they would need to implement.[67] Some educators did not agree with her plans or her implementation approach, but they trusted that she wanted the best for the students in SDP.[68]

Clayton and the Board of Education took on several controversial issues during her tenure. As one of the oldest urban public high schools in the nation, Central High School admitted only young men, while Philadelphia High School for Girls, its fellow single-sex institution, was less than two blocks away. In 1984, young women were admitted to Central, and the board opted not to oppose the court's ruling, despite requests to appeal, not just from those who wanted to keep Central all-male but also from those who feared the elite Philadelphia High School for Girls would suffer a brain drain as a result of this ruling.[69] The board also adopted policies that acknowledged AIDS as a public health issue of grave concern, as well a policy to keep pregnant girls in school while being cognizant of their needs.[70] The Adolescent Health and Sexuality policy of 1991 allowed for the distribution of condoms in high schools, twenty years after students first petitioned the board to do something about the rising cases of sexually transmitted diseases that impacted students as early as 1970.[71] This policy also encouraged teens to wait for a "mutually monogamous relationship" before having sex.[72] There were continual protests regarding the distribution of condoms in Philadelphia high schools from those who said it was taking too long versus those who said should not happen at all.[73] Conservative protesters also sought an abstinence-only approach that urged marriage as the sole mutually monogamous relationship.[74]

School Desegregation

Philadelphia had been working on its voluntary school desegregation plan for two decades before Clayton arrived, and one year after she became superintendent, she released her highly anticipated modified school desegregation plan.[75] Board member Helen Oakes commented that Clayton's was the first plan since Mark Shedd's plan of 1968, which focused on student learning, not just the physical rearrangement of students' racialized bodies. Clayton lauded her plan as being realistic and morally sound.[76] The Pennsylvania Human Relations Commission approved this revised desegregation plan, and the board president, Herman Mattleman, gave Clayton credit for achieving what the school district had been attempting since 1968.[77] But the plan was not without its drawbacks, critics, and lawsuits.[78] Parents came repeatedly to board meetings to voice their concerns over the desegregation plan and to offer suggestions for improvement.[79] When this plan was enacted, the School District of Philadelphia was comprised of 64.4 percent Black students, 8.4 percent Latino/Hispanic students, 2.3 percent Asian students, and less than 1 percent Indigenous students, which made the district approximately 75 percent students of color.[80] The district had seventy-one desegregated schools in 1985 and eighty-four in 1987.[81] By 1993, the Human Relations Commission filed suit arguing that the district had not adequately desegregated the majority of its schools, and they wanted mandated busing. The district's argument was that it was impossible to fully desegregate given the racial composition of students in Philadelphia's schools.[82] The idea that white students would leave the Northeast section of the city to desegregate schools incensed many residents, including City Controller Jonathan Saidel, who remarked, "I would never approve sending children to parts of the city that looked like 'East Beirut.'"[83] By April 1993, Judge Smith rejected mandatory busing, but the desegregation lawsuit with the Human Relations Commission would continue until 2009.[84]

As state institutions that often uphold white supremacy amid claims of racial neutrality and equality, public schools can be oppressive for marginalized people. There is a gap in the ideology of correcting America's racism: it is that distance between racism and the social pressure to remediate racism with race-neutral color evasiveness. As Philadelphia's first Black school superintendent, Clayton was expected to be the lead representative of the state and its oppression as delivered through the public schools. Thus, her desegregation plan was problematic for a number of reasons. Clayton's modified desegregation plan increased "opportunities for children to interact across racial lines," but mere interracial social interaction represents a tepid, surface-level misconception that racial mingling will solve racism.[85] It demonstrates either a gross misunderstanding of racism as the nefarious result of prejudice combined with state power, or it reflects an avoidance of that knowledge by using interaction to substitute for changing the racist power structure. Too much of the district's work under the modified desegregation plan fostered color-evasive multiculturalism that did not take into consideration the real and material structural barriers created by white supremacy that are part and parcel of every iota of school districts.[86] As such, Clayton's approach to school desegregation did not disrupt the racially or economically stratified school system, its resources, or its power arrangements.[87]

Budget Cuts

By the late 1980s, neoliberalism was gaining traction in Philly schools by way of bond deals, private philanthropy paying for public school elements, and the outsourcing of maintenance and nursing services at some schools.[88] In order to meet the annual balanced budget requirement of Philadelphia's home rule charter, Clayton reduced management structures and costs to yield a more efficient school system, just as Superintendent Marcase had done.[89] Early on in her tenure, Clayton reduced positions in some departments, eliminated positions in others, and instituted some forced demotions.[90] These cuts could be evidence that the superintendent was a hatchet woman, but they could also be evidence that she was removing people who were unqualified and had been given patronage posts by her predecessor. The budget situation from 1988 and beyond was particularly difficult. On May 31 that year, Clayton said the school district and the Philadelphia Federation of Teachers had reached a tentative agreement that included both educational improvement and fair wages. She, Mayor Goode, and the Board of Education's president, Mattleman, were in agreement, and they expected City Council to deliver new tax revenue that would have generated $325 million through 1993. That would have still left the district with a shortfall of $253 million that Clayton expected to make up through management shifts—like school consolidations, local district reorganizations, and professional downsizing—she had already implemented throughout her time at the helm. It would have left the school district needing another $143 million, which Goode, Mattleman, and Clayton expected to get from city, state, and federal funds. City Council members Burrell, Clark, Ortiz, and Tasco supported this plan, but the thirteen other members of City Council did not. Council approved forward funding instead of year by year in language but not in the deed of guaranteeing multiyear revenue. City Council wanted the district not to honor its contract with the teachers' union, but Clayton was unwilling to renege on the agreements she had made with the union because it could jeopardize her ability to continue to stave off strikes. She had already gone public with her position that teachers "need and deserve a salary increase." The district had forged an agreement with the union in 1985 with which board members struggled. On the one hand, many people were still traumatized by the bitter strike of 1981, when school did not start until November. Some voted against the ratification of the 1985 contract and issued a resolution stating they knew they could not fund the second and third years of the agreement unless City Council increased tax revenues by $9 million by May 29, 1986.[91] Most board members knew that if the revenue was not secured by 1988, mayhem could ensue in the city once again. Clayton had been pushing the mayor and City Council on this point and had enjoined business leaders and community advocates to urge this point on their behalf.[92] Because the City of Philadelphia was in financial disarray, City Council did not generate the additional funds the school district needed.[93] Clayton responded with cuts in services and programs and said the following:

> Let me be clear, the program deferrals and program reductions will hurt. There is no easy or painless way to take that amount of money out of this budget. But we will because we must. ... As I said in my testimony to City Council, what we have proposed is a very modest beginning to the obvious need to improve our facilities. This need will not go away. With delay the need simply grows more urgent. Even more urgent are the needs of the children who would have been served by full-day kindergarten and the families who would have been served by the family support workers. These were not items on a wish list—they were responses to very real needs and concerns. However, the fiscal constraints require otherwise. ...The elected leadership of this City has responded. We are duty bound to abide by that response.[94]

For the rest of that year and the remaining years of her tenure, citizens continued to bemoan programmatic and service cuts. Parents complained about proposed or suspected cuts at two neighborhood comprehensive high schools and one special-admission magnet high school.[95] People fought a reduction in the music programs at Girls High and at Central High School, two special-admission magnet programs. But the district had moved into school-based budgets and decentralized management, so Clayton could not be blamed for the specific choices principals made with their budgets at this point.[96] When people came to ask that guidance counselors not be cut, Clayton responded that there would be a realignment of guidance counselors, not a reduction.[97] In 1991, the eight neighborhood districts that comprised the School District of Philadelphia were condensed into six regions. Clayton made it clear that that reorganization was not her recommendation.[98] People rejected the elimination of the cooperative education work program at Germantown High School, particularly concerned with the harmful impacts these cuts would have on students of color.[99] Clayton explained, "We have tried to use the most skillful scalpel possible in maintaining the educational program."[100] Fully resolved in the reality of no additional funding for Philly's schools, Clayton asked everyone involved with the district to do more with less, as that was the mandate she had been given.

The Race Woman

By 1987, Clayton's national reputation as an urban education leader was well-established. She was active in the Council of Great City Schools and would become its president in the next few years.[101] In a review of her work, the Board of Education "determined that Dr. Clayton's performance as Superintendent has been exemplary in all respects and that her comprehensive school improvement and education reform programs have fostered a restoration of public confidence in and support for public education in general, and this School District in particular." They extended her contract again and increased her annual salary, from $68,000 to $85,000 to $100,000 to forestall the departure of this national education star to an urban district faced with challenges similar to those in Philadelphia.[102] New York City was considering her for its schools' chancellor position, but late in December 1987, Clayton removed herself from consideration, explaining that she was

> a native Philadelphian with deep affection and strong commitment to this city. And while this school district has traveled a great distance over the past five years, there is still a long way to go. ... There are also matters of the unfinished agenda. ... In focusing on student success, we must resist the temptation to embrace a one-dimensional view of success: Complex problems rarely have simple solutions. While simple solutions might be beguiling, they are too often misleading and just plain wrong. This School District will not be

measured, nor we will allow the success of our children to be measured by any one single indicator—

Not solely by scores on any individual test

Not solely by Drop-out rates

Not solely by the number of desegregated schools.[103]

Toward the end of the summer of 1988, the reverence and respect widely held for Clayton dissipated rapidly when she went under fire for using race- and class-based ideology to guide her budget priorities and racially coded language to explain budget cuts. A budget shortfall and showdown that year elucidated Philly's longstanding racial divide, left Clayton at odds with white people in the Northeast part of the city, and led Philadelphia business leaders to lose confidence in her. Budgets are always political; they always represent the prioritizing of finite resources toward infinite needs.[104] That 1988 moment brought back to the forefront Clayton's racial allegiance to Black people. White Philadelphians—particularly white ethnics in South Philly, some areas of Southwest Philly, and throughout the Northeast part of the city—had tolerated her racial identity, provided it was absent of racial allegiance. When she revealed her loyalties, their zero-sum ideology charged back at her forcefully. The racial politics of white Philadelphia had long held that any educational advance for Blacks represented a loss for them and their children.[105] Thus, it was unsurprising that white Philadelphians who had trusted her, if only superficially, abandoned her after that summer 1988 moment. Linda recalled the instance this way:

> I feel very sad [that] truth telling gets you in trouble. … Connie Clayton made a statement that was authentically true, but Black women have always gotten in trouble for telling the truth, and I feel as though she got in trouble for telling the truth. … She used the phrase *historically privileged*, and they crucified her for that. That she was gonna concentrate on resources going places where the need is, that there were some historically privileged areas that always got *dadada*, and she wanted to have some balance to that.[106]

Philadelphia's City Council had passed a budget with less than what the district needed for full funding. In order to balance the budget and honor the contract with the teachers' union, Clayton needed to cut some district programs or services. She proposed cutting busing programs that paid for students who lived in Philadelphia but attended private schools, as well as closing six daycare centers, five of which were located in the Northeast section of the city.[107] Northeast Philadelphia had been known to be mostly white and more affluent than most other parts of the city. Clayton's rationale for making cuts that targeted this section of the city was that parents there were better able to pay for private daycare than were those in other sections of Philadelphia. Furthermore, though the state legislated that the local public school system must provide buses for public and private school students who live in Philadelphia, the state did not provide enough funds to Philadelphia to cover the cost of this requirement. The *Philadelphia Tribune* estimated that following this mandate, busing cost more than $12 million but the state contributed only $5 million. City Council people from the Northeast were furious.[108] Clayton explained that she and the school district would be committed to all children but that there had to be a special allegiance to children who had the fewest resources, "children who are most at risk and most in need." Clayton attempted to present this as a financial management problem:

> This one-year-at-a-time / ignore-the-future approach to fiscal management is myopic and irresponsible. It may make good copy and seem like good politics, but it is bad management and even worse policy. Too many of us remember too well the trauma associated with that approach. We remember talk of bankruptcy and bailouts. We remember a school district unable to pay its bills and unable to fulfill its contractual obligations. Most of all, we remember a school district where education of our children was constantly disrupted by programmatic fits and starts, layoffs, and labor strife. … There are those among us who will always choose in favor of the historically privileged. That is a luxury the school district, this city and our society can ill afford. When compelled to choose, we must choose in favor of those children most at risk and most in need, even if they are not the loudest or most connected.[109]

Clayton's public articulation of her commitment to underresourced children and communities marked the turning point in her tenure. She substituted racial identifiers with the coded language of "historically privileged," but Northeast Philly residents knew to whom she was referring. Beyond the socioeconomic issue inherent in these budget constraints, Clayton's chosen cuts made her racial allegiance evident, and her racial allegiance angered many whites.[110]

Black educators and community members had long been concerned that school resources and opportunities were based on where one lived and attended school in Philadelphia, and Clayton shared this concern.[111] She tried to present her budget allocations as a social justice issue; she saw herself as an advocate of the marginalized and disadvantaged. While some Black community members hailed Clayton for being brave enough to say in public, from her elevated position, what Black people often spoke privately, Clayton's comment brought pushback and criticism from white people, highlighting the discrimination they believed they had experienced. Northeast Philadelphia Democratic City Council member Joan Krajewski commented, "I'm tired of this nonsense. We've got to get rid of her."[112] According to white veteran district administrator, June Smith, many whites in the Northeast held onto the notion that the schools in their section of the city were neglected as long as Clayton was at the helm:

> But that really was how the Northeast felt. And you could see it on the Board, the Board politics. Lurie and Mills were the two white men on the Board of Education at the time. And I think when Dr. Clayton left, there was a bit of, *okay, finally now the Northeast would get its fair share.*[113]

Due to calls for Clayton's resignation and increasing harassment at her home and office, the Philadelphia Police Department assigned officers to escort and protect her.[114] Northeast Philly politicians rejected Clayton's cuts and comments. Republican State Senator Frank Salvatore claimed, "She's polarizing the city with her remarks. I don't think she's ever going to be fair to us. We want our fair share of services here."[115] An editorial in the *Philadelphia Inquirer* remarked,

> The reason that her remarks have caused a minor squall—and that her decision to close the day-care centers has caused such furor—is that, in truth, there are very few people in this city who can credibly be called historically privileged. (And just about all of them send their kids to private schools.) Most white Philadelphians are the recent descendants of immigrants, people who fled poverty and persecution in their homelands and found no red carpet awaiting them on Ellis Island. They worked their way out of poverty—in some cases, just barely—encountering no shortage of discrimination along the way. While the immigrant experience certainly compares favorably with the black experience, privileged is not the word that leaps to mind.

Ms. Clayton's rhetoric would hardly be worth comment if it were coming from a speaker at a street rally. But she is in a position of power in this city and has to be extra careful not to give the impression that she has any racial axes to grind. Earlier in her remarks to the board, she reaffirmed her commitment to "serving all children entrusted to our care," a view "by no means inconsistent with our recognizing a special obligation to those children who are most at risk and in need." If only she'd stopped talking then.[116]

Northeast residents and the mainstream newspaper resisted the notion that whites were in any way privileged. Their use of words like "fair share" and articulating the Ellis Island immigration experience as only slightly better than the lives of those captured in Africa, the Middle Passage, slavery, and Jim Crow experience demonstrated their demand for a race-neutral evasive ideology to which Clayton did not subscribe.[117]

Clayton led the district for five more years after this incident, but this episode highlighted the racial lines that had always been a part of Philadelphia. Despite weathering her "historically privileged" moment of 1988, Clayton never fully regained the trust of white people in the Northeast or the confidence of business leaders in Philadelphia. Corporate executives and foundations that once supported her leadership began questioning her judgment and wanted more say in the direction of their partnerships.

Private-Public Access and Accountability

Part of the way that Clayton brought public confidence to and faith in the school district was by inviting businesses to be involved with the city's schools. In 1984, she began the Adopt a School program, where organizations could make contributions of funds, resources, or services to individual schools.[118] The Board of Education seemed to value this shift toward neoliberalism: private funds supplementing needs the public funds did not meet.[119] Local banks gave money to fund the district's JobSearch Program, Philadelphia Alliance for Teaching Humanities in the Schools (PATHS), and Philadelphia Renaissance in Science and Mathematics (PRISM).[120] The William Penn Foundation (led at the time of giving by a Black former school district administrator, Bernard Watson), Pew Memorial Foundation, and Pew Charitable Trusts gave several multimillion-dollar grants to the district.[121] Valuing corporate partners became a feature of Clayton's tenure.[122] But after her public indictment of the "historically privileged," many of her cabinet members left their posts, and concerns grew over her ability to maintain strong relationships with her colleagues and business leaders.[123] Critics claimed she wanted the support of the business community but did not want their input on educational matters. Business leaders wanted her to be more accountable to them—focused on outward accountability and not just the inner accountability of educators.[124] Though some Black educators believed students performed better academically during her tenure, widespread student achievement did not improve the way people had hoped it would despite her standardized curriculum and citywide testing programs.[125]

Clayton and the Board Presidents

Throughout her leadership, Clayton worked with the Board of Education through three presidents: Herman Mattleman (1983–1990), Ruth Hayre (1991–1992), and Rotan Lee (1993–1994). Mattleman often sang Clayton's praises and acknowledged the strengths and diligence she brought to her work.[126] But Clayton's strongest relationship was with Hayre. Hayre was the first Black senior high school principal in Philadelphia, and after her retirement in 1976, she served as a consultant on the search committee that ultimately brought Clayton to Philly's top schools' post.[127] As Hayre wrote in her memoir *Tell Them We Are Rising*:

> My desire to ensure that she had at least one firm friend on the board led me back to the school system. Dr. Clayton encouraged my interest in a seat on the board, the mayor approved, and in due time they appointed me. ... In December 1990, I was persuaded by Mayor Wilson Goode with the board's overwhelming backing to accept its presidency—the first woman to head the board of education.[128]

What distinguished Mattleman's relationship with Clayton from Hayre's relationship with her is the sisterly, mutually reverent way they described one another, referring to each other as "mentor." Additionally, while Mattleman always spoke well of Clayton in public, Hayre often took the lead on articulating the need for controversial policy herself. She made it clear that she stood with Clayton, beside her always and in front of her, to block opposition for her, if need be. Although Hayre had no intention of becoming board president, Lee nominated her for the position in 1990:

> When Rotan Lee came to me and announced that he wished to be a candidate and asked me for my support, I agreed. I believed him to be exceptionally bright, competent, and able to sustain the level of leadership to which the Board has grown accustomed. When it became evident that he could not effect political relationships necessary to be the Board's President, he, along with Mayor Goode, Dr. Christine Torres-Matrullo, and the leaders of the Parents Union encouraged me to seek the presidency.[129]

Given Hayre's assessment of Lee's political relationships, it makes sense that the he and Clayton had a difficult relationship.[130] An ambitious Black attorney, Lee helped the Board of Education create its affirmative action plan in 1984.[131] Mayor Goode nominated him to the board in 1989.[132] In 1991, Lee and Clayton displayed tension publicly during a board meeting. Black community members came to the meeting requesting a revised curriculum guide for Black studies that would be published by 1992, an infusion of African-centered content, and the reexamination and implementation of effective Afrocentric goals.[133] Lee responded that African studies was very important to him, specifically bringing in Black achievement into history curricula. He said that the community should continue to "force and cajol [*sic*] to make sure this process takes place." Clayton appreciated the speakers but responded, "it is not necessary to force and cajol [*sic*]," and she assured the audience that Black studies mattered to her.[134] That brief interaction seemed to call into question who between them was more committed to Black people and the process by which advocacy should happen. Lee seemed to advocate force. Clayton advocated a milder stance, perhaps offended at the notion that her administration would need to be pushed into concern for Black students. As Clayton was the public face and highest representative of the school district, she needed to defend her administration, and thus, she had to straddle between defending and protecting Black people, managing Black folks' impressions of her commitment to them, and advocating for her administration.

Clayton credited Lee for the key role he played during the 1992 contract negotiation between the school district and the teachers' union, calling him "the man of the hour," more involved in negotiations than members of any previous Board of Education. Lee also lauded Clayton for being a visionary.[135]

Though there were rumors of a rift between Clayton and Lee, a letter to the *Philadelphia Tribune* challenged that characterization, saying, "there is nothing that can separate Clayton and Lee except mountains and water. ... Their dedication and responsibility in producing and fertilizing the minds of present and future generations is beyond the muddy waters of faction and disunity."[136] But a staff member at the *Tribune* saw the Clayton-Lee situation differently. He referred to Lee as both the Clarence Thomas and the Bugs Bunny of the district; he criticized him for being disrespectful to Clayton and for trying to usurp her authority, for not deferring to her opinion, for conspiring with Mayor Rendell to exaggerate white fears about school integration in the city, and for advancing his own political agenda instead of representing the consensus of the board.[137] While Clayton had never let on that she was considering retirement, Lee alluded to the potential for it on more than one occasion.[138] The *Tribune* wrote, "the superintendent was wearied out of her responsibility and wanted out."[139] LeRoi Simmons described Clayton's exit this way:

> She kind of took charge in a good way, in my view, and she was kind of empowered by the sisters, the brothers and sisters on the Board, because she was making a difference. ... And when they really started messing with her is when she realized she wasn't going to be able to educate anymore and she stepped down. I don't think she was removed. I think she stepped away. And that's why I called it a reign, 'cause she decided when she was going to leave. She decided when she was going to go. I think she had full control. And I think she's the last one that had full control. They might've broke it up because of her. But she had full control and she really cared. ... She had a whole lot of stuff that she never got done. But she got a lot of stuff done. I loved her, you know. And we rumbled, because you know, ain't nobody gonna get along with Connie every day. You know. But I never challenged her heart. I never challenged her desire to lift children. I never challenged that 'cause I could see that. There were others that I challenged on that.[140]

In July 1993, she announced that her resignation/retirement would be effective August 31, 1993. Despite the length of time of service and her successes, no board member asked Clayton to withdraw her resignation.[141]

4

Ready to Die

Last Rites for Philly's Schools, 1994–2001

*If Mr. Hornbeck is not able to radically reform education
in Philadelphia, it will demonstrate that education
reform cannot be facilitated from the inside out
and perhaps will open the door to school choice.*

*—Rotan Lee, president,
Philadelphia Board of Education*[1]

*I don't like it one bit when Bob Dole starts kicking
around teachers and their union for his self-serving
purposes. But if we don't shape up and pay some
attention to that sentiment, I'm not at all certain
that either the PFT or the District—as we know
them—will be here when it is time to sit at the
bargaining table four years from now.*

*—Debra Kahn, member,
Philadelphia Board of Education*[2]

*July 1, 1998 is the date that the School District
[of Philadelphia] will cease to exist in any
recognizable form.*

*—David Hornbeck, superintendent,
School District of Philadelphia*[3]

avid Hornbeck knew a little about Philly. As executive director of the Philadelphia Tutorial Project, he witnessed the student uprising at the School District of Philadelphia's headquarters in 1967.[4] He had also served as deputy counsel to the governor of Pennsylvania and executive deputy secretary of education in the 1970s.[5] By the time Hornbeck returned to Philadelphia to lead its public schools in 1994, in addition to his education work at the state levels in Maryland and Kentucky, he had been the chair of the national commission on Title I and chair of the board of trustees for the Children's Defense Fund.[6] Despite his national reputation of fighting for all children, he was unprepared for what was happening in and to Philly's public schools or the city's adversarial relationship with the Commonwealth of Pennsylvania.[7] The *Philadelphia Tribune* lamented that student achievement was abysmally low in 1994 and that too many adults were looking for ways to milk the school district for its spoils instead of focusing on children and student achievement.[8] As this chapter explores, David Hornbeck was hailed as a "white knight" by the *Baltimore Sun* one year after he arrived in Philly, but his saviorism ultimately led to the district's disbanding and virtual demise.[9] While he raised consciousness regarding the pervasive low expectations many had for Philadelphia's children, Hornbeck employed deficit discourses to raise this consciousness. His approach to school reform lacked dialogue, coalition building, and local context, and it was not inclusive of those most affected by reform.[10] Hornbeck was a Philly outsider, a white savior who had good intentions he could not deliver on and reforms he could not fund.[11] When the Pennsylvania General Assembly wouldn't budge on its funding formulas, he accused Assembly of racism. But this accusation would prove to be an ineffective motivator for state officials to increase funds. And the school district would pay for Hornbeck's miscalculation well into the next century.

The 1990s

The president of Philadelphia's Board of Education, Rotan Lee, bemoaned implementing budget reductions yet again. After cutting $90 million from the budget, the district would need to cut another $30 million by the end of May 1994 if it did not receive additional funds from the city or the state. Plus, federal Title I funding was being cut.[12] Lee hoped for the "restoration of revenues" and said the board would begin more adamant political advocacy for other ways to fill funding holes.[13] He said, "The District cannot continue to cut. The City government must decide where education falls within its priorities and to fund public education."[14] The school district was struggling with itself, with the city, with the state, with taxpayers, and with community members. There was an ominous sense that a miracle was needed for Philly's public schools to survive. While Constance Clayton had made improvements to the district after the disarray and dysfunction she inherited from Michael Marcase, all was not well in this school system of 195,000 students in 256 schools in 1993.[15] Shared governance and school-based management had proven complicated in implementation.[16] Decentralization made principals more responsible for programmatic, resource, and people cuts at their schools.[17] The results were mixed. Some parents spoke of insufficient instructional materials, school security, and building maintenance as the result of fiscal inequity rampant within and throughout the district, while others discussed school overcrowding.[18] There was also concern about poor air quality in schools, insect and rodent control, painting and plastering, bathroom renovations, glass pane replacement, and unsafe gyms.[19] Black parents and community members were concerned about neighborhood violence; children being educationally, physically, and emotionally mistreated by school personnel; and the underfunding of African American studies.[20] The Board of Education adopted a multiracial-multicultural-gender education policy "to foster knowledge about and respect for those of all race, ethnic groups, social classes, genders, religions, disabilities, and sexual orientations."[21] Though this new policy was developed while the district was still cutting programmatic funding, Lee said the cuts would have the least impact on instruction and the offices focused on Black, Latinx, and Asian students.[22]

The 1990s were a wild time for racial tensions. The nation watched major racial events unfold on their television screens: the Anita Hill/Clarence Thomas case showed a highly educated Black woman interrogated by powerful white men about the violations she experienced from a highly educated Black man who would soon be a US Supreme Court justice. Video footage looped constantly of Black Rodney King being beaten by white Los Angeles police officers, followed by King imploring people of different races to "get along" once LA erupted with violence when those police officers were acquitted. White Reginald Denny was beaten by Black rioters on the streets of LA without police intervention. Black adolescent Latasha Harlins was shot in the head on video in LA, and the Asian store owner who killed her was convicted of manslaughter but received no prison time. America watched Black O. J. Simpson in the slow-moving white Bronco after his white former wife and her friend were found dead. Many Black Americans rejoiced when Simpson was acquitted of their murders, while most white people felt that justice had not been served. During this cultural and political moment, Black storytellers came into the mainstream depicting the complex challenges and beauty of Black lives in America, while Louis Farrakhan brought Black men to Washington, DC, from across the country for a public day of atonement. At the same time, liberals and conservatives wrestled on the ideological plane regarding political correctness, personal responsibility, and ways to meet the needs of various racial and ethnic groups extending beyond the Black/white binary. In Philly, the Board of Education was looking to be in compliance with the latest desegregation order for its public schools.[23] Despite the Black student majority in Philadelphia's public schools, the multiracial-multicultural-gender education policy seemed like an effort to persuade people of color to get along, despite having little to no power analysis of the insidious, dangerous nature of white supremacy. Many Black Philadelphians involved with the school district wanted and expected more of a focus on Black people in leadership and in every facet of its schools.

After having had the first Black mayor (from 1984 to 1992), the first Black police chief (Willie Williams, who left Philadelphia for Los Angeles after the Rodney King uprising in 1992), the first Black fire commissioner (Harold B. Hairston), and the first Black woman superintendent of schools, with a Black Board of Education president and vice president (Floyd Alston), there were those who believed the school district should be led, once again, by a Black educator.[24] One finalist for the position was Black, one was white, and both were Philadelphia outsiders. The African-American Chamber of Commerce of Pennsylvania, New Jersey, and Delaware chose the Black candidate, Arthur L. Walton of New York. When Walton withdrew his name for consideration, the Chamber and District Council 33 of the American Federation of State, County, and Municipal Employees (AFSCME) withheld their support from David Hornbeck, believing that Hornbeck's experiences in state education governance had not prepared him for the unique challenges of urban education in general and the specific needs of the majority Black student population in Philadelphia.[25] Hornbeck's school reform work in Kentucky and Maryland were not interpreted as useful to the Philadelphia context, and in 1991, though he had been considered to lead Baltimore City's public schools, that majority Black school district chose a Black educator.[26] Additionally, many were frustrated by what appeared to be the interference of "America's mayor" in the superintendent hiring process. Hornbeck was Mayor Ed Rendell's choice. City Council members and the leader of AFSCME District Council 33 did not feel they had been included in the process. It seemed as though Rendell wanted Hornbeck, and that's who it would be.[27]

Navigating the Landscape

Philadelphia was facing a bleak population forecast and political situation in the 1990s. The city had lost 61,000 people between 1990 and 1994, and in 1992, the city lost 40,000 jobs. Though the city's public school rolls had fallen in the 1980s, enrollment had started increasing at a rate of 3 percent per year. School district leaders estimated the 1994 school year would begin with 15,000 more students than had been enrolled the previous school year. The city's needy population was increasing exponentially, while city revenues and federal subsidies declined.[28] On the national political scene, during a campaign speech, independent presidential candidate Ross Perot referred to the National Association for the Advancement of Colored People audience as "you people," a comment met with disgust and annoyance. Democrat Bill Clinton pandered to Black voters by playing his saxophone on *The Arsenio Hall Show* and then ousted Republican George H. W. Bush from the presidency on the promise of a "change." Two years later, tainted by rumors of his marital infidelity and sexual harassment, a failed attempt at healthcare reform, and accusations of corruption, Clinton had lost much of his popularity.[29] The impact of his administration was local: when it was time for the reauthorization of Title I, which provided funds to poverty-stricken students, funding was slashed, and the threshold for students in poverty was increased to 79.2 percent, devastating cash-strapped school districts in urban centers like Philadelphia.[30] Though the mayor and governor were Democrats when Hornbeck was appointed Philly schools' superintendent in the summer of 1994, Newt Gingrich's national "Contract with America" campaign led to the Republican Revolution that fall, when Republicans swept offices across the country during the midterm elections.[31] At the federal level, they seized control of the Senate and won majorly in the House of Representatives. In Pennsylvania, Republican Tom Ridge won the gubernatorial race, upsetting Lieutenant Governor Mark Sigel, who was ahead in the polls until Ridge ran a racist campaign ad, Pennsylvania's version of the Willie Horton race-baiting television spot Bush the elder ran against Michael Dukakis in 1988.[32]

Philadelphia's political scene was full of its own messiness. As the school district attempted responsiveness to the social needs of the 1990s, personal responsibility and selective moralism were hot-button issues. While President Clinton encouraged heteronormativity in the military with his "Don't ask, don't tell" policy, in Philadelphia, there were disputes over sexuality and gender in public schools, essentially about morality and whose identities mattered.[33] Some fought the multicultural-multiracial-gender education policy's assertion that homosexuality was acceptable.[34] While high-powered automatic machine-gun-toting teens, gangs battling over drug territories, and crack addiction pushed President Clinton to sign the Violent Crime Control and Law Enforcement Act of 1994 (the 1994 Crime Bill), Black educators in Philadelphia were advocating for video cameras in classrooms, in hopes they would ensure better classroom management and deter violence.[35] On the fiscal front, the discord was consistent. Five previous years of forced budget reductions amounted to $158 million and a loss of 2,425 positions from the district. The board supported the city's sin tax—increased taxes on alcohol sold by the drink—though the revenue was not enough to make up for what had been lost.[36] Board President Lee, Mayor Ed Rendell, and Council President John Street agreed to find the needed $30 million.[37] Recognizing the money from City Council was like using a cotton ball to fill a sinkhole, Lee said the district would pursue litigation against the Commonwealth of Pennsylvania regarding inadequate funding. In preparation for the lawsuit, board members met with Philly's state legislators, noting that Philly's own Dwight Evans was the chair of appropriations for the State House. Lee proclaimed, "Representative Evans is an advocate for education and has a budget package that will benefit the School District on the table."[38] This would become debatable when Evans wrote the legislation that ultimately dismantled the school district.

Hornbeck's Theory of Change

There was a lot of pressure on Hornbeck to produce positive results.[39] Problems were plentiful, and the resources were limited. Shortly after Hornbeck assumed the school superintendency, the *Philadelphia Inquirer* lamented public education in Philadelphia. Lee responded the public could "do nothing and watch the demise of public education," or it would restructure the school system, which would cost money.[40] Hornbeck believed precluding poor children from achieving high learning standards was an injustice. He believed both the will for all students to succeed as well as accountability for those responsible were required.[41] Hornbeck deliberately chose Philadelphia in which to operationalize his theory.[42] Philadelphia was the site of the writing, signing, and adoption of the Declaration of Independence, and Hornbeck said that his Children Achieving plan could become "the second Declaration of Independence. … Philadelphia is the place where change in American public education can take place."[43]

Hornbeck began his work as superintendent of schools by promising to change the culture of the district. His attempts at cultural shifts included increasing opportunities to learn since all students could learn at high levels, just not necessarily at the same pace.[44] He also advocated an educator accountability system, which included himself, with merit pay built into his contract. If his performance was unsatisfactory, the Board of Education could decrease his salary by 5 percent each year.[45] This new accountability system for educators would give Hornbeck the authority to create "keystone" and "quest" schools. A "quest" school had "for a variety of reasons, difficulty achieving success with its students." A "keystone" school would be considered "academically distressed," and at least 75 percent of its faculty would be required to transfer. The school would then get a new principal and new teachers (appointed by Hornbeck). This new group and community members would work together to overhaul the school. Keystoned schools would get more resources in the form of counselors, teachers, support services, and supplies.[46]

Children Achieving

Hornbeck's school reform plan for Philadelphia was called Children Achieving.[47] Its tenets were as follows:

1. Set high expectations for everyone by establishing a set of rigorous, challenging graduation standards.
2. Design a system of accountability for everyone.
3. Shrink the centralized bureaucracy and let schools make more decisions.
4. Provide intensive and sustained professional development to all staff.
5. Make sure that all students are ready for school.
6. Provide students with the community supports and services they need to succeed in school.
7. Provide up-to-date technology and instructional materials.
8. Engage the public in shaping, understanding, supporting and participating in school reform.
9. Ensure adequate resources and use them effectively.
10. Be prepared to address all of these priorities together, starting now.[48]

With high expectations as Hornbeck's call to action, the board adopted academic content standards, benchmarks, and performance examples for English language arts, math, science, and the arts; citizenship, communication, multicultural competence, problem-solving, school-to-career readiness, and technology.[49] Hornbeck intended Children Achieving to be phased in starting with the 1995–96 school year and be fully operational by the fall of 1996 at the start of the school year.[50] He wanted Children Achieving enacted urgently.[51] When parents complained that the needs of their students were not being met in schools, Hornbeck would respond with selling points on Children Achieving, stating why it was necessary and positioning it as a balm for everything ailing the city's students.[52] In an effort to show that Children Achieving could yield results when funded, Hornbeck opted to implement it in only a portion of the city's schools at a cost of $40 million. He needed to show results somewhere even though he could not get full funding.[53]

Few people doubted Hornbeck's intentions were to improve the academic outcomes of Philadelphia's students. However, Children Achieving evoked both accolades and cautions. Many Black educators and other community members believed that Hornbeck cared passionately about children of color.[54] Some Black educators and community members saw Children Achieving as revolutionary for American public education at the time, though funding for it was a citywide concern.[55] It took some time before Hornbeck would address how much this plan would cost the school district to implement, but he insisted that full implementation was required if real reform was to take place.[56]

Hornbeck Versus Black Philadelphia

It did not take long for the insider-outsider tensions inherent and apparent with Hornbeck at the helm of Philly's schools to become visible.[57] He had some early missteps, such as this one Torch Lytle described:[58]

> At the Convocation in August—Convocation is when you bring in all the principals in Central Office, senior administrative staff and the Superintendent, sometimes they go for three days, for a week, whatever. But they are the sort of kicking off for the coming school year. And at the Convocation, which Hornbeck was appointed in June and began officially in mid-August, although he was around in July, but at the Convocation at the end of the August, you know, he did one of these trumpets and fanfare routines and gave his ten points of *Children Achieving* thing, talked about another new era and blah, blah, blah, he didn't mention Connie's name at any point at all in his remarks. Which stunned me. Because—and I knew, my number was already up, so that wasn't personal in that regard. But Connie had, she was the first, she had been incredibly successful, she had balanced the budget for every year she'd been here, there'd never been a teacher strike despite all the strikes that had happened during the Marcase era, she had developed a core curriculum, she had put in place a strong assessment program, on and on and on. The District had made incremental gains during the whole time she was superintendent. And it's a sort of textbook case of leadership transitions. You know, how hard is it to say something nice about your predecessor? It's highly symbolic. And here's a guy, a white guy, coming in who is going to take over a predominantly African-American district, who does not honor his predecessor.

Hornbeck did not publicly acknowledge Clayton's work until a year and a half into his position. She mattered to Black Philadelphia, and he either did not consider or misinterpreted how important acknowledging her would be to the educators (especially Black educators) who had worked under her and appreciated her. The tardiness of his acknowledgment was a missed opportunity for him to persuade Black educators to support his leadership. At the same time, Hornbeck was challenging white educators' racism. As Theresa, who worked closely with him, recalled:

> He did a professional development for administrators, principals or whatever. And in his speech he talked about white male privilege. ... Girl, if you had looked around the room and saw, first of all, the number of white men who got up and walked out. ... And the faces of some of the other white folks that he had the nerve to put it out there. That's absolutely white male privilege! I mean, what they thought, that we didn't know? If you're female, you didn't realize that? If you're a man of color? But if you had seen the people. I think that just helped them just go ahead and they just sent him out the door. Because he was sensitive and aware of that stuff.[59]

Black educators' views on Hornbeck's leadership were mixed.[60] Joe recalled, "I really liked Hornbeck. Of course, Hornbeck was really child-centered, to the extent that he would really fight and do everything that he could to help children."[61] Missy, a Black educator who began working in the school district as a Central Office administrator, shared this reflection:

> I loved my job. I enjoyed working under Hornbeck. He was open, willing to hear the teams, like they like to speak often, offer input, was willing to accept the assistance of the experts that he had surrounded himself with. You were just free to do what needed to be done. ... We had professional development. ... We were able to travel and learn, experience new things. ... So under him it was just, we just had this feeling of constant learning and growth. As a professional you felt honored and needed and recognized and part of the process. So it was a great experience.[62]

Other Black community members questioned how his being a minister and attorney qualified him to lead the fifth-largest school district in the nation.[63] As he was never a traditional school-based educator and he was a Philly outsider, there was also significant pushback from various sources on Children Achieving. Reverence for and allegiance to Clayton may have contributed to its lackluster support among Black educators. There were those who did not believe this reform plan could make improvements like Clayton had.[64] Marsha reflected, "I think that he rode on the coattails of Connie, and his idea of change was to destroy what she had created."[65] Elizabeth, a Black educator who relocated to Philadelphia, commented:

> *Children Achieving* made sense to me. But you know, I didn't have all that baggage and history of other people in Philadelphia. People loved Connie and nobody else was gonna get a shot. I didn't have all that. So, if somebody stands in front of me and presents a reasonable platform that's child-centered and wants to get rid of the people who aren't doing their jobs and, you know, isn't part of this good old boy network, I thought he was a decent man.[66]

There was also the concern from some Black educators and community members that Children Achieving was missing a very important high school focus.[67] This was disconcerting, considering less than half of the students who started high school in Philly in 1989 finished high school in four years.[68] Betty, a Black high school administrator shared the following:

> I didn't see anything on his platform that was doing the kinds of things that moved high school instruction. ... It was good in terms of the top, you know, synergy. But it didn't have a specific focus. It didn't have a strategy-based focus. And so I'm in the trenches, now, and saying, *Okay, you've got these ten points now, you know, but where is the actual specific focus? Where are the strategy-based instructions? Where's the corrective reading? ... Where's the specific skill-based intervention that will move these children?* And he didn't have it. I understand he was a nice man. You know, but at that point ... we needed specific interventions to move these children. ... And so what he did was he took the graduation requirements from 21.5 to 23.5 what we have today. He did do that. But that didn't mean rigorous instruction happened in the class-room. All that did mean, then, for the population I was serving at that time at Simon Gratz was give us another hurdle to jump.[69]

Additionally, Hornbeck's processes were unclear.[70] Jim was an administrator responsible for "keystoning" schools during Hornbeck's superintendency. He explained:

> We had no idea what was going on. ... We didn't know what keystone was. We just knew it was the worst thing that could happen to the school. But we had to go in and take over the schools. ... I felt it was punitive because to go to a school like Olney High School and say you're gonna *keystone* that school, you're gonna close it down and do whatever you're going to do, that's more punitive instead of bringing resources in.[71]

Community members also had concerns. If a neighborhood high school was "keystoned," would parents be involved in that process?[72] Hornbeck attempted transparency and community input, but there was a chasm between shared governance of the district in theory and in practice.[73] District policy seemed to preclude parent participation.[74] A parent told the board that when parents ascertained how schools were operating, they were no longer welcomed in the schools. When parents pushed against being banned from the schools their children attended, they also worried about retaliation against their children.[75]

Other critiques of Children Achieving centered on its relationship to school desegregation. While Hornbeck believed there was alignment between Children Achieving and Judge Smith's school desegregation ruling in the district's ongoing litigation, a Black parent complained that Hornbeck was removing programs and structures Judge Smith ordered to stay. The judge wanted all available funds directed toward racially isolated schools. Hornbeck wanted to fund Children Achieving.[76] Some saw Children Achieving as not committed to racial justice and as in conflict with the district's multicultural-multiracial-gender education policy.[77] Others complained that after working for twenty-five years on the issues Judge Smith addressed in her 1995 ruling, the school district needed to prioritize ending the use of uncertified substitute teachers, to encourage parental presence in schools, and to restore vocational education.[78] Children Achieving was mute on culturally appropriate curriculum and materials. Black community members appealed to the board for inaccuracies about Black people to be removed from the curriculum and coursework on African history and culture, as well as African American studies.[79] They were also concerned about school safety, and with the Million Man March a not too distant memory, some community members urged "an Islamic security force would be both an economical and successful means of ending violence in schools."[80] Black community members were also concerned with how Black people were being regarded in schools: Black educators were being unfairly targeted for micromanagement and removal from their positions, and Black parents alleged their children were being placed in closets as a disciplinary measure.[81] While board members complained of parents not being involved enough in the district, one community member reprimanded them to "stop using the lack of parental involvement as an excuse for its failure to properly educate

Black children. ... [C]hildren of inactive parents deserve the same quality education as children of active parents."[82] Community members also described school-based personnel using Hornbeck's Small Learning Communities to racially segregate students.[83]

Another Hornbeck era reform that aroused concern was the shift from six local districts within the school district to twenty-two clusters. There was a lack of communication between the district's central office and the clusters, and this structure did not provide problem-solving or a sense of cohesion.[84] Some school-based educators felt overwhelmed and overly burdened by Hornbeck's reform approach. Reform overload was pervasive, particularly because reforms were top down and local educators were not consulted about how reforms should be implemented. School-based educators often experienced decentralization as getting more responsibility without the requisite input, support, or resources.[85]

One major sticking point for some Black educators was their belief that Hornbeck sought to dismantle Philadelphia's stratified system of special-admission schools.[86] He considered this systemwide tracking and a threat to equity, while many Black educators and community members saw special-admission schools as providing opportunities for exceptional Black students.[87] Some Black educators recognized Hornbeck's efforts were about equity in the distribution of resources.[88] He disputed the narrative that special-admission schools would be neglected with him as superintendent, arguing he would hold special admissions schools at their same level of support while neighborhood high schools would get additional attention. In truth, they needed it. Black students were struggling in neighborhood high schools.[89] Legendary Black Philly educator John Skief objected that West Philly High School received a high number of adjudicated youth whose unique needs surpassed what faculty could provide.[90] Another community member bemoaned that students transferred for disciplinary infractions were being sent to West Philly High, William Penn, Olney, and Ben Franklin, all neighborhood high schools, which further doomed their images as mere warehouses for youth without other options.[91] Hornbeck wanted to create opportunities for the masses rather than the privileged few.[92] While he was working in earnest on behalf of those who had been marginalized and disregarded by this inequity, disrupting this system was perceived as an affront to those who benefited from these special academic schools and programs, including some Black students, educators, and families. Secondary public schooling in Philadelphia thrived on a Darwinian type of stratification.[93] Hornbeck was trying to dismantle a system that disadvantaged the masses, but Black educators and community members knew, perhaps better than he did, that inequity would persist in Philadelphia's schools, regardless. And if he was able to equalize neighborhood high schools, somehow, Black students would still be shortchanged.

Board Politics

In 1994, Philadelphia's Board of Education had four Black members (Rotan Lee, Floyd Alston, Ruth Hayre, and Dorothy Sumners Rush), one Latinx member (Christine Torres-Matrullo), and four white members (Jacques Lurie, Andrew Farnese, Debra Kahn, and Thomas Mills). White Philly powerbrokers were elated with Hornbeck.[94] June Smith, a white veteran school district administrator, recalled his whiteness as giving him credibility with white board members who believed their interests had been neglected during the Clayton administration:

> I think in general, having a white man coming in after having an African-American who ran the District for a very long tenure, I think David was seen—and he was Southern, too—so I think he was seen very much as an outsider. And I think initially the white establishment gave him a lot of lee-way. And the African-American establishment didn't. They were suspicious. And I think by the end of his tenure that actually flipped. And I think the African-American establishment and the African-American community re-ally saw him as a champion for what I would call traditionally underserved populations—Black, Latino, poor. And the white community felt that he was not their champion. And it's probably accurate. The Northeast, for exam-ple, there was always this conversation about the Northeast. And I think the Northeast initially thought, *Oh, finally a white man is coming to town, we're finally going to get ours.* And by the end I think they were, like, *There was nobody worse for the white community than David Hornbeck.* ... And I really do think that flipped over time. ... Lurie and Mills were the two white men on the Board of Education at the time. ... And David came and did not give them the time of day.[95]

Black board members were hesitant with their initial support of Hornbeck to be superintendent of Philly's schools. Hornbeck ultimately won over Hayre by linking accountability for schooling outcomes to better outcomes for Black students.[96] Not long after Hornbeck assumed the helm, the board's president, Lee, rumored to be exploring a mayoral campaign to unseat Ed Rendell in 1995, left to become executive vice president and chief executive officer of a computer technologies company.[97] Rendell replaced Lee with a white woman, Deborah Parks, which shifted the racial balance of the nine-member board to from four Black members to three Black members, one Latinx member, and from four white members to five white members.[98] Five votes were needed for resolutions to pass. Board votes on hot-button issues were often along racial lines, with the exception of Debra Kahn, who usually voted with Black board members. The Latinx board member was often the swing vote.

In 1995, Floyd Alston became president of the Board of Education with Andrew Farnese as the vice president, which made for interracial leadership.[99] By the end of that year, the Latinx woman on the board was replaced by a young Latinx man, Pedro Ramos.[100] White board member Parks nominated Farnese to be president of the board, saying he deserved it because there had never been an Italian American president. Board member Hayre challenged that nomination, urging the board president share the racial identity of the majority students in the district. She wanted current board president Alston to remain in the position, and Black members, joined by white member Kahn, gave their four votes to Alston. The other four white board members were joined by Ramos to give Farnese the presidency and Parks the vice presidency.[101] White powerbrokers, disappointed that Hornbeck had not represented their interests thus far, attempted to shut Black people out from influence on the board in 1996.[102] At the end of that year, Kahn nominated Alston to be president of the board again while Mills nominated Parks to move from her post as vice president to president. In turn, Parks nominated Mills to be president and vice president of the board. Hayre nominated Ramos to be vice president. Ramos, who had voted with white board members to elect Farnese president the year prior, cast his vote with the three Black members and Kahn, reinstating Alston as president. The only white board member who voted for Ramos to be vice president was Kahn.[103] Control of the board meant having some control over the district's budget. With the high cost of Children Achieving, the high needs of Philadelphia's students, combined with an ever-shrinking tax base and limited government support in a racially segregated and economically stratified school system, the budget situation in Philadelphia grew dire. Whoever controlled the budget determined the fate of the city's schools.

Funding

School funding is never neutral. It is always political and ideological. Education funding determined primarily by local taxes in large urban centers with high poverty and a shrinking tax base yields underfunded schools, consistently. For years in Philadelphia, many who could afford to send their children to private school did so.[104] Politicians wrestled with privatizing Philly's public schools and issuing vouchers because the school situation was viewed as driving middle-class families out of Philadelphia.[105] City Council member Angel Ortiz said he hoped the city and state would understand they needed to provide additional funds to make Children Achieving happen.[106] There was a gap of $115 million for the 1995–96 school year, precisely when Children Achieving was scheduled for implementation.[107] Children Achieving was supposed to lead to additional funds, but there were fewer funds available under Hornbeck's program.[108] Confounding this situation were cuts to federal funding through Title I and desegregation. Hornbeck did not plan for these funding troubles to converge on Philadelphia all at once, and whether or not he was to blame, the public was upset. Like Clayton did earlier, he modified the budget in a Robinhood-esque manner. He moved program funds from privileged areas of the city to the underresourced, prioritizing schools that would increase racial balance in the next school year.[109] He instituted split-grade classes, combining students from two grades in one classroom with one teacher.[110] He apologetically rescinded teacher sabbaticals.[111] Parents, students, community members, and teachers opposed these shifts in funds.[112] Community members from northwest Philly threatened to leave the school district and to pursue school vouchers.[113] Others suggested a management audit and cuts to central administration to find needed funds.[114]

Hornbeck looked for various solutions because he did not want local groups bickering against each other for funding of their programs.[115] Though he secured funds from corporations and philanthropic foundations, Children Achieving was still short the money it needed to be fully funded.[116] He said the school district needed a state-level program similar to the federal Title I program, and he initially believed the city and state would provide the additional funds.[117] Budget solutions varied depending who was board president. When Farnese was board president, the board did not press City Council for additional funding the public schools desperately needed, which is what happened when Thomas was board president more than twenty years earlier. Rizzo was in his first term as mayor then; Rendell, in his second mayoral term at that point, sought to balance fairness with austerity, especially since his profile was rising with the national Democratic Party. Rendell refused to raise city property taxes to increase funding for the schools. He believed it was the responsibility of the state to increase the funding to the district.[118] City council members Angel Ortiz and David Cohen both implored board members to request the money the schools needed anyhow. Ortiz noted that the state lawmakers saw that Hornbeck and the board had not requested more money from the city. Further, he opposed Rendell's stance and decried the city for providing corporate tax cuts at the expense of funding public schools.[119]

During the years Alston was president of the Board of Education, he and Hornbeck encouraged people to pursue City Council and state representatives for additional funding.[120] Hornbeck began repeating an argument, more intensified every time he made it: that he first came to Philly in 1966 and there had been no change in students' achievement levels and no change in the funding formula from Harrisburg; that Philly had $1,500 to $2,000 less per child than sixty-two other school districts in the state; and that Philadelphia had 44 percent of the state's welfare recipients and the state should compensate for Philly's concentration of poverty amidst its declining tax base.[121] Using a Jonathan Kozol *Savage Inequalities*–type comparison, Hornbeck told audiences the following:

> This translates into $45,000 less, basically, for every classroom on this side of Stenton and City Line Avenues in contrast to the same classroom on the other side, making it unfair purely on the basis of residence or birth. If Philadelphia had the $1,500 that the sixty-one surrounding suburban school districts have, we could fund day care, academies, music—every single thing that has brought people here tonight. We could fund every part of Children Achieving and we could still have $171 million left over. The fact is that the hand that the State Legislature and the Governor (both past and present) have dealt with Philadelphia is plain unfair. ... The District does not ask for more than others have, We ask for only the average of what others have.[122]

Hornbeck also asserted that the school district had 12.1 percent of the state's public school children but was receiving only 11 percent of the state's funding for public schools and that this 1.1 percent gap represented $118 million.[123] Alston announced that the district's lawsuit against the Commonwealth "for fair and equitable funding for our students."[124] Hornbeck referred to the funding relationship between the district and the state as "a modern form of slavery" and "apartheid."[125] He attempted to get money from the state by campaigning against the state, insinuating its leaders were racist.[126] After this battle ended, Hornbeck said, "I never called anybody racist. I think the funding system in fact is a racist system. There's no doubt that it discriminates against kids of color. For some reason, a lot of people took that personally."[127]

Playing Chicken

There was an already longstanding contentious relationship between the school district and the state legislature. In the 1970s, this beef became apparent when the state legislature lowered its requirements for Philadelphia's superintendent in order to put Michael Marcase in place.[128] In 1981, Mayor Green supported state legislation to dissolve Philadelphia's Board of Education.[129] And at the end of the 1990s, Hornbeck—with the support of Mayor Rendell, the school board, and City Council—tangled with Governor Ridge and the state legislature for the bulk of the time he was superintendent of Philly's schools. Hornbeck had only partially delivered on the legislature's expectations. For instance, the Commonwealth approved the development of charter schools in 1997, and granting them began slowly under Hornbeck.[130] Leaders of the Republican legislature also wanted concessions from the Philadelphia Federation of Teachers. Hornbeck had won a provision to lengthen the school day to bring it on par with teachers across Pennsylvania, but he had more difficulty with the accountability measure whereby any teacher rated "unsatisfactory" would not get wage or step increases. Board member Kahn said Philly could not get the money it desperately needed for its schools because people were tired of the bickering and lack of student outcomes. She said the teachers' union did not like Hornbeck before he became superintendent and that the union's negotiation behaviors fueled the desire for vouchers.[131] But Hornbeck's own rhetoric further damaged a relationship that was already on life support.[132] He and the Commonwealth were at an impasse.

Hornbeck threatened that Philly schools would close in March 1999 without additional funds from the state, a threat that had been made by board president Dilworth in 1969.[133] Governor Ridge responded to the threat by signing legislation—written by Philly's own Representative Dwight Evans, who Rotan Lee had called "a friend of public education"—that would allow the state to take over the school district if it either did not have a balanced budget or had a school year that lasted less than 180 days.[134] City Council members lost faith in his ability to effectively work with the state to increase its funding to Philadelphia.[135] By May 2000, the state had hired a search firm to look for a replacement for Hornbeck in the event a state takeover happened.[136] The next month, Hornbeck offered his resignation effective August 2000.[137]

State Takeover

Throughout the constant battles between Hornbeck and the state, calls came for Pennsylvania to assume control of Philadelphia's public schools. Members of the Philadelphia delegation, State Senator Vince Fumo and State Representative Dwight Evans, both put forth plans to reorganize the district.[138] There were complaints that with the state running schools in Philadelphia, there would not be greater outcomes, that this was not an educational endeavor, and that the state takeover would not be the result of fiscal mismanagement or declining academics.[139] It was mere political action.[140] Black state lawmakers wanted to see a better working relationship between city officials and state officials, especially with regard to the governance of school district. State Senator Anthony Hardy Williams saw the district's problems as steeped in politics, and he wanted to see the issues move from politics to policies. Williams supported schools remaining under local control with significant state funding assistance. State lawmaker Vincent Hughes wanted the conversation to be about state-of-the-art schools, and State Representative Leanna Washington did not want to see the state participate in governance of the school district at all.[141]

Years later, reflecting on what motivated him to craft Act 46 of 1998—which also precluded the Philadelphia Federation of Teachers from striking—State Representative Evans would tell an audience of charter school advocates, "I want to implode the Philadelphia School District and I want to redefine how education is done. I want to change governance, I want to change management, I want to change recruiting, I want to do everything."[142]

Mayor Street stalled the state takeover when Hornbeck resigned, but it happened the next year.[143]

The state takeover of public schools that ensued in 2001 made Philadelphia the first school district of its size to come under state control while simultaneously privatizing the management of many of its chronically underperforming schools.[144] State takeover of public schools in Philadelphia was not about schools' or students' accountability.[145] The state sought to depose the school district of its own authority and impose a conservative political agenda.[146] The state's takeover of Philadelphia's public school was about financial management and power: whoever controls the money controls the district. The business community in Philadelphia and in the state had not had the influence on the district that it sought. These business leaders had also not been educated in the public schools of Philadelphia. Most were graduates of its Catholic schools and therefore were less inclined to allocate additional funds for the schools.[147] Governor Tom Ridge and his successor, Mark Schweiker, demonstrated little faith in the city's school system and wanted, instead, to contract it out to private management companies.[148]

After battles between Mayor Street and Governor Schweiker, the new School Reform Commission replaced the long-standing Board of Education as the schools' governing body as of December 2001. It included five members—two appointed by the mayor and three appointed by the governor.[149] While the details of the state takeover were worked out, the district hired one of the cluster leaders Hornbeck had appointed, a Clayton protégé, to be its first chief academic officer, Deidre Farmbry. Phillip Goldsmith, who had been Mayor Green's deputy in the 1980s, was hired to be the interim chief executive officer. This new structure was seen as eliminating the superintendency, dividing the post among a chief executive officer, a chief academic officer, a chief financial officer, and a chief operating officer. School systems in the major urban centers of New York, Los Angeles, and Chicago were already using this model of governance.[150]

The Grim Reaper

Constance Clayton said "historically privileged." While she did not have the luxury of using the words *racist* or *apartheid*, the very white privilege that Hornbeck did professional development sessions on, the cachet affiliated with his whiteness and his maleness, allowed him to point out these issues. And his naming them led to a state takeover of city schools. Hornbeck had a racial analysis of schooling in Philadelphia, but he lacked a concomitant strategy for mitigating the racism embedded in the school funding nexus so Philly schools could get what they needed. Hornbeck's fatal flaw was miscalculating the Philadelphia context, misunderstanding *why* children were allegedly not achieving in schools.

Hornbeck and board president Alston ascribed to a social mobility ideology where they viewed schools as the great equalizer and sought funding to make that reality for Philadelphia's public school students. But those who fund Philly schools operated from a personal responsibility standpoint, which absolved them from liability for equalizing opportunity for Philly's students.[151] Hornbeck tried to bring equity to a school system that thrived on stratification and inequity at both the local and state levels. His method of persuading the state to fund Philly's public schools seemed to be aggravation and public embarrassment. But the legislature would not be shamed into increasing funding.

Though Hornbeck was right about the state legislature's entrenched racism, being correct is not the same as being victorious. By the time he left his post in 2000, he lost the showdown with the state, and the next year, Philly lost its right to self-governance of its public schools. Philadelphia's residents, educators, and public school children were left to cope with the state's oversight for the next sixteen years. And Hornbeck returned to his home in Maryland.

He was not innocent in his miscalculation of the racism embedded in Philadelphia's context, especially his own.[152] How did Hornbeck expect to urge equity and be supported by the white power structure? Because of his shared racial identity with many state lawmakers and local businesspeople? Because he was a white man who could identify racism? Hornbeck had worked on behalf of poor children in Philadelphia, many who were Black, but he also alienated many Black adults, including Black educators and lawmakers. It is significant that Dwight Evans, a Black lawmaker and charter school advocate who represented Philadelphia in the state legislature, wrote the school district's death sentence.

5

Things Fall Apart

The Paul Vallas Project, 2002–2007

The days of parental disappointment and poor academic performance are over. ... New schools, with exciting reforms, will make Philadelphia's schools the finest urban learning centers in the nation.

> —Mark Schweiker, governor,
> Commonwealth of Pennsylvania, 2001 to 2003[1]

We have a school system that was in cardiac arrest. We had to make a serious intervention. ... We are now in a state of triage. We are in the process of stabilizing the patient.

> —James Nevels, chair,
> School Reform Commission, 2002 to 2007[2]

Wait a minute. The books are closed. How is the deficit rising?

> —Rev. LeRoi Simmons, community activist[3]

Everybody's upset. We are really upset about it. We thought we were OK. We thought that with the state takeover, we wouldn't be here. No one knows out of the clear blue why we are here.

> —Jannie Blackwell, member,
> Philadelphia City Council[4]

89

The Commonwealth of Pennsylvania won a pyrrhic victory against School District of Philadelphia. The school reform scheme imposed on Philadelphia in 2002 was the result of decades of state underfunding; an inherently classist and racist system of funding schools with property taxes while old homeowners fled to the suburbs and new homeowners received tax abatements; untaxed corporations and universities; and the national standards movement's evolution into nationalized education policy.[5] Once the state took over Philly's schools in 2001 as the No Child Left Behind Act of 2001 became the law of the land, synergistic forces ushered the city's school district into a program of destruction and wealth extraction. The district now had the money previous superintendents had so desperately wanted, but the School Reform Commission (SRC) and Paul Vallas funneled those funds to corporations, nonprofits, and universities for their interventions. This chapter argues that state-controlled governance and Vallas's leadership merged with the federal government's market ideology to enact racial capitalism—the process of extracting wealth from someone's (usually someone else's) racial identity—in Philadelphia's schools.[6] Racism *and* capitalism were significantly at play and inextricably linked once the state took over Philadelphia's schools in the early 2000s. Publicly unaccountable private businesses made millions off the well-publicized, alleged failure of Philadelphia's public schools, especially its Black and Brown students.[7]

The school district was subject to capitalist logic prior to state takeover when banks and foundations granted and loaned funds *to* the district. But under state control, corporations, universities, and nonprofits filled their coffers with money *from* the school district, money that was available only because of the perception of Philly's Black and Brown students as failures.[8] Vallas and the SRC had a fundamental misunderstanding of the primary problems that plagued the school district. They acted as if their work was race-neutral while they used racist ideology as their rallying call, which furthered white supremacy. While minor improvements came to the district through Vallas and the SRC, the costs outweighed the benefits. The solutions they crafted to the problems they misunderstood exploited Black students for the wealth of external service providers. In this money grab, there was limited improvement for Black and Brown students' lives. The commission's and Vallas's corporate solutions deepened and widened the financial problems they were sent to ameliorate. What initially looked like improvement was a shell game that left the district more fiscally distressed under state control than local control.

The (Im)Perfect Storm

The early years of the new millennium were fueled by uncertainty and fear. Public schools wrestled with school safety after the Columbine High School mass shooting. Republican George W. Bush had won the presidency of the United States after the hanging chads election debacle in Florida, where his brother, Jeb Bush, was governor. Within a year of Bush's presidential inauguration, the nation went into a tailspin with the September 11, 2001, attacks. The United States hunted for alleged weapons of mass destruction and declared war on Afghanistan in 2001 and Iraq in 2003, Bush's biggest international policies. His most important domestic policy was the reauthorization of the Elementary and Secondary Education Act of 1965 (ESEA)—No Child Left Behind (NCLB). Bush hailed it as educational accountability to confront "the soft bigotry of low expectations."[9] It claimed it would close so-called achievement gaps between white, Spanish-speaking, Black, and Asian students, but it leaned heavily on a system of spectacle and surveillance, monitoring test scores and delivering ever-increasing consequences for chronic underperformance, such as publishing school performance rates, restructuring school staffs, removing school leadership, and the reallocation and/or withholding of federal funds, among other components.[10] NCLB also provided supplemental educational services to students whose schools were labeled "failing" by paying private service providers with public funds and investing private businesses in the failure of traditional public schools.

Ultimately, NCLB was extensive, expensive, and destructive. Locally implemented, it was racist and unjust. High standardized test scores were the primary marker of success. Low standardized test scores were interpreted as failure for students and schools. The federal government's pressures on states to yield higher test scores led states to decrease the rigor of their learning standards so they could more easily meet federal mandates and led local educators to find other ways to game NCLB's high-stakes system of rewards and punishments.[11] After the September 11, 2001, attacks, Pennsylvania Governor Tom Ridge became Bush's chief adviser on homeland security (2001–2003). With the authority and financing provided via NCLB, Ridge's successor, Governor Mark Schweiker, continued Ridge's remaking of the School District of Philadelphia.[12] He promised things would get better.[13]

The first appointment to the state-controlled SRC in 2002 was James Nevels, a suburban Black Republican banker who was already on the Board of Control for the Chester-Upland School District, a nearby Black school district that was the only other district under state takeover at that time.[14] Before the other commission members were named, Nevels authorized contracts in the millions of dollars for consultants to the School District of Philadelphia. The next three SRC members were white men—Daniel Whelan, James Gallagher, and Michael Masch. Governor Schweiker named Whelan, then president and CEO of Verizon Philadelphia, and Gallagher, then president of Philadelphia University.[15] Mayor John Street named Michael Masch, then vice president for budget and management analysis at the University of Pennsylvania, and Sandra Dungee Glenn, a Black woman, then president of the public policy organization, American Cities Foundation.[16] All original SRC members served on this body throughout Vallas's term except for Masch, who left to become Ed Rendell's secretary of the budget in 2003, when Rendell replaced Schweiker as Pennsylvania governor.[17] To fill Masch's seat, Rendell appointed Martin Bednarek, CEO of the Washington Savings Association, a Philadelphia bank.[18] Both Dungee Glenn and Bednarek had previously served on the Board of Education in 2000.

An important part of the district's new governance model, in addition to the newly formed School Reform Commission, was the leadership structure.[19] State and local business leaders wanted another outsider to be the new school, chief. A skilled politician emerged, and he espoused the virtues of impression management through accountability—Paul Vallas.[20] He came to Philadelphia fresh from losing a primary-election bid to be governor of Illinois.[21] He had been CEO of the Chicago Public Schools since 1995 and was referred to by some there as a "miracle worker" and "a walking encyclopedia" who "would find sources of money to do things that were miraculous."[22] Vallas's money magic and miracles would catch up to him by the time his tenure in Philadelphia came to an end.[23] In the beginning, though, Vallas was regarded, with excitement, as "outspoken" with a "can-do attitude," a "straight-shooting practical idealist … ready to give Philadelphia schools the shake-up needed for serious reform."[24]

Many Black educators and other community members bemoaned Vallas's ability to lead Philadelphia's public schools given the questionable success of Chicago's public schools.[25] Their impressions of him ran the gamut: a snake oil salesman and a hustler, a conflicted politician who wanted to do well and to do good, a master communicator concerned with managing the impressions others had of him and his administration, a community-minded businessman who knew nothing about teaching and learning and who made huge promises but left the district in severe debt, a hype man whose substance had dissipated.[26] Vallas consistently overpromised and underdelivered.[27] LeRoi Simmons described Vallas as "smooth" yet able to lie with a straight face. Another community activist chided Vallas for having said he would "dismantle racism in the school district" but he had "broken his word."[28] And another community member remarked that Vallas failed "to change the destructive culture imbedded [*sic*] in the school system, take on upper-level education, and work on discipline and curb violence in schools."[29] As Judy recalled, "Paul's downside is that, depending on who was talking to him, he would promise everything. And staff had to figure out how to deliver on Paul's promises."[30] Vallas confirmed this characterization when he told a commission member, "I promise more than I can deliver, absolutely. … If I promise ten things and deliver six or seven, I'm still ahead of the guy who promises two things and delivers one."[31] He made powerful friends in the state legislature and City Council, and his political skill, combined with the SRC's mandate to recreate the school district while the state legislature held the purse strings, made the perfect combination for the neoliberal agenda in Philly's schools.[32]

Structure and Chaos

By 2002, the school district was struggling with old school buildings and insufficient space for students in various schools.[33] The distribution of resources throughout the district was unequal and inequitable. School libraries (called instructional materials centers) often lacked books and librarians.[34] Programming for academically gifted students was limited.[35] Privately run disciplinary programs operated like small prisons, warehousing students with little to no academic programming.[36] Vallas and the SRC had different ways of responding to these conditions. The SRC issued its list of goals, called the Declaration of Education of 2004, aspiring to close "education gaps" and ensure "equity across all schools in terms of resources." While the SRC paid thousands of dollars to inform and invest the public in their education agenda, Vallas had a different leadership approach.[37] June Smith described it this way: "Paul had a gut instinct and he operated within the gut instinct. ... And I think at base, there was a method behind Paul's madness but he didn't lead with that. He didn't say, *Here's the theory and here's how we're going to implement.* He said *Do this.*"[38] Dave described Vallas as "more like a cowboy, like John Wayne. ... Cowboy diplomacy was his tactic."[39] Still, both the SRC and Vallas operated from faulty assumptions and generated solutions that created more problems.

The SRC employed the terms of school-reform jargon as neutral instead of recognizing their histories and implications as political choices with lasting consequences for communities that have long been underserved and dispossessed. Nevels employed an "expert" who could help the commission "sharpen its focus" "to reduce the achievement gap," an ideology rooted in racism.[40] An explanation of Black students' *performance* differences absent the history of structural barriers promulgates anti-Black ideology, which is what the commission did in Philadelphia.[41] The only SRC member who challenged this ideology was Dungee Glenn, the lone Black woman in the group, when she explained, "a significant portion of the District's achievement gap is an opportunity gap. There are very clear differences in what and where resources are available. The District must eliminate the opportunity gap."[42]

Changes Afoot

In the spirit of No Child Let Behind, Vallas and the School Reform Commission instituted a new graduation and promotion policy, provided dual enrollment of district students in local postsecondary programs, gained International Baccalaureate status for five neighborhood high schools, and adopted new curricula with aligned assessments and culturally relevant materials.[43] While some Black educators appreciated the new curriculum, others questioned its validity since it was suspected that it came from Vallas's friends in Chicago.[44] Still, the most significant curriculum innovation in the Vallas era was instituting an African American history class as a graduation requirement, something that Black educators and activists had pursued for almost thirty years.[45] Vallas and the SRC also created "boutique schools," small high schools that had an average enrollment of four hundred students and new instructional options with technical assistance from private companies that would receive massive financial contracts.[46] The US Army Cadet Command gave the district half a million dollars to establish the Junior Reserve Officer Training Corps (JROTC) at five high schools.[47] As Jim recalled:

> I came back to the United States in 2004. And at that time, Paul Vallas was in contact with me all the time. He said *I want to start a military academy.* I said *Well, I don't wanna start a military academy that is a disciplinary school.* He said *No, it's an academic school. It's gonna be one of the smaller concepts that I want to do.* ... We opened up the military academy, and Paul didn't explain to me that the military academies, when he opened them up in Chicago, got a lot of grief because people thought you were trying to send their kids to war. Well, just coming off active duty, I was the best person to say *I'm not trying to send anybody to no wars.*[48]

With the United States at war in Afghanistan and Iraq, the apprehension was warranted.[49] Commissioners also had questions about small schools' access to athletic programs, after-school clubs, and music and arts programs and about whether the principal or the service provider would be responsible for underperformance. This plan created uncertainty and instability. If enrollment fell below 50 percent, the district could close that school, a Darwinian approach to school reform. Vallas and the SRC sacrificed stability in the lives of students and city dwellers, many who were already vulnerable, for a false sense of choice.[50] Vallas and the SRC created new schools, restructured neighborhood high schools, assigned a region of "failing" schools that had been managed by education management organizations (EMOs) in the early days of the state takeover back to district control, changed grade arrangements at existing schools, planned new magnet schools, and gerrymandered catchment areas, all in the name of school choice.[51] Which home addresses were slated for which schools (known as *catchment areas* in Philadelphia) was a constant concern of parents and community members.[52] "School choice" is political, historically lobbed to subvert school desegregation.[53] High-quality school programs were poorly distributed throughout the city, and the commission conflated *equity* and *equality.*[54] Schools could have equal resources but still be inequitable as needs vary by school.[55]

Vallas and the SRC also reformed faculty and staff policies. They rescinded the 1983 policy that required school district employees to live in the City of Philadelphia.[56] They expanded school-based teacher hiring and hired new principals, which pleased some Black educators.[57] Others were more concerned with who was moved and removed due to these new appointments, with movements seemingly arbitrary, harmful to the school district's professional culture, and in some ways undoing Clayton's legacy of bestowing powerful district positions on Black educators.[58] Joe, Marsha, and Nina all left the district during Vallas's tenure or shortly thereafter. Here is how they described their concerns:

> He wanted to bring his own people in to run things. And those people that he did bring in, and those people that he could get on his side that were already here, he kept them. And the other people had just to go. He did a lot of shifting people around here and there. And it made for a bad situation.[59]

> He brought in parasites that didn't know the culture of the city and didn't have respect for what existed.[60]

> I found him to be such an ego-centric person, and I felt like he treated veteran educators here so disrespectfully. … He may have been here for a matter of months before he just fired all kind of folk. … These educators that had given their hearts and souls and were having an impact, at least, in my view.[61]

They were not alone in their exodus. Between 1978 and 2008, the school district's Black teaching force decreased from 36 percent to 29 percent.[62] June Smith described Vallas as "much more loosey-goosey about credentials and much more about *did you have the right values and were you willing to work hard.*"[63] Perhaps this lack of transparency and understanding of what qualified people for positions was what caused some Black educators and community members to tell of a professional culture riddled with nepotism and favors during the Vallas era. According to them, Vallas built relationships with key people and players who had leverage in the district or those who had resources by exchanging favors with them.[64] Latifah shared, "he was also a politician because he also [paid] a lot of people off. … Every time there was a complaint, somebody got a contract to do something within the District."[65] As Missy recalled:

> As a matter of fact, one of the management people [for the company that manages the District headquarters building] now has a [position in the same office] higher than mine! And I don't know how that kind of stuff happens.

I never saw it advertised. But it was this new position created. ... And the next day she thought she was my boss and could tell me stuff. But she caught me on a bad day.[66]

Marsha said, "The total morale began to chip away. See, there's a number of us who were hired all around the same time. And we were talking about, *I can't wait to get out of here*. And then people you don't expect to retire came out when I retired. It's like a brain drain of sorts."[67] Elizabeth, who left the School District of Philadelphia for a promotion in another district, shared, "But for me, the Vallas reign was the worst. It brought out the worst in the sabotagers. There just didn't seem to be any ethical character, you know? It just was like power-mongers and power plays. ... He brought other people in who were like that, which is really what my problem was."[68]

While some Black educators viewed Vallas as fearless and brave, other Black educators viewed him as a bully who facilitated a tense professional culture that silenced veteran Black Philly educators.[69] As Belinda reflected:

I didn't want to come off as being negative, so therefore, silence for me was better. And I became a watcher of behaviors as opposed to a doer in those meetings. I couldn't wait to get out of them. And that probably hurt me. I probably should have spoken up more in certain things, but that part wasn't important for me. The job was. And results were. And not necessarily PSSA [Pennsylvania System of School Assessment] because they knew my feelings about that. I said we need to develop the whole child not a test-taking machine, but that's what they forced us to do, so.[70]

Schools for Sale

Programmatic cuts and selling district-owned property was also a significant part of Vallas and the School Reform Commission's agenda in Philly.[71] District officials claimed they would sell the buildings to pay for new construction of school structures that were fifty years old or more. The district's headquarters at 21st Street and the Benjamin Franklin Parkway, the John F. Kennedy Center, and the Stevens Administration Center sold for a total of $25 million and were slated to become high-end residential properties.[72] But for veteran Black educators and community members, the sales of these buildings were not just financial transactions. Since 1930, the school district's headquarters building was the symbol of educational leadership, an impenetrable fortress into which Black professionals were not allowed.[73] Access to the district's grand edifice indicated upward mobility for many elder Black Philadelphians. Instead, the SRC sold the building, a move interpreted by some as devaluing veteran Black Philly educators.[74] The headquarters held a long, tangled history of politics over education.[75] Regardless, there were questions about whether it made financial sense. The purchase of the new headquarters at 440 North Broad Street would cost more than what the buildings were sold for, but Nevels justified this with, "We want to move this operation into the 21st century. We are reformers. It is terribly inefficient and not a good message to the public."[76] LeRoi Simmons balked:

> There was doors in 21st and Parkway worth $1 million. Them big brass doors in the front? Those doors were worth $1 million with all the carving on them. … People don't know how much they got for it to this day! I can't get an answer about *How much did you sell that building for?* Where the money went. … the School District [sold] 21st and Parkway in a package with Kennedy Center. There were brand-new trucks parked at Kennedy Center they had forgot were in there. There was a printing press in the Kennedy Center could print all new magazines and they never used. There were books and calculators and every time I went through there, there were boxes and boxes of *unused* stuff in the Kennedy Center. And nobody knew. And they sold that and the contents in a package with 21st and the Parkway. And nobody knows how much that was. There was some art that was priceless on the walls at 21st and Parkway, and nobody can find that art. There were priceless pieces of art hanging in schools across the city. And all that was sold in a package and nobody saw where it went. … That is pure flim-flam, in my view. They just took this money from these children, and they didn't care nothing about that.[77]

A few district schools were also targeted for closure. Two schools had interesting postclosure lives. Thomas Durham Elementary School closed in June 2003, and John Wanamaker Middle School closed in August 2005. Both schools needed repairs so extensive they were not worth salvaging.[78] But the Wanamaker property was used to house displaced Hurricane Katrina survivors who had been relocated to Philadelphia.[79] If the school was that uninhabitable, why would vulnerable people who survived a deadly storm be housed there? The Durham School property was a little different. Located close to Center City Philadelphia, it was prime real estate. The SRC authorized its sale for $6 million as-is, and Independence Charter School was interested in buying Durham Elementary School property for $1.1 million instead. Vallas objected to Independence Charter's low-ball offer, but the charter school was protecting its own interests, as is a standard feature of capitalism.[80] The SRC also closed two schools in June 2006 to reopen them as small high schools in the fall of 2007.[81] While Ada Lewis Middle School students, parents, and teachers pled with the SRC to keep their school open and intact, the CEO/headmaster of Multicultural Academy Charter School declared his interest in taking the building for the new location of his charter school while at the same meeting.[82] Moves like this made it hard to see charter schools as partners peacefully coexisting with traditional district schools. Plotting to subsume a functioning school building while its inhabitants were fighting for it to remain open was predatory.[83]

The Charter Big Bang

When the state's commission to govern Philly schools was formed, Governor Schweiker wanted the education management organization (EMO) Edison Schools to manage the majority of the district's schools. However, the School Reform Commission opted for the diverse provider model of district management, in which a combination of EMOs and charter school proliferation was paramount.[84] The first charter schools in Philadelphia were authorized in 1997 during David Hornbeck's tenure as superintendent, but they expanded massively under Vallas and the SRC.[85] In 2005, the commission's charter policy was updated so charters would be prioritized in neighborhoods with overcrowded schools and low test scores to compete with private schools.[86]

Some charters were successful and complicated, such as Laboratory Charter School, the 2004 NCLB Blue Ribbon school whose founder was prosecuted but acquitted of defrauding the school of $6.7 million.[87] Other Philly charters had troubles, too. For example, Dave sent one of his children to a charter school that was closed "because of embezzlement and misuse of funds."[88] The former principal of Raising Horizons Quest Charter School told the SRC there was "unethical, illegal, and unfair treatment of staff and students" from the school's CEO.[89] This charter school is now closed. A parent accused Freire Charter School of "racial discrimination ... misappropriation of funds, illegal disenrollment, blocked due process, Ferpa [*sic*] violation, record non-compliance, negligence, and cruelty."[90] This school is still open. Commissioner Dungee Glenn was concerned that the SRC did not have a coherent charter policy detailing how charters would be assessed and evaluated. She wanted charter applications to be deferred until the charter policy was in place.[91]

In addition to authorizing new charters, during the Vallas/SRC era, the conversion of traditional district schools to charters, managed by charter management organizations (CMOs), began. Thomas Middle School in South Philly was the first conversion by Mastery Schools and was followed by Shoemaker Middle in West Philly and Pickett in Germantown.[92] Conversions of traditional district schools to those taken over by CMOs would take off under Vallas's successor.

Big Pimpin and Spending Cheese

Significant federal money was tied to NCLB for students attending schools deemed underperforming.[93] Under state control, there were massive amounts of money coming in and going out of the School District of Philadelphia. By August 2007, $200 million in educational contracts had been paid out, not including payroll or the capital fund.[94] The state's financing provisions mandated the district have private, external service providers.[95] While external service providers included some local entities, the majority were corporations capitalizing on the alleged failure of Philly's majority Black and Brown students, while Black and Latinx people were shut out from getting much from these contracts.[96]

Under the diverse provider model, seven external organizations initially received five-year contracts to manage public Philadelphia schools, which was more outside providers than any other school district used in the nation at that time.[97] Throughout the Vallas/SRC era, additional service providers for schools were added.[98] This was an expensive venture, as the SRC contracted these schools to private managers and then financed support programs for these private managers, as well.[99] Furthermore, despite an increase in per-pupil expenditures, student achievement at EMOs was not any better than at other district schools.[100]

Vallas and the SRC were undeterred. They diversified how they worked with private managers. Camelot Schools of Pennsylvania was paid $4 million to manage Daniel Boone School's four hundred students and $3.2 million to manage Shallcross School's three hundred students.[101] Cornell Abraxas, Inc. was paid $2 million to operate a therapeutic program with third and fourth graders.[102]

Universities also fed on the school district. The SRC contracted with the University of Virginia, $560,000 for a professional development experience for twelve turnaround school principals during the 2006–07 school year.[103] The commission authorized $61,000 to Johns Hopkins University's talent development program at Beeber and Vare Middle Schools.[104] Temple University managed four North Philly schools for $450 per child, $300 less per child than what was paid to Edison, Victory, Foundations, and Universal.[105] Temple also received an additional $43,290 for its work at Meade Elementary.[106] The University of Pennsylvania was paid $450 per student for three West Philly schools and an additional $160,000 for its work at Lea Elementary.[107] The commission authorized $600,000 to Drexel University for school-based support in the 2004–05 school year, which doubled for the 2005–06 school year, and $500,000 to St. Joseph's University for its school-based support.[108]

When some SRC members questioned the usefulness of the professional development contracts, Vallas claimed that "universities are bringing tremendous resources into the schools" in the form of student teachers, student counselors, and student co-op workers.[109] But these institutions were receiving funds *from* the school district while not paying taxes *to* the City of Philadelphia, thus being complicit in the lack of local tax funding available for the district so that it could rely less on the salvation of the state. Instead, they allegedly provided payments in lieu of taxes (PILOTs), courtesy of Mayor Rendell's 1994 executive order.[110] But they didn't actually provide PILOTs consistently.[111]

Community-based organizations also cashed in on the school district in the Vallas era, though to a lesser extent. For example, the SRC contracted with the historic Black Philadelphia organization Opportunities Industrialization Center (OIC) for $1.125 million to provide programs for 150 students, ages seventeen to twenty-one, who were out-of-school youth, formerly adjudicated returning from court placements, or were enrolled in school but were not earning enough credits.[112] The commission contracted with International

Education and Community Initiatives to do the same work with the same number of students as the OIC for $1.875 million.[113] Fourteen other local groups—including ASPIRA, Congreso de Latinos Unidos, Philadelphia Anti-Drug/Anti-Violence Network—received a combined $2.17 million to give support around school attendance and truancy issues.[114] With Vallas and the SRC at the helm, the school district widened its engagement of external services through corporate and nonprofit organizations, thus expanding the district's neoliberalism.[115]

The SRC paid over $7 million to SchoolNet to provide Benchmark Assessments created by Princeton Review's Homeroom.com for privately managed district schools.[116] This meant the district paid EMOs a per-pupil fee *plus* paid for their test-preparation materials. The commission also paid $50,000 to Princeton Review for Praxis test-preparation services for five hundred teachers so they could be considered "highly qualified."[117]

One of the SRC's most problematic contracts was with K12, Inc. for $3 million to "provide academic and curriculum development support, access to K12's online curriculum and assessments, academic enrichment via summer and extended day programs, professional development, teacher planning and training materials, and community involvement activities."[118] Conservative radio talk show host, William Bennett, was the founder of K12, Inc. He had been an adviser to former presidents (Ronald Reagan and George H. W. Bush). During a show in 2005, he said the following:

> If you wanted to reduce crime, you could—if that were your sole purpose—you could abort every black baby in this country and your crime rate would go down. That would be an impossibly ridiculous and morally reprehensible thing to do, but your crime rate would go down.[119]

Bennett insisted he was not racist and refused to apologize for his comments. Commissioner Dungee Glenn did not "believe K12's interest in urban education is one that matches what is in the best interest of the School District of Philadelphia." She put forth a formal motion to terminate the K12, Inc. contract.[120] The school district was 70 percent Black. Community members protested against the contract with K12, Inc. and regarded Bennett's remarks as "genocidal."[121] However, Commissioner Gallagher had stock in K12, Inc. and said the organization had performed in a satisfactory manner. He, Nevels, and Whelan voted to keep K12 Inc., defeating Dungee Glenn's resolution. With their vote, the SRC decided the racism of K12's founder was nowhere near as important as the multi-million-dollar contract the company had with the district or the returns it yielded for its investors, like Gallagher.[122] Commissioners had so little regard for Black children that they funded a company affiliated with someone who casually hypothesized about their deaths, further demonstrating the SRC's commitment to racial capitalism in Philadelphia.

In addition to the district's plentiful corporate contracts, Teach For America (TFA) and the Broad Foundation began its Philly work and the New Teacher Project (TNTP) increased its work in Philly during the Vallas/SRC era.[123] The commission paid TFA $321,000 in 2005 and $414,000 in 2006 to support TFA teachers in Philly.[124] The SRC increased its work with TNTP with $525,000 for the 2005–06 school year and $385,000 to fill midyear vacancies and teachers for the start of school in the fall of 2007.[125] The Broad Foundation granted the district $200,000 to subsidize the salaries of two participants in the Broad residency in urban education program from August 2004 to July 2006.[126] Numerous scholars have pointed to the ways TFA has worked with other organizations to facilitate neoliberal school reform in cities around the nation.[127]

Bills, Bills, Bills

Vallas's initial CEO contract was for five years, ending June 30, 2007. In 2006, questions emerged about whether he should be retained in Philadelphia.[128] Two commission members even initiated a national search to replace Vallas, while city and state Black politicians and the *Philadelphia Tribune* supported his staying.[129] At that time, Vallas was seen by many as one of the top urban schools administrators in the nation.[130] Nevels credited Vallas with the recent progress and success of the school district.[131] By August 2006, Vallas's contract had been renewed for two additional years, so he would stay into 2009. Nevels told the *Tribune*, "The contract is designed to retain a gifted human being, a gifted professional."[132] Within a month, praise for Vallas became confusion and rage when a significant budget issue was revealed. Earlier that spring, Vallas said the budget was "structurally balanced" despite federal cuts and no increases from the city or state.[133] Nevels followed Vallas's budget comments with these comments:

> the purpose of today's discussion is to alert the political decision makers to the tightness of this budget and that if the reforms are to continue at an ongoing robust pace, it becomes critical that children in Philadelphia and throughout the Commonwealth receive the benefits of that financial support locally and from the State.[134]

These comments were eerily similar to statements prior board presidents Dilworth, Alston, and Lee made before state takeover. But there were concerns about money management, the SRC's expenditures, and Vallas's misuse of funds.[135] For example, according to NCLB legislation, 15 percent of Title I funds were for tutoring. Vallas was accused of doing only after-school tutoring, which cost $6 million, in order to save money for the district.[136]

Theresa argued that Vallas's choices may have been inappropriate but were not unethical:

> He may have misused funds, but guess where it went? Schools, children and community organizations. And if that's wrong, then he's wrong. I can truly say that he *never* misused funds to hire people. It was always about *How can we get the extended day?* He used money like in a way he wanted to use it.... It was all about *how do we get the resources out to schools? How do we get kids more services?* And it really didn't matter to him what the rules were. His finance person was eating his fingers off because you had to manage Paul and the budget, too.[137]

In October 2006, the budget was found to be in deficit of $21 million, then $70 million, then $73 million.[138] The commission, especially Vallas's biggest supporters, Nevels and Gallagher, could not explain how their miracle man had the budget in such crisis.[139] The solution was, once again, extensive budget cuts. On this, Gallagher remarked, "the proposed resolution is difficult and painful, and has to be considered. ... the School District deficit was avoidable if the Commission had been given the proper heads up last spring. ... a clear message from the Mayor and other leadership that the Commission must balance its books and create a coherent five year plan."[140] Mayor Street said he had been unaware of the financial crisis the district was in.[141]

To avoid ending the school year with a $29 million deficit, Vallas recommended that the SRC implement "contract cuts and the reduction in force."[142]

The commission authorized the sale of four school buildings in North and West Philly, one that was built in 1902 and was on the historical registry.[143] To much community uproar, the SRC also considered selling off other assets, such as an art collection estimated to be worth $15 million to $20 million.[144] A failure at managing the budget once again meant shortchanging Black Philadelphians. Community members, students, and families had been promised a new building for West Philly High School, but those plans were now on hold.[145] In this racial capitalist context where Black students' alleged failure was a hot commodity that funded many external service providers, Black students in West Philly were still left with little to show from all the money that had come in and gone out from the district. And then Vallas was gone, replaced in the interim by his Broad-trained chief operating officer.[146]

6

Black on Both Sides

Perils of Neoliberalism, 2008–2017

*Change is hard. People have benefited from this system,
and it's not fair, and it's not equitable. People are going
to be mad at me and the SRC. There are the 'haves'
and the 'have-nots.'"*

—*Arlene Ackerman, chief executive officer,
School District of Philadelphia,
2008 to 2011*[1]

*The SRC is a racist institution. If one teacher is devalued
and disrespected that is one too many. If one parent
is bullied, disrespected or retaliated against, that is one
too many. If one qualified Philadelphia educator
is overlooked in favor of an out of town stranger, that
is one too many. If one citizen is denied the right
to elect a local school board, that is one too many.*

—*Leroy Warner, community member*[2]

*It is very important to talk about minority children and
ask that why, at the schools that are serving minority
children, we have not been able to determine or figure
out how to teach them to read and do math.*

—*William Hite, chief executive officer,
School District of Philadelphia,
2012 to present*[3]

This final chapter of this book begins amid "the worst economic crisis since the Great Depression," the year a young*ish* Black man became the first Black president of the United States.[4] And this chapter ends the year that first Black president's chief detractor succeeded him as president. These are perfect bookends as this chapter chronicles the challenges imposed both by and on Black leaders over a majority-Black school district with which they had little prior knowledge, contact, or context. When Arlene Ackerman came to Philadelphia in 2008, she generated the sense of possibility and hope that many Black people initially experience when Black people are in positions of power. However, Ackerman and her successor, Bill Hite, were both outsiders to Philadelphia and affiliated with the Broad Superintendents' Academy who were brought into Philadelphia to deepen and widen neoliberal school reform. While these Black educators had some Black support, some Black people opposed their plans to further decimate public schooling in Philadelphia. Similar to how some Black people supported the idea of Barack Obama as the first Black president while being less than moved by his centrist orientation and his preservation of the American empire, some Black people were happy with the School District of Philadelphia having Black leadership while bemoaning how they led.

What does it mean to be a Black educator overseeing the systematic defunding of the majority-Black school district you were entrusted to lead? Two Black Philadelphia outsiders were deliberately chosen to advance neoliberal public schooling in Philadelphia. Their presence gave a veneer of representation that made more palatable the state's dismantling of Philly's public schools as democratic institutions with the capacity to improve life conditions for the Black, the Brown, and the most vulnerable. In the new millennium, where liberals touted claims of a "postracial America," they elected, appointed, and rewarded Black officials who bought into anti-Black, deficit-laden ideologies, policies, and practices. This chapter exposes what happens to a majority-Black school district when the mayor is Black, the chairs of the state-controlled School Reform Commission are Black, and the chief executive officers of the school district are Black. Ackerman's and Hite's identities as Black education leaders gave credibility to their neoliberal ideologies and practices. But whose interests would be privileged and prioritized throughout their tenures? Tensions between the embeddedness of structural barriers versus individual efforts and personal responsibility abounded in these years.

Ackerman took on the white power structure in Philadelphia on behalf of Black businesses. She valued educators individually but begrudged educators collectively. She attempted solidarity with families in a hierarchical way. She wanted to *give* education to underresourced parents and insisted parents have access to schools. But she struggled with accepting parents' insights into her school reform plans. When she refused to play politics, the politics demanded her ouster and paid her well to go. Her successor was an expert politician. Hite built relationships with leaders regardless of political affiliation. Instead of rebuffing Philly's white power structure, Hite rhetorically wrestled with Black mothers as he defended neoliberal reform, and he did little to hold off attacks on Black-led charter schools. Ackerman's and Hite's tenures in Philly harken the age-old Black question: *At what point is this selling out or buying in?*

Importing Reform

Shortly after Vallas left to lead New Orleans's Recovery School District, the School Reform Commission's (SRC) inaugural chair, James Nevels, exited the commission.[5] Its next chair was Sandra Dungee Glenn, the lone Black woman who had served on the SRC to that point.[6] While many Philadelphians were left with little to no confidence in Nevels after Vallas's multimillion-dollar budgetary miscalculations, the homegrown Dungee Glenn was perceived differently by many Black Philadelphians.[7] Under her leadership, the commission considered weighted student funding, expanded early childhood, reduced class size for the youngest students, and authorized incentives for teachers in critical needs subjects.[8] Most notably, though, Dungee Glenn helped to usher in the second Black woman to lead Philly's public schools, Arlene Ackerman.[9] In some ways, coming to Philly was seen as Ackerman's last stand for kids.[10] Throughout her brief tenure, Ackerman maintained some of the standard features of neoliberal school reform.[11] She gave greater control of public schooling to corporate education nonprofit organizations, such as the Broad Foundation, Teach For America, and the New Teacher Project.[12] Ackerman's successes seemed so remarkable that the Council of Great City Schools gave her its award for the nation's best urban schools leader while she led Philly's public schools in 2010.[13] She also demonstrated commitments to Black people that ultimately led to her exit, run out by politicians who could not manipulate her for their purposes.[14]

Ackerman had been superintendent of the District of Columbia's public schools prior to coming to Philadelphia.[15] She had also been the first Black person and first woman superintendent of schools in San Francisco, California.[16] She retired from being an education practitioner when she left San Francisco, but she resurrected her practitioner status for Philly.[17] Her Philadelphia school reforms were similar to those she had implemented in DC and San Francisco, such as weighted student funding, where schools got resources according to students' needs.[18] She hired new Black teachers, provided extra time for students' learning, and paid teachers for their extended time.[19] But these additions came at a cost.[20] Promise Academy teachers were mandated to wear the school uniform to work every day.[21] Empowerment schools' teachers were forbidden from customizing scripted curriculums.[22] Lead Academic Coaches for the Arts were cut, and the Office of African American Studies was subsumed under the American History Office.[23] Given the African American history course graduation requirement Black Philly folks had fought for thirty years, this shift seemed like a demotion in the significance of that work. Charter schools were an essential part of Ackerman's reforms, though the landscape was messy. The SRC granted charter approvals with conditions, but this status made it difficult for conditionally approved charter school to conduct business.[24] Charter operators believed they were constrained by the school district's approval process. But charter critics demanded more stringent accountability given their costs.[25] By 2009, the district's sixty-three charter schools had cost $350 million, though six charter schools opened and twenty received enrollment increases (which drove up costs) between 2009 and 2011.[26]

Ackerman's flagship reform was Imagine 2014.[27] It advanced smaller class sizes, more school counselors, and additional resources for the district's most racially isolated, lowest academically performing schools, which allowed the district to settle its decades-old school desegregation case, something the prior six superintendents had not done.[28] Imagine 2014 had major drawbacks, though. While "empowerment schools" would receive targeted interventions and additional resources due to sustained poor academic achievement, faculty at "renaissance schools" would have to reapply for their jobs or be force transferred.[29] Renaissance schools were turned over to external providers, mostly through charter management organizations.[30] Under Ackerman's leadership, private management of public schools expanded, while the district's management of its own schools shrunk. Charter schools were not subjected to the Philadelphia Federation of Teachers' collective bargaining agreement and its work rules, so the union balked at the Renaissance process amid their already contentious relationship with Ackerman.[31]

The Ackerman administration also pursued school closures as financial reform.[32] They said the district had lost eleven thousand students from 2006 to 2011. But this loss occurred as charter seats and costs increased.[33] Ultimately, the SRC's rightsizing policy and adaptive reuse policy were school closure plans to foster charter expansion.[34] They facilitated a predatorial, parasitic relationship where traditional public schools were deemed "failing" and then taken over by independent charter schools in need of space and charter chains looking to expand their brands.[35] Giving closed buildings to charter schools or selling these buildings and land to the highest bidder was defunding publicly accountable schooling and abdicating responsibility for the people of Philadelphia.[36] The commission claimed closing schools would lead to the distribution of resources in equitable ways, but that was slow to materialize.[37]

Crucial Conflicts

Black Philadelphians had long viewed the City and the school district as old boys' networks that were difficult for anyone who was not white and male to penetrate.[38] Before 2003, only 2 percent of district contracts were going to businesses owned by people of color and women.[39] By 2010, the tally was 20 percent. This displeased many Black Philadelphians, including State Representative Ron Waters, who argued, "In a school district with 88 percent children of color, minority participation leaves much to be desired."[40] To address this disparity, Ackerman steered a no-bid contract for security camera installation at nineteen "persistently dangerous" schools to IBS, a Black-owned business and district-approved vendor. Ackerman allegedly commented about being tired of contracts going to white people, and some of her white staffers who leaked that comment and documents around these contracts to the media were terminated. Some white business owners claimed reverse discrimination and filed suits against Ackerman and other administrators.[41]

Commissioners Archie and Irizarry grilled district leaders over the extent to which those getting lucrative contracts were people of color or woman-owned businesses.[42] Cody Anderson, president of ACG Associates, said that the district's business culture relegated people of color to subcontractor status. He asked Ackerman "to stand strong in her position of inclusion."[43] Hundreds supported Ackerman in this conflict, and Archie commended her implementation of an "anti-discrimination policy and extended his support to 'level the playing field for all Philadelphians.'"[44] Ackerman did receive criticism, however, for putting students under the surveillance of installing cameras at their schools.[45]

While Ackerman and Archie were on the same side of that situation, things changed with Martin Luther King High School in 2011.[46] Foundations, Inc, had managed King since the School Reform Commission became the governing body for the school district, a contract worth $12 million annually. State Representative Dwight Evans wanted Foundations to continue managing King and told the commission he felt excluded from the decision-making process with an iteration of, "if I do not feel a part of it, it will be difficult for me."[47] King's School Advisory Council wanted Mosaica Education to manage the school, but Evans was unwilling to work with Mosaica.[48] At the public commission meeting, since Commissioner Archie's law firm represented Foundations, Inc., Archie recused himself from the vote; the remaining commissioners approved Mosaica as King's turnaround partner.[49] Later that night, though, Leroy Nunery, Ackerman's second in command, orchestrated a meeting between Evans, Archie, and John Porter of Mosaica.[50] The day after the SRC's vote for Mosaica and the subsequent surreptitious meeting, Porter withdrew Mosaica from consideration to manage King. But then Foundations, Inc. also withdrew its bid for King, citing "unrelenting hostility."[51] An investigation by Mayor Nutter's chief integrity officer soon revealed that secret meeting between Archie, Evans, and Porter, as well as continued pressure on the School Advisory Council members and Ackerman.[52] Melonease Shaw, the lobbyist with lifelong ties to Evans who was hired to acclimate Ackerman to Philly, told her, "Evans could hurt her career if she did not steer the MLK contract to Foundations." Another friend warned Ackerman if she didn't get on the same page as Evans, information about her delinquent taxes would be leaked to the public, which local news outlets soon released.[53] Since Mosaica and Foundations both withdrew from consideration to manage King, King came back into district management.[54]

Ackerman's departure began brewing when Tea Party Governor Tom Corbett devastated Philly by slashing education funds across Pennsylvania.[55] To manage a $610 million budget gap, the school district laid off more than three thousand employees, including 1,523 teachers, in 2011.[56] Ackerman refuted rumblings of her departure, but she was absent from the commission meeting on August 10.[57] At the first meeting with principals for the 2011–12 school year and Ackerman's last meeting with them, Sade's "Is It a Crime" played in the background, and Ackerman rhetorically asked, "Is it a crime to stand up for children instead of stooping down into the political sandbox and selling our children for a politician's campaign victory? … Is it a crime to believe that all children can achieve? … So sentence me, I dare you. Or set me free."[58] By its next public meeting, the SRC authorized a $905,000 buyout of Ackerman's contract, which incensed many Philadelphians.[59] Still, there was a ground swell of Black people unprepared for her abrupt departure and worried about what and who would come next.[60]

In Recovery

Almost all commissioners left within two months of Ackerman's departure.[61] Between Ackerman's exit and Bill Hite's entrance, much of the new commission's work was destructive. They expedited school closures and property sales in predominantly Black North Philadelphia and Germantown, despite research that school closures did not yield financial savings.[62] Interim district CEO Leroy Nunery worked with charter management organizations and foundations to decide how to manage the district moving forward, a collaboration called the Great Schools Compact. This was an agreement between the commission and charter school advocates to decrease and defund traditional public schooling and increase charters.[63] But expanding charter seats did not make financial sense. In 2012, the commission approved an additional 4,500 charter spaces, which was seven times the cost of new renaissance school seats annually.[64] With charter school payments like these and the neglect of education funding from Corbett's state government, the SRC was anticipating a budget deficit, which meant the school district could not make payroll in June 2012.[65] The commission also suspended the section of

Pennsylvania's Public School Code to allow them to lay off district employees unrepresented by a union.[66]

City Council member Bill Green (son of former Mayor Bill Green) proposed that the school district become a "Recovery School District," and the SRC mostly followed Green's proposal.[67] The new leadership structure would have a chief recovery officer and acting superintendent, former Philadelphia Gas Works executive, Thomas Knudsen, for $25,000 per month.[68] They implemented furlough days for all nonrepresented employees making more than $50,000.[69] Knudsen's five-year financial plan that included borrowing $300 million to finance debt and "closing a number of school buildings because they are underutilized and in poor condition." This move made possible the unprecedented damage they would do in June 2013.

Mass Layoffs and School Closures

As a new superintendent, Bill Hite's greatest task would be "overhauling the workings of the infrastructure of the school district."[70] Hite came from Prince George's County, Maryland, where he froze all salaries, cut thirteen hundred positions, enforced furlough days, increased class sizes, and closed schools, which made him perfect for furthering neoliberal school reform in Philadelphia.[71] LeRoi Simmons believed, "Hite came in with the next phase, because [Ackerman] was on the board of the Broad Foundation.... He came in with the next phase which was to cause chaos."[72] A number of veteran Black Philly educators were lukewarm and felt conflicted about Hite. As Bryton explained, "I think that he is a more natural politician. ... I think that when he gets up and he speaks, people are like, *Oh, okay. I like what he's saying.* But I don't know if it necessarily translates to truth."[73] Novaturience echoed that sentiment, describing Hite as "Shyster, and I like him personally, I do."[74] Dave explained, "I call Dr. Hite 'Teflon" because it just comes off ... the vitriol."[75] Bryton was right: Hite continued neoliberal school reforms, called for a recommitment to Ackerman's Renaissance and Promise Academies, and pursued more school closures to "right size the District."[76] The worse was to come at the end of his first year in Philadelphia.

In the spring of 2013, political gaming created local disaster. Though Hite said his obligation was "to expose students to safe, clean and well-maintained environments, quality teaching, effective leadership, technology upgrades, curriculum resources, and enrichment activities," there was a $304 million gap for the upcoming school year.[77] Hite said no new revenues were coming and that the budget for the 2013–2014 school year "in no way fits his idea of public education."[78] Commission chair Ramos claimed, "Philadelphia students deserve a safe high quality education … but [the SRC] cannot fulfill its duty to children if funding is so dramatically inadequate." Commissioner Pritchett believed the sparse funds provided by the city and state were unconstitutional and unacceptable.[79] And Commissioner Dworetzky blamed charter funding for a big portion of the district's financial problems, saying it "has become impossibly severe at the present."[80] Whoever and whatever was to blame, this represented the worst time in the history of the School District of Philadelphia since it began in the early nineteenth century.[81] It was no longer in good enough financial standing to borrow money. Despite massive outcry that schools had long been neglected, defunded, and then labeled failures; despite various plans for improvement, concerns about safety and the distance young students had to travel to their new schools after their neighborhood schools closed; and despite data showing academic gains and suspension decreases, Hite and the SRC closed twenty-three schools and laid off almost four thousand educators, including counselors, assistant principals, teachers, secretaries, nurses, and school police.[82] These school closures impacted mostly Black students and low-income communities, compounded by decades of city neglect.[83] Under the 2013–2014 budget, traditional public schools would have no art, no music, and no sports. Educators and schools were pitted against one another as they begged the SRC not to close their schools and implored them to take the limited resources the district had from one school and give them to another. Schools receiving hundreds of new students would not have suitable employees to make students' transitions to their new school experiences peaceful. Bryton described this situation as "a shitshow."[84] He, Novaturience, and LeRoi Simmons believed Dwight Evans's connections to King High was why Germantown High was closed and why King became the receiving school for former Germantown students.[85] As Ceage argued:

> The same schools that were in Renaissance, that were Promise, that would "turnaround," they're all the same freaking schools every single year is the same, exact schools, until we turn over the charters, they'll be closing. Same exact schools in all poor neighborhoods. … Yeah, poor people being preyed

on, again when you look at test data to determine how successful the school is, then you don't care about schools. You just want to see the kids out there. Every educator in the world would tell you testing does not determine how good a school is. We all know it, we do but we still allow it to be the determining factor in how we rate the schools, how we rate teachers, how we rate principals.[86]

While the state allowed Philadelphia public schools to endure a $300 million deficit, it allocated an additional $400 million to build a new prison for Philadelphia residents.[87] Mayor Nutter told the nation the SRC was right to make these unfathomable cuts.[88] Black community activists and educators challenged the commission and school district administration on these school closures.[89] Though the district closed twenty-three schools at the end of the 2013 school year, combining that number with the closures from the Ackerman era meant that a total of thirty schools had closed. With the previous faculty and staff layoffs, the decrease in staffing was between 3,800 and 5,000.[90] These policies and practices pushed families out of district schools and into charters that appeared more stable. And they pushed educators to seek work in surrounding districts and even in Philadelphia charters where they were less likely to worry about being laid off every time the district was in manufactured financial distress.

Making matters worse, the SRC and Hite temporarily accomplished something Ackerman attempted but failed: they suspended parts of the Pennsylvania School Code directed at labor, charter schools, and property.[91] Several community members, district educators, education activists, and students opposed this move.[92] Suspension of the Public School Code meant removing workers' longstanding and hard fought for rights, such as steps raises, and a major point of contention was how educators would be brought back to work: by seniority or by "need."[93] Hite said Mayor Nutter and City Council President Clarke would give the district $50 million to hire back laid off essential faculty in time for school to open in the fall of 2013.[94] The public would later find out that money was not a gift but instead was a loan that came at a high cost. Students and community activists told the SRC that $50 million was not enough to open schools sufficiently and that students and teachers should boycott the first day of school. Helen Gym pushed the SRC on what school would look like with the split classrooms, few guidance counselors, and without nurses and librarians.[95] As Shanee Garner recalled:

> Any semblance of equity vanished in 2013. … Schools lost so many teachers, schools don't have nurses and counselors, we can't even get to trauma informed care or safety, when nurses are only actually there two days a week, when kids don't have arts and music or paper in September, it's pandemonium and it's going to take us a long time to realize what the impact of this. To put that in context, could this have happened to rich white people?[96]

The damage was irreparable.[97] Sixteen school counselors were assigned to cover 120 schools with 48,000 students.[98] By October 2013, Governor Corbett agreed to release $45 million to the school district. Hite said that money would let them hire back more people who were laid off in June, but the funds were being released depended on "fiscal and academic reforms." That was too late for Bryant Elementary's LaPortia Massey, who had an asthma attack that began at school where there was no nurse and later died.

During that school year and going forward, the district funded schools by donation, which exacerbated inequity.[99] Some donors did not specify which schools were to receive their contributions; others did.[100] There was of a tier of schools that would never be considered for closure and would never see a significant dip in resources because they would be boosted with private monies.[101] Drexel University's School of Education was already providing $206,000 for Powel Elementary for instructional personnel, professional development, and technology upgrades.[102] The University of Pennsylvania contributed $700,000 annually to Penn Alexander Elementary, with its gerrymandered catchment area, since the school was developed in 1999.[103] Parents from Albert Greenfield Elementary donated $300,000 to pay for personnel and activities that had been cut.[104] Philadelphia's Children First Fund donated $210,000 for salary and benefits for two full-time librarians, one at Central High and one at Masterman High, both special admissions schools. Central High's alumni association gave the district more than $260,000 for technology upgrades.[105] Meanwhile, the district's fiscal situation deteriorated more with an expected $28.7 million shortfall.[106] To provide the minimum for the most vulnerable, the district would need at least $100 million.[107] At the end of that nightmarish school year, Hite and the commission refused to approve a budget until they had more certainty of increased funds from the city and the state.[108]

Hite's Marketplace

Hite expanded the school district's neoliberal course by creating new district schools to compete with charters, outsourcing services once provided by the district, consolidating existing traditional schools, and selling closed school buildings.[109] Community activists and educators were concerned about the control and authority that Mastery Charter Schools and the Philadelphia School Partnership exerted over the district.[110] Mastery expanded through the conversion of traditional District schools. Then the district contracted with Mastery to pilot their teaching practices and coaching model in four schools.[111] As this program expanded, community members questioned why services previously provided by district employees were being outsourced "to private, low-ball bidders to give the illusion of servicing the needs of our children."[112] One retired educator told the SRC, "There are still hundreds of teachers in Philadelphia traditional public schools that could provide invaluable, scintillating, and effective staff development."[113] While Hite wasn't the first to lead the district this way, after years of defunding the district, devaluing its educators, and giving lucrative contracts to private businesses, the public had grown frustrated over the poor performance of these outside contractors, particularly its sources of substitute teachers.[114] The district was also shifting from K–5 schools to K–8 schools and creating new boutique schools. Leeds and Beeber school programs were closed; special admission schools would occupy those school buildings. The West Philly campus of Science Leadership Academy would occupy all of Beeber and add a middle school component.[115] Hill-Freedman World Academy would move into the Leeds building, and the SRC approved $6.5 million in renovations at Leeds for Hill-Freedman.[116] The Building 21 school opened in 2014 and relocated to the old Kinsey School building with $4.75 million of renovations to that building.[117] Such moves gave credence to complaints that the district defunded its traditional schools and, in some cases, left them to rot and then invested in special admission schools and charters.

The most notable of corporate practices was selling properties where schools had been closed.[118] Community members were concerned about blight and wanted to have input on what would happen with the shuttered schools in their neighborhoods.[119] Some of these buildings were historic properties, built at the beginning of the twentieth century. Germantown was preparing to celebrate its ninety-ninth year when it was closed.[120] And Wilson Elementary had housed an art collection bequeathed to it worth more than the building was actually sold for. What's worse, the proceeds from these sales did not create resources for the school district. In 2017, Commissioner Green said City Council had insisted that, in order for the district to get that $50 million for the rehiring of laid off essential employees in 2013, the SRC had to sell "inventory of existing schools and pay them back the $50 million they were giving us. … some of these school sales were unfortunate."[121]

Hite and the SRC also further expanded charters, though the cost of these expansions were untenable. By the spring of 2014, 35 percent of Philly's public school students were attending charter schools, and 29 percent of the school district's budget was consumed with the per-pupil costs of charters.[122] Traditional SDP schools had not been given the resources they needed to thrive, but resources were infused with charter conversion.[123] Thus, some parents supported conversions while others were concerned about charter fraud and mismanagement of funds with little commission oversight.[124] Several community members requested a moratorium on new charter schools, as advocated by the NAACP, while other community members requested the district focus on community schools.[125] Kia Philpot Hinton of Action United said her organization was not anticharter but antifraud.[126] Parent and community organizer Tomika Anglin lamented, "Neighborhood schools are starved of resources." Hite charged back that the district's Black students "were not performing even when we had the resources," seeming to justify the neglect and defunding of traditional schools.[127] But with no institutional memory prior to his arrival in 2012, it is difficult to know to what period of resource abundance Hite was referring. Predominantly Black schools in Philadelphia had been neglected since at least the 1960s. Hite's claim was uninformed, ideological, and mythical. By 2016, many traditional public schools in Philadelphia were still so neglected that many lacked safe drinking water and clean air unencumbered by asbestos, let alone adequate resources for teaching and learning.[128] Still, there was Black pushback against charter school proliferation. While Hite and the SRC successfully converted district schools Cooke, Huey, and Wister to charters in 2015, parents, teachers, and community organizers stopped the conversion of Steel Elementary School into a Mastery school.[129]

Despite Black leadership, the neoliberal marketplace did not value Black charter schools. Leaders of Black charter schools unattached to corporate charter management organizations suspected the SRC sought to eviscerate them. Ayesha Imani, CEO of the African-centered Sankofa Freedom Academy Charter School, criticized the commission's plans for "the School District to turn over independent neighborhood charter schools to corporate charter franchises."[130] Other Black Philadelphians noticed a pattern.[131] The African-centered Imani Education Circle school was recommended for nonrenewal in the fall of 2013.[132] The SRC authorized the surrender and forfeiture of African-centered charter school, Wakisha Charter School in 2014, as well as the Walter Palmer Leadership and Learning Partners Charter School, a Black charter named for one of the key organizers of the massive school protest at school district headquarters in 1967.[133] The commission revoked the African-centered Khepera Charter School's charter in 2017.[134] It seemed while the SRC was laxed with the oversight of most Philly charter schools, it had no qualms about holding Black-led charter schools unaffiliated with corporate CMOs to the letter of charter regulations. Though Black-led charters made up 19 percent of Philadelphia's charter schools, they represented 87 percent of the charters targeted for closure between 2010 and 2020.[135]

Fight the Power

The Epilogue

R esearch on schooling in the United States has been historically viewed
through the lens of psychology, which is rooted in pathology—always
in search of a problem to be fixed. Education researchers are usually asked
to situate our work with the *statement of the problem*. In school districts like
Philadelphia, many assume the "problem" is Black people—Black students,
families, and communities, the languages Black people speak or don't speak
with precision, the wealth Black people don't have, what Black people don't
know—as if schooling could be compulsory yet impotent to actually educate
Black students. White supremacy, anglonormativity, and anti-Blackness in
ideology, policies, and practices render Black people insurmountable problems for schools. These elements are features built into American schooling
to maintain oppressive schools and schooling systems. In his foundational
text, *The Education of Blacks in the South: 1860–1935*, James D. Anderson
wrote, "it is difficult to comprehend how a subordinate institution such as
a state-controlled public education system might advance a class of people
against the racist oppression of government and other dominant social
institutions." It was true for the descendants of the enslaved in the late
1800s, and it is true today: American schools are ill-equipped to educate, let
alone advance, the very people they demean. Such an education would be
counterproductive to these allegedly United States of America. Public schools
will likely always reflect the poisonous ideals of this racist, capitalist nation.

Since the modern reform era began in Philly in 1967, racial school reform
has consistently been sabotaged by racism, capitalism, and constant political
combat. Claims of liberal ideals are mythical and farcical for the masses, even
if they have applied to some individuals and a few circumstances. Liberal

claims cannot absolve the United States of the permanence of racism or its capitalist reality. White supremacy and capitalism pervade our social, economic, and political systems—including school districts—in the hierarchical exploitation of anyone who is not white and/or wealthy. In the context of schooling, capitalism renders social mobility Herculean for multitudes of students who are underserved by underresourced public schools in stratified systems with tracked classes, special-admission magnet schools, comprehensive neighborhood schools, and philanthrocapitalist-funded charter chains. Schooling for social mobility is available only to some while educators purport false notions of meritocracy. This holds true for Black students even when the mayor is Black, the police chief is Black, the head of the Board of Education or the School Reform Commission is Black, and the superintendent of schools or chief executive officer is Black. The elevation of Black people to positions of prominence does not eliminate racism and cannot outdo capitalism, not in society at large and not in the work undertaken by these prominent Black people. Even when Black people led, racism was still weaponized. Public school inequities persisted. There have been constant doing and undoing in the School District of Philadelphia, such that there are surface-level changes, but the core issues that existed in 1967 remained in 2017. The shift from the Board of Education to the School Reform Commission did not change the highly political nature of Philadelphia's public schools, nor did it change the state-imposed fiscal issues that plagued the school district for years. The state's usurping of Philly's public schools was supposed to make public schooling in the city better. It did not. There were new initiatives, repackaged reforms, and new curriculums for students, schools, and communities narratively constructed as failures, which enriched corporations and corporate nonprofits. The district was used as a laboratory for venture capitalists and wealthy foundations that sought to improve education by destroying public schooling. There was also an abundance of financial mismanagement that culminated with the largest school closing and staff layoff in the more than two-hundred-year history of the district. Political entrenchment and fiscal malfeasance actually deepened and widened under the School Reform Commission.

Policy remedies that attempted to redress racism actually expanded racism. In Philly, as in many large urban centers around America, state-sanctioned desegregation efforts replied to endemic racism and racist practices of school systems by addressing school-level issues and not systemic, structural issues.[1] School desegregation policies and plans prioritized white desires for comfort over confronting racism. Black Philadelphians had been the victims of racial discrimination, and then their children were tasked with fixing it with their schooling. Busing Black students from Black neighborhoods to attend school in white neighborhoods was dangerous, physically and emotionally, and no white students were forced to attend Black schools for racial integration. Busing did nothing to address the historic, pervasive ill-regard with which Black students, families, communities, and professionals had been handled in Philadelphia. Black educators opposed the district's racial balance policy for faculty for two reasons. First, the policy meant eliminating critical masses of Black educators in schools throughout the district, and far too often, integration meant tokenism. Second, the faculty racial-balance policy reduced Black educators to second-class status when it withheld a key benefit afforded to other members of the Philadelphia Federation of Teachers: seniority. That meant the racial balance of school faculties was more important than Black educators' rights. This policy made desegregation the responsibility of Black educators who neither caused nor benefited from state-enforced segregation. Whether it was through busing Black students or forced transfers of Black educators, making Black people responsible for remedying racist problems they did not create centers whiteness and allows white educators to remain prioritized and unscathed. What were white people ever asked to surrender? How would white people adjust for antiracism? Policies and practices that hinge on Black people facing the water cannons first, offering themselves on the front lines to correct oppression, are racist and perpetuate white supremacy.

Shifting the people in power to redress racism has not ended racism. Philly does not value enough who and what it has, its own richness. Too often, changes in leadership meant institutional memory was lost and what *was* working was devalued and dumped. Philly's strong insider-outsider tensions are homegrown love prevailing. Philly insiders lived within the city limits when its neighborhoods were not hot commodities, were educated in its public schools, and/or worked within the School District of Philadelphia. Even suburbanites only get conditional insider passes on a case-by-case basis. Outsiders cannot fully discern the local context, whether that context is geographical or racial. Insider-outsider tensions impacted perceptions of school reform. Constance Clayton's shifts were easier for Black educators, Black activists, and the Black press to digest and navigate than those enacted by David Hornbeck and Paul Vallas. But Arlene Ackerman and Bill Hite being Black was not enough for Black educators, community members, and activists to view and respond to them in ways similar to Clayton. Ackerman was more beloved by Black educators and community members than Hite, likely because she championed *some* Black people—namely, the Black upwardly mobile. Maybe because of the love for her, maybe because of how she was essentially pushed out of the district by powerful Black men after only three years at the helm, maybe because she died from cancer less than two years after she left Philadelphia, some Black educators and community members still hold reverence for Ackerman.

It is important to note the criticisms of Ackerman that were tied to how people perceive highly visible Black women.[2] Given the controlling images associated with Black women over time, it is not surprising that critiques of her policies seemed to be of less concern than her demeanor. Hite continued Ackerman's policies but was nicer, more obsequious, more political, and male. When she became superintendent, Ackerman expected to have camaraderie, connection, and covering with Black people running the city—School Reform Commission Chair Robert Archie, Mayor Michael Nutter, State Representative Dwight Evans. But when she stood up to them, they turned on her. The Black mayor abandoned his public schools' Black chief executive officer because he valued his political career and public persona more than what solidarity with Ackerman could offer. In 2015, Hite contracted with Foundations, Inc., the company Evans favored and over which he fell out with Ackerman, to fill the positions of two assistant superintendents. Though the transaction appeared to be pay to play, Hite claimed there was no such impropriety.[3]

The damage produced from the investment in corporate school-reform models cannot be overstated. Corporate, neoliberal school reform renders impossible public schooling as democratizing institutions. These models use the masses' tax dollars to fund contracts with corporations that have no public accountability. Corporate, neoliberal schooling takes intractable issues confronting school districts and solves them in the most cynical, makeshift ways. Instead of figuring out how to retain excellent Black educators, it is easier to contract with Teach For America and TNTP (formerly The New Teacher Project) to send a steady crop of newbies, regardless of how long they stay in the district and how disinvested they are in the communities. Instead of spending time developing teachers' capacities for critically analyzing instructional frameworks, practices, ideologies, outcomes, it is easier to give them a scripted curriculum they are mandated to parrot in the classroom. Instead of developing instructional leaders' capacity for relationship building, problem-solving, and reshaping school culture to center the marginalized, it is easier to send them to programs that spew technical skills and behaviors for corporate school leadership. While beneficial to some Black people, market ideology in school reform is harmful and problematic for the most school-dependent and least resourced Black people in Philadelphia. Market-based reforms also did not and do not move urban America any closer to the purported democratic, liberal ideals of the United States. Even if Ackerman's and Hite's intentions were pure, their impacts were devastating. They signed on to manage a system and structure that was built to dispossess and disempower the most vulnerable, the poorest, and the Blackest residents of Philadelphia. Ackerman did attempt to shift resources to people who had the least, but she was challenged in these efforts at every turn. Hite seemed more committed to satisfying his bosses, seeming measured, middle-of-the-road, and political enough to stay in the role almost as long as Clayton's eleven years at the helm. This is the challenge of Black leadership of white institutions: aspiring ascendance to improve the organization on behalf of Black people is often muffled by the ascendance in the organization. The higher that people climb in an institution, the more they represent that institution and work for its preservation and their own preservation within that institution. Institutional improvement for justice usually moves down in its priority, especially when the organization is steeped in and accountable to the ideals, desires, and trappings of white supremacy and capitalism.

Black educators—and any educators committed to collective improvement, justice, and liberation, not just individual advancement—have to be particularly mindful of whose interests they serve as they do their work and who benefits from their policies and practices. Educators who aspire to be freedom fighters must free themselves of the white gaze and consider the larger social purposes for the work. This requires informed empathy for the dispossessed, the marginalized, the Black, the Brown, the poor, and the underresourced, not just sympathy, charity, and philanthropy. Any educator with a lackadaisical commitment to disrupting systems of oppression is complicit in the system of oppression.

To be an educator is a privileged position, even if that privilege is relative to the racial, economic, and political realities. It is the responsibility of the privileged to challenge power and policies on behalf of those who have been marginalized, oppressed, and dispossessed. Any educators unwilling to use their position on behalf of those who have been marginalized, oppressed, and dispossessed is not worthy of their position. Any educator more concerned with job security than with the lives of the students, families, and our collective humanity is a self-serving educator. Any educator who prioritizes temporary compliance rather than challenging the oppression embedded in schools and school systems is merely reproducing our inequitable, unjust society. Any educator not actively working to dismantle systems of oppression (and our schools are systems of oppression) is complicit in maintaining these systems of oppression. After the George Floyd uprisings of 2020, many school systems claimed an antiracist orientation, only to relent in 2021 with trumped-up tales of lessons about critical race theory in schools. Educators must disrupt the harm that has been done to the most vulnerable and marginalized through our schools and school systems. Being an antiracist, anti-oppression educator supersedes interrogating identity. It requires interrogating the systems and structures that organize schools and school systems and that oppress those who are not white and wealthy and looking for ways to resist, disrupt, and dismantle those oppressive systems and structures. The charge is clear: Don't become what you first aimed to disrupt.

Methodological Appendix

This book brings together thirteen years of research. *Not Paved for Us: Black Educators and Public School Reform in Philadelphia* uses the narratives of Black educators, the Black press, the Philadelphia Board of Education minutes, and the School Reform Commission minutes as its primary sources to ask: What were the reform policies and practices in the School District of Philadelphia that impacted Black educators, specifically, and Black Philadelphians, more broadly, from 1967 to 2017? How did they experience and respond to these school and school system politics, policies, and practices? Given a changing racial, sociopolitical, and economic climate—in the school district, in the City of Philadelphia, throughout America, and in the sphere of urban education reform across the nation during these fifty years—how did Black educators and community members navigate the persistence of racism embedded in the school district over time? How did the narratives created by Black educators and community members—about the policies, practices, and politics of superintendents, chief executive officers, other district administrators, the Board of Education, and the School Reform Commission—shape their work as educators? How did changes from mayoral control to state control—from the Board of Education to the School Reform Commission, from superintendents to chief executive officers— impact Black educators' perceptions of district governance and practices within the district? The specific experiences of Black educators are of importance to the historical record of Black education in Philadelphia, but this research also asks larger questions and draws conclusions regarding the experiences of a racialized group of educators within a large, urban, underresourced school district with a history of racist practices and racial politics, and thus it locates this case within a larger context regarding issues of inequity in schools.

This research began with a pilot study in 2008, an oral history of three retired Black Philadelphia educators who discussed their memories of and experiences with the School District of Philadelphia's voluntary teacher-transfer plan to deal with faculty racial isolation in the 1960s. Using what I discovered from that initial inquiry, between 2010 and 2018, I met with and interviewed twenty-eight Black Philly educators whose work in the district spanned at least two superintendents or chief executive officers between 1967 and 2018. Purposeful sampling was used to determine self-identified Black educators from the district. This sampling strategy was used because of the participants' particular insights into the experiences of Black educators in Philly.[1] Separate, in-depth, semistructured, one- to two-hour oral history influenced interviews were conducted of those twenty-eight Black educators.[2] As key narrators, these Black Philly educators spoke on the condition of anonymity, so they were each assigned a single-name pseudonym to obscure their identities in this text.

A second group of narrators was interviewed for this study. In this group were eight educators and/or education activists who worked in or alongside the district throughout the time period being studied. The purpose of this set of interviews was to corroborate the data secured from the key narrators and from the historical record. Interviews were audio-recorded using a digital voice recorder and were transcribed.[3] The second group of narrators did not speak with the assumption of anonymity. However, for the publication of this book, one did request and receive anonymity so as not to risk retribution for her insights.

Transcripts were then cleaned and edited, and throughout this process, themes and topics emerged. Analysis was conducted by reviewing interview transcripts multiple times for salient points, ideas, and perspectives that emerged across narrators and other sources. Trustworthiness was ensured through constant corroboration across the multiple sources and through narrators' reviews of their transcripts. Newspaper accounts were examined and used to create the cultural and historical context of the school district during each era examined. Newspaper accounts were also used to support the stories and ideas conveyed by key narrators within this research.

To complicate these narratives, from 2018 through 2021, I poured over and through the public meeting minutes of the School District of Philadelphia's

Board of Education and School Reform Commission, examining the record from 1963 through 2018. Each year of the Board of Education's minutes are housed in its own book, and each book of minutes is between 700 and 1,100 pages. Those books reside in the Office of the General Counsel for the School District of Philadelphia. The School Reform Commission's minutes are online, and the links to those minutes were provided to me by a representative of the Office of the General Counsel. Other sources for this research are mainstream news sources, testimonies of Philadelphia public school activists and cultural workers, reports, and scholarly articles.

Critical race theory (CRT) is the epistemological lens through which I have studied this research examining the experiences of Black educators within an urban school district engaged in reforms over a period of fifty years. This study focuses on the following components of critical race theory: the endemic nature of racism to American society and its institutions, interest convergence, the importance of storytelling and counternarratives, and objectivity, neutrality, colorblindness, and merit as falsehoods.[4] Gloria Ladson-Billings and William Tate initiated the use of critical race theory in education. They argued that class and gender alone were insufficient to explain the variances in schooling experiences and performances for students of color. They problematized the ways that the law has attempted to correct racist educational practices (for example, with the US Supreme Court's holding in *Brown v. Board of Education*), specifically how its inability to separate democracy from capitalism has left these corrections incomplete.[5] In the context of schools and systems of schooling, capitalism urges social reproduction while democracy suggests meritocracy, though these are competing constructs.

An analysis of education through a critical race theory lens views schools as tools of social reproduction that purport false notions of meritocracy.[6] This speaks directly to Derrick Bell's work on interest convergence—the notion that white people will consent to legal or policy changes for marginalized groups of people only as long as it benefits them.[7] Because of this need for interest convergence, the work of rectifying racist practices and social ills through education has not been fully implemented. The privileged do not easily participate in their dethroning. The role of interest convergence is paramount in rethinking schooling systems.[8] Interest convergence is oppositional to justice. Thus, when there are no benefits for whites who operate from the standpoint of interest convergence, the racially, economically, and politically marginalized and disenfranchised will have little to no access to opportunities to advance, enhance, shift, or rectify their positions in life, which thereby maintains the system that keeps the white, the wealthy, and the powerful in control of American life.

To complement critical race theory, narrative identity theory—specifically, the work of Jerome Bruner and Pablo Vila—serves to explicate how the aspect of CRT that involves storytelling and counternarratives is understood and is used in this study.[9] Narrative identity theory argues that people make sense of their lives through the stories they tell about themselves.[10] Whether their stories are comprised of actual facts does not matter. Facts make sense when they are organized into a narrative; they matter only because of how they fit into our larger understanding of an entire story. Facts live only in context.[11] What matters most is the story that was created by the lived experience.[12] Experiences are organized through narratives; narratives are an accepted version of reality that do not need "empirical verification and logical requiredness."[13] Narrative has power to shape our understandings of the world.[14] Through the organization of facts into stories, human beings construct reality.[15] Vila argued that identities are socially and historically constructed and that the context of the storyteller matters. If identity is relational and has the capacity to shift based on circumstances, one needs a narrative in order to process one's identity.[16] Edward Taylor has also argued for the significance of narratives within specific historical contexts in order to contradict the master narratives that have dominated the education discourse, a narrative replete with the facade of liberalism and meritocracy.[17] As such, these stories within a community have the capacity to construct the knowledge of what it means to be a Black educator encountering the endemic racism within the School District of Philadelphia over time. However, this book takes no interest in attempting to redress the existing grand narrative with an alternate grand narrative and singular voice of Black educators.[18] Of course, Black people are diverse, not monolithic.

This book is about how Black Philadelphians encountered public schooling in Philadelphia, whether as teachers, administrators, community organizers, or agitators. This book is not a history; it is about Black educators and the politics of racial school reform over time. This book does not focus on

Black children, nor does it examine other marginalized populations who have also been oppressed in public schooling, though similar research examining reforms, impacts on students or students' activism in Philly over time is a worthy pursuit. In the process of reviewing these meeting minutes, there were many times I came across issues involving bilingual education and issues specifically pertaining to African and Caribbean students and families navigating the School District of Philadelphia that are worthy of exploration. This book does not explore the politics of the Philadelphia Federation of Teaching (PFT) beyond the teacher strikes until 1981. This book does, however, serve as a foundation for an inquiry around what teacher unions could look like, especially considering the success of the Chicago Teachers' Union in 2012. The PFT is ripe for additional research on its racial politics, its old-guard faction (whose members really shine in the areas of due process and collective bargaining), and the more radical newbies (such as Caucus of Working Educators, who pushed the Black Lives Matter Week of Action in Schools). This research does not explore those tensions.

Notes

Foreword

1. I use the term *progressive* to describe a superintendent considered an "outsider" to what had been a very insular district. He brought new and seemingly progressive ideas to teacher development and curriculum change.
2. Isabelle Wilkerson, *The Warmth of Other Suns: The Epic Story of America's Great Migration* (New York: Random House, 2010).

Introduction

1. Throughout this book, I use *Black* to represent the vast identities belonging to those of us in the African diaspora. I also use *Black* and *African American* interchangeably.
2. See Barbara Sizemore, *Walking in Circles: The Black Struggle for School Reform* (Chicago: Third World Press, 2008); Jerald Podair, *The Strike that Changed New York: Blacks, Whites, and the Ocean Hill-Brownsville Crisis* (New Haven: Yale University Press, 2004); Daniel Perlstein, *Justice, Justice: School Politics and the Eclipse of Liberalism* (New York: Peter Lang, 2004); Marion Orr, *Black Social Capital: The Politics of School Reform in Baltimore, 1986–1999* (Lawrence: University Press of Kansas, 1999); Jeanne Theoharis, "'I'd Rather Go to School in the South': How Boston's School Desegregation Complicates the Civil Rights Paradigm," in *Freedom North: Black Freedom Struggles Outside the South*, ed. Jeanne F. Theoharis and Komozi Woodard (New York: Palgrave MacMillan, 2003); Jack Dougherty, *More Than One Struggle: The Evolution of Black School Reform in Milwaukee* (Chapel Hill: University of North Carolina Press, 2004).
3. Mari J. Matsuda, Charles R. Lawrence, Richard Delgado, and Kimberle Williams Crenshaw, *Words That Wound: Critical Race Theory, Assaultive Speech, and the First Amendment* (Boulder: Westview Press, 1993).
4. Gloria Ladson-Billings, "From the Achievement Gap to Education Debt: Understanding Achievement in U.S. Schools," *Educational Researcher* 35, no. 3 (2006): 3–12; Asa G. Hilliard, "No Mystery: Closing the Achievement Gap Between Africans and Excellence," in *Young, Gifted, and Black: Promoting High Achievement Among African-American Students*, ed. (Boston: Beacon Press, 2003); Camika Royal, "Please Stop Using the Phrase 'Achievement Gap,'" Good, November 8, 2012, retrieved August 19, 2021, from https://www.good.is/articles/please-stop-using-the-phrase-achievement-gap.
5. The School District of Philadelphia was established in 1818.
6. Vincent P. Franklin, *The Education of Black Philadelphia: The Social and Educational History of a Minority Community, 1900–1950* (Philadelphia: University of Pennsylvania Press, 1979); Ruth Wright Hayre and Alexis Moore, *Tell Them We Are Rising: A Memoir of Faith in Education* (New York: Wiley, 1997).
7. See Adrienne D. Dixson, Camika Royal, and Kevin Lawrence Henry, "School Reform and School Choice," in *Handbook of Urban Education*, ed. H. Richard Milner and Kofi Lomotey

(New York: Routledge, 2014); Anne E. Phillips, "A History of the Struggle for School Desegregation in Philadelphia, 1955–1967," *Pennsylvania History: A Journal of Mid-Atlantic Studies* 72, no. 1 (2005): 49–76; Kenneth K. Wong and F. X. Shen, "Big City Mayors and School Governance Reform: The Case of School District Takeover," *Peabody Journal of Education* 78, no. 1 (2003): 5–32; Larry Cuban and Michael Usdan, eds., *Powerful Reforms with Shallow Roots: Improving America's Urban Schools* (New York: Teachers College Press, 2003); Jon S. Birger, "Race, Reaction, and Reform: The Three Rs of Philadelphia School Politics, 1965–1971," *Pennsylvania Magazine of History and Biography* 120, no. 3 (1996): 163–216.

8. See also Kelli Sparrow Mickens's *Philadelphia Freedom Schools* (On the Wings of Margaret Sparrow Publishing: Philadelphia, 2016).

9. See also Lester Spence's *Knocking the Hustle: Against the Neoliberal Turn in Black Politics* (Punctum Books: Brooklyn, 2015).

Chapter 1

1. School District of Philadelphia (SDP) Board of Education (BOE) Minutes, May 25, 1970, 405.

2. Jon S. Birger, "Race, Reaction, and Reform: The Three Rs of Philadelphia School Politics, 1965–1971, *Pennsylvania Magazine of History and Biography* 120, no. 3 (July 1996): 168–169, 163–216.

3. SDP BOE Minutes, December 12, 1966, 727. The School District of Philadelphia's Board of Education Minutes for January 23, 1967, backdated Mark Shedd's appointment as a consultant to November 28, 1966, and stated that he would be paid at a rate of $150 per day plus expenses.

4. Matthew Countryman, "'From Protest to Politics': Community Control and Black Independent Politics in Philadelphia, 1965–1984," *Journal of Urban History* 32 (September 2006): 813–860.

5. Subini Ancy Annamma, Darrell D. Jackson, and Deb Morrison, "Conceptualizing Color-Evasiveness: Using Dis/ability Critical Race Theory to Expand a Color-Blind Racial Ideology in Education and Society," *Race Ethnicity and Education* 20, no. 2 (2017): 147–162.

6. Larry Cuban and Michael Usdan, eds., *Powerful Reforms with Shallow Roots: Improving America's Urban Schools* (New York: Teachers College Press, 2003); Harvey Kantor, "Education, Social Reform, and the State: ESEA and Federal Education Policy in the 1960s," *American Journal of Education* (1991): 47–83. Per SDP BOE Minutes, May 29, 1969, 348, SDP had received "$31,489,000 for Federal Education and Anti-Poverty Programs."

7. Yvonne Reynolds, "ADL Claims 'Ethnic Patronage' Blocks Jewish Promotions," *Philadelphia Tribune*, January 4, 1983, 7; Anne E. Phillips, "A History of the Struggle for School Desegregation in Philadelphia, 1955–1967," *Philadelphia History: A Journal of Mid-Atlantic Studies* 72, no. 1 (2005): 49–76; Conrad Weiler, *Philadelphia: Neighborhood, Authority and the Urban Crisis* (New York: Praegar, 1974).

8. SDP BOE Minutes, June 25, 1963, 221.

9. Jon Shelton, *Teacher Strike! Public Education and the Making of a New American Political Order* (Urbana: University of Illinois Press, 2017), 15: "Desegregation became a major battlefield in the North as well by the end of the 1960s, and the busing of school students to achieve integration was a hot-button issue in national politics over the course of the long 1970s."

10. William W. Cutler III, "Public Education: The School District of Philadelphia," *The Encyclopedia of Greater Philadelphia*, accessed March 5, 2015, doi: http://philadelphiaencyclopedia.org/archive/public-educationthe-school-district-of-philadelphia/; Rene Luis Alvarez, "'There's No Such Thing as an Unqualified Teacher': Unionization and Integration in the Philadelphia Public Schools," *The Historian* (2003): 837–865; SDP BOE Minutes, June 13, 1966, 266.

11. "Nichols, Hutt Battled to Help Negro Pupils," *Philadelphia Tribune*, January 24, 1967, 1.

12. "Most Strikes CAN Be Averted by Thinking, Acting in Advance," *Philadelphia Tribune*, January 16, 1967, 7; "Board of Education Submits to Pressure of Teacher Segregationists," *Philadelphia Tribune*, January 24, 1967, 7.

13. "Agencies Fighting Racial Imbalance of Teachers Here," *Philadelphia Tribune*, November 14, 1967, 3; "NAACP Suing to Bar Teacher Transfer Plan," *Philadelphia Tribune*, January 31, 1967, 1; "Voluntary Teacher Transfers Necessary, Mr. Dilworth Says," *Philadelphia Tribune*, February 11, 1967, 7; Mark Bricklin, "Teachers Union Called 'Blatantly Biased,' Strike Threat to Block Transfers Blasted," *Philadelphia Tribune*, January 24, 1967, 1.

14. John Brantley Wilder, "Slurs Heaped on Children at Schools, Parents Claim," *Philadelphia Tribune*, January 14, 1967, 20; John Brantley Wilder, "Can School Parks Foster Pupil Integration Here?," *Philadelphia Tribune*, January 17, 1967, 20; John Brantley Wilder, "No White Children Being Bused to Negro Schools," *Philadelphia Tribune*, January 21, 1967, 24; John Brantley Wilder, "Claim Education Park Plan Will Assure Only Minimum School Busing," *Philadelphia Tribune*, January 24, 1967, 20; John Brantley Wilder, "Claim Lack of Sincerity 'Bad' for Busing Program," *Philadelphia Tribune*, January 31, 1967, 20; John Wilder, "Urban League Urges School Board to Reject Study Report Opposed to 'Educational Parks,'" *Philadelphia Tribune*, February 7, 1967, 4.

15. Wilder, "No White Children Being Bused to Negro Schools," 24.

16. Wilder, "Claim Lack of Sincerity 'Bad' for Busing Program," 20.

17. "Slurs Heaped on Children at Schools, Parents Claim," 20.

18. Wilder, "North Phila. Group Calls Program 'Colossal Flop,'" 20; Camika Royal, "Reflections of Three Black Philadelphia Educators: An Oral History," paper presented at the Annual Meeting of the American Educational Research Association, Division F, History and Historiography, San Diego, CA, April 2009.

19. Wilder, "Slurs Heaped on Children at Schools, Parents Claim,"20.

20. SDP BOE Minutes, January 28, 1974, 76.

21. "Editorials & Comments: Board of Education Lavishes Thousands on Experts; Short-Changes Students," *Philadelphia Tribune*, March 18, 1967, 9.

22. Jon Birger, "Race, Reaction, and Reform: The Three Rs of Philadelphia School Politics, 1965–1971," *The Pennsylvania Magazine of History and Biography* 120, no. 3 (1996): 163–216.

23. Rene Luis Alvarez, "'There's No Such Thing as an Unqualified Teacher': Unionization and Integration in the Philadelphia Public Schools," *The Historian* 65, no 4 (2003): 837–865.

24. Peyton Gray Jr., "Peyton's Place: Shedd's Seven Subtleties of Racism," *Philadelphia Tribune*, March 16, 1968, 6.

25. Birger, "Race, Reaction, and Reform," 163–216.

26. "Editorials & Comment: Dr. Mark Shedd Is Doing a Commendable Job as School Superintendent," *Philadelphia Tribune*, March 27, 1971, 8.

27. "Protest Principal Leaving School for $15,000 Post," *Philadelphia Tribune*, March 21, 1967, 5; "Urge Negro Woman for Board of Education," *Philadelphia Tribune*, September 30, 1967, 1; Alvarez, "'There's No Such Thing as an Unqualified Teacher'"; "School Bd.'s Teacher Will Cost $707,080," *Philadelphia Tribune*, April 25, 1967, 4.

28. J. Donald Porter, "Public School Setup Is Loaded with Negroes in High Positions," *Philadelphia Tribune*, March 14, 1967, 4.

29. School District of Philadelphia, Department of Superintendence, "Colored Teachers Appointed in Senior, Junior, and Vocational Schools," Temple University Urban Archives, 1944.

30. John Wilder, "Robert Poindexter Heads School Board Until Fall, Signs First Pact with Custodial Workers," *Philadelphia Tribune*, May 20, 1967, 6; John Wilder, "Poindexter Now Top-Ranking Negro School Official in US," *Philadelphia Tribune*, July 18, 1967, 1.

31. "Editorials & Comments: Board of Education Lavishes Thousands on Experts; Short-Changes Students."

32. William W. Cutler III, "Public Education: The School District of Philadelphia," *The Encyclopedia of Greater Philadelphia*, accessed March 5, 2015, doi: http://philadelphiaencyclopedia.org/archive/public-educationthe-school-district-of-philadelphia/.

33. "Whittier Raps Bickering in School System," *Philadelphia Tribune*, May 23, 1967, 1. Per SDP BOE Minutes, August 13, 1967, 150, Whittier had been superintendent of schools in Philadelphia since August 1, 1964. His tenure would end on August 1, 1967, and he would be paid as a consultant from that date until December 1, 1969 at a rate of $1,400 per month and would be reimbursed for travel expenses.

34. Per SDP BOE Minutes, January 27, 1969, 25, Marcus Foster was commended at the Board of Education meeting "for his exceptional leadership at Gratz, his superior relationships with his students and staff, and for his eminent record in human and community relations." Per SDP BOE Minutes June 30, 1969, 434, on this day, Marcus Foster was named associate superintendent. Per SDP BOE Minutes April 13, 1970, 274, Marcus Foster submitted his resignation from his post with the district, and Shedd expressed his regret at losing him. For more on Marcus Foster, see John P. Spencer, *In the Crossfire: Marcus Foster and the Troubled History of American School Reform* (Philadelphia: University of Pennsylvania Press, 2012).

35. "Editorials & Comments: A Fair Chance for Dr. Shedd's Ideas," *Philadelphia Tribune*, June 3, 1967, 7.

36. John Wilder, "Frank Sullivan Speaks Before Shedd Arrives," *Philadelphia Tribune*, April 19, 1969, 1, 29.

37. "Peyton's Place: Shedd's Seven Subtleties of Racism," 8.

38. John Brantley Wilder, "Fired Teacher Rehired; Let Students Read About Sex," *Philadelphia Tribune*, June 27, 1967, 1.

39. Wilder, "Fired Teacher Rehired; Let Students Read About Sex."

40. John Brantley Wilder, "Educators Rising Rapidly But Can't Keep Up with Soaring Numbers and Hopes of Students," *Philadelphia Tribune*; February 17, 1968, 17; Vincent P. Franklin, *The Education of Black Philadelphia: The Social and Educational History of a Minority Community, 1900–1950* (Philadelphia: University of Pennsylvania Press, 1979).

41. "Editorials & Comment: Philadelphia School Segregation Exposed by Government Agency," *Philadelphia Tribune*, June 22, 1971, 8.

42. See, for example, William H. Watkins, *The White Architects of Black Education: Ideology and Power in America, 1865–1954* (New York: Teachers College Press, 2001; James Anderson, *The Education of Blacks in the South, 1860–1935* (Chapel Hill: University of North Carolina Press, 1988); Michelle Fine, *Framing Dropouts: Notes on the Politics of an Urban Public High School* (New York: State University of New York Press, 1991).

43. "Editorials & Comment: Dr. Mark Shedd Is Doing a Commendable Job as School Superintendent."

44. Bricklin, "Teachers Union Called 'Blatantly Biased'; Strike Threat to Block Transfers Blasted."

45. Wilder, "Educators Rising Rapidly But Can't Keep Up with Soaring Numbers and Hopes of Students."

46. Latifah, interview with the author, July 22, 2010; "School Changes Favor Negroes," *Philadelphia Tribune*, January 2, 1968, 1.

47. Interview with Nina, July 12, 2010; interview with Constance Clayton, September 30, 2010.

48. SDP BOE Minutes, June 26, 1967, 423. Per SDP BOE Minutes on June 28, 1968, 415, Bernard Watson would be promoted to associate superintendent as of July 1, 1969.

49. "277,500 Students Will Find Many New Changes When They Go Back to School" *Philadelphia Tribune*, August 26, 1967, 16. Per SDP BOE Minutes, June 26, 1967, 475, Robert Poindexter was appointed acting superintendent of schools until Shedd's appointment as school superintendent in Philadelphia was finalized.

50. "Protest Principal Leaving School for $15,000 Post," *Philadelphia Tribune*, March 21, 1967, 5; "Fight to Keep Two Principals Won by Parents," *Philadelphia Tribune*, March 28, 1967, 1.

51. Wilder, "Educators Rising Rapidly But Can't Keep Up with Soaring Numbers and Hopes of Students."

52. "Protest Principal Leaving School for $15,000 Post," *Philadelphia Tribune*, March 21, 1967, 5; "Fight to Keep Two Principals Won by Parents," *Philadelphia Tribune*, March 28, 1967, 1; Joe Hunter, "Hamilton School Parents Demanding Principal Stay. Petition School Board on Behalf of Negro Rate Inexperienced," *Philadelphia Tribune*, June 27, 1967, 2.

53. Floyd Logan, "Negro Leader Demands Action from Mayor Tate," *Philadelphia Tribune*, May 9, 1967, 24.

54. "Woods Declares Mayor Tate Won't Name Negro Woman to School Board," *Philadelphia Tribune*, October 10, 1967, 1; "Urge Negro Woman for Board of Education," *Philadelphia Tribune*, September 30, 1967, 1–2; Mark Bricklin, "*Tribune* Gets First Nomination for Negro Woman on School Bd," *Philadelphia Tribune*, October 3, 1967, 1, 3; Mark Bricklin, "Nominations for Negro Woman on School Board 'Flood' *Tribune* Office," *Philadelphia Tribune*, October 10, 1967, 4; Mark Bricklin, "Back Negro Women for School Board," *Philadelphia Tribune*, October 14, 1967, 23; Mark Bricklin, "Baptists Back Negro Woman for Education Board, Blast Rioting," *Philadelphia Tribune*, October 17, 1967, 1, 3.

55. Per SDP BOE Minutes, March 23, 1970, 231, the district appointed two thousand teachers who had failed the National Teacher Exam to be part of a two-year study to see if these teachers would perform significantly better or worse than those who had passed the test and had similar training. For more information on the National Teacher Corps, see Stephen D. Lerner, "The Teacher Corps," *Harvard Crimson*, May 24, 1966, retrieved on January 24, 2020, from https://www.thecrimson.com/article/1966/5/24/the-teacher-corps-pthe-national-teacher/. See also Sarah Anne Eckert, "The National Teacher Corps: A Study of Shifting Goals and Changing Assumptions," *Urban Education* (2011): 1–21.

56. John Wilder, "1,000 Teachers Here Facing Loss of Jobs," *Philadelphia Tribune*, June 10, 1967, 1.

57. R. Scott Baker, "The Paradoxes of Desegregation: Race, Class, and Education, 1935–1975," *American Journal of Education* 109, no. May (2001): 320–343; Samuel B. Etheridge, "Impact of the 1954 *Brown v Topeka Board of Education* Decision on Black Educators," *Negro Educational Review* 30 (October 1979): 217–232.

58. Wilder, "Fired Teacher Rehired; Let Students Read About Sex"; Lawrence Geller, "400 Substitute Teachers Get 'Reprieve' from Firing," *Philadelphia Tribune*, July 4, 1967, 3.

59. "Long-Term Subs Say They Won't Be Flunkies to School Teachers," *Philadelphia Tribune*, July 15, 1967, 4; "348 Long Term 'Sub' Teachers to Get the Ax," *Philadelphia Tribune*, August 22, 1967, 3.

60. "Teachers were clear representatives of the state." Shelton, *Teacher Strike!*, 16.

61. J. Brantley Wilder, "Rev. Nichols Nearly Quit School Post," *Philadelphia Tribune*, October 3, 1967, 1.

62. John Wilder, "Accuse White Man of Urging Son to Beat Woman Teacher," *Philadelphia Tribune*, May 13, 1969, 1.

63. "School Changes Favor Negroes," *Philadelphia Tribune*, January 2, 1968, 1.

64. Interview with Mary, August 2, 2010.

65. "School Changes Favor Negroes; System Changing Radically."

66. "Shedd Administration Counts Its (Own) Blessings … But Remains Cursed with Crowding, Violence, and Segregation," *Philadelphia Tribune*, February 16, 1971, 6.

67. "Grant Classroom Teachers Here Greater Latitude," *Philadelphia Tribune*, November 4, 1967.

68. Interview with Mary, August 2, 2010.

69. Interview with Theresa, July 29, 2010.

70. Interview with Torch Lytle, August 18, 2010; "Editorials & Comment: Dr. Mark Shedd Is Doing a Commendable Job as School Superintendent."

71. "West Philly High Demonstration School for Micro-Teaching Plan," *Philadelphia Tribune*, July 25, 1967, 5; "$77,112 to Be Spent to House Student Teachers," *Philadelphia Tribune*, August 22, 1967, 3; interview with Jolley Christman, August 19, 2010.

72. "School District to Open Sat. Morning Voc. Program," *Philadelphia Tribune*, November 4, 1967, 10.

73. "Shedd Administration Counts Its (Own) Blessings; … But Remains Cursed with Crowding, Violence, and Segregation."

74. "School Program Gets Special Grant from US," *Philadelphia Tribune*, November 11, 1969, 1, 3.

75. "School Changes Favor Negroes; System Changing Radically"; SDP BOE Minutes, June 27, 1994, 475: "WHEREAS, In 1969, by administrative directive, every School District of Philadelphia school was required 'to provide a well-rounded program on African and Afro-American history and culture for every child in all areas of the curriculum as an integral part of his total school experience. …"

76. "School Changes Favor Negroes; System Changing Radically."

77. Andrea K. Rorrer, Linda Skrla, and James Joseph Scheurich, "Districts as Institutional Actors in Education Reform," *Educational Administration Quarterly*, 44 no. 3 (2008): 307–358; Arnetha Ball, "Three Decades of Research on Classroom Life: Illuminating the Classroom Communicative Lives of America's At-Risk Students," *Review of Research in Education* 26 (2002): 71–111; Jean B. Wellisch, Anne H. MacQueen, Ronald A. Carriere, and Gary A. Duck, "School Management and Organization in Successful Schools (ESAA In-Depth Study School)," *Sociology of Education* 51, no. 3 (1978): 211–226; Jean Anyon, *Radical Possibilities* (New York: Routledge, 2005); Wellford W. Wilms, "Altering the Structure and Culture of American Public Schools," *Phi Delta Kappan* 84, no. 8 (2003): 606–615; Richard Ingersoll, *Teacher Turnover, Teacher Shortages, and the Organization of Schools* (Seattle, WA: Center for the Study of Teaching and Policy, 2001); Frederick M. Hess, *Spinning Wheels: The Politics of Urban School Reform* (Washington, DC: Brookings Institute Press, 1998).

78. Per SDP BOE Minutes, September 4, 1970, 703, President Richardson Dilworth commented, "at the moment, there is no money with which to grant any salary increases; also that we could not hope to look for any more money from City Council. They having just given us an additional twenty-eight million dollars in order to just stand still." Per SDP BOE Minutes, January 26, 1969, 58–60, Board of Education President Dilworth complained that the board was forced into three major budget reductions within eighteen months.

79. Interview with Mary, August 2, 2010.

80. Interview with LeRoi Simmons, October 14, 2010.

81. John Wilder, "Poindexter Now Top-Ranking Negro School Official in US," *Philadelphia Tribune*, July 18, 1967, 1.

82. John Wilder, "Costly School Experimental Programs Have Poor Pay-Off," *Philadelphia Tribune*, September 13, 1969, 4.

83. John Wilder, "Mark Shedd's School Work Gets Barely Passing Grade," *Philadelphia Tribune*, May 8, 1971, 2.

84. "Logan Gives School Bd. an 'F' in Integration," *Philadelphia Tribune*, October 28, 1967, 3.

85. "Segregation Feared in 'Model Schools,'" *Philadelphia Tribune*, July 15, 1967, 1.

86. Thomas Burress III, "Good Negro Schools Are Better Than Poor Integrated Schools," *Philadelphia Tribune*, August 1, 1967, 7.

87. Per SDP BOE Minutes in 1968 (no date and no page number), the Overbrook Park Community Council opposed the decentralization of Philadelphia schools. Per SDP BOE Minutes, January 11, 1971, 32, the Home and School Association representative from South Philly High requested more input on the principal selection process, insisting that Shedd and the Board of Education live up to the community participation and decentralization claims they have made. Per SDP BOE Minutes, April 12, 1971, 239, there was tension around decentralization that involved community control versus community involvement.

88. John Wilder, "Frank Sullivan Speaks Before Shedd Arrives," *Philadelphia Tribune*, April 19, 1969, 1, 29; "'275 Sub-Boards of Education' Seen Looming in New Proposal," *Philadelphia Tribune*, March 13, 1971, 19; "School Decentralization Proposals Will Fail, Local ACLU Branch Says," *Philadelphia Tribune*, February 27, 1971, 4.

89. John Wilder, "Paxson Parkway School Closed as of January 1st" *Philadelphia Tribune*, November 25, 1969, 1, 5. The Paxson Parkway School was later reopened without the knowledge of the school board under the name "Project LEARN." John Wilder, "Paxson-Parkway School Has New Home; Reopened Without Knowledge of Board," *Philadelphia Tribune*, March 31, 1970, 1, 2; SDP BOE Minutes, November 24, 1969, 955–956.

90. Wilder, "Mark Shedd's School Work Gets Barely Passing Grade"; "Editorials & Comment: Philadelphia School Segregation Exposed by Government Agency."

91. Derrick Bell, "*Brown v. Board of Education* and the Interest-Convergence Dilemma," *Harvard Law Review* 93, no. 3 (1980): 518–533; Derrick Bell, "Learning from Our Losses: Is School Desegregation Still Feasible in the 1980s?," *Phi Delta Kappan* 64, no. 8 (1983): 572–575; Derrick Bell, "The Politics of Desegregation," *Change* 11, no. 7 (1979): 50–53; Marvin Lynn, "Race, Culture, and the Education of African Americans," *Educational Theory* 56, no. 1(2006): 107–119; Edward Taylor, "A Critical Race Analysis of the Achievement Gap in the United States: Politics, Reality, and Hope," *Leadership and Policy in Schools* 5, no. 1 (2006): 71–87; Gloria Ladson-Billings, "Landing on the Wrong Note: The Price We Paid for Brown," *Educational Researcher* 33, no. 7 (2004): 3–13.

92. Anne E Phillips, "A History of the Struggle for School Desegregation in Philadelphia, 1966–1967," *Pennsylvania History: A Journal of Mid-Atlantic Studies* 72 no. 1 (2005): 49–76.

93. SDP BOE Minutes, June 10, 1968, 370–371.

94. Tommy Cross and Len Lear, "Black Pupils Bussed to Furness School Stoned and Stabbed," *Philadelphia Tribune*, June 20, 1970, 1.

95. Mark Bricklin, "Teacher Strike Looms over Forced Racial Transfers; Union Says Plan Would Shift 339 Negroes, Only 6 Whites," *Philadelphia Tribune*, January 23, 1968, 3.

96. "Human Relations Unit Launches State-Wide Investigation of Racial Imbalance in Schools," *Philadelphia Tribune*, November 7, 1967, 3.

97. SDP BOE Minutes, June 30, 1969, 454.

98. SDP BOE Minutes, August 11, 1969, 622.

99. "Philadelphia Lags Behind Many Large Southern Cities," *Philadelphia Tribune*, June 19, 1971, 1, 4.

100. Wilder, "Mark Shedd's School Work Gets Barely Passing Grade."

101. Matthew Countryman, "Community Control of the Schools," *Up South: Civil Rights and Black Power in Philadelphia* (Philadelphia: University of Pennsylvania Press, 2006).

102. Countryman, "Community Control of the Schools," 226.

103. Wilder, "Mark Shedd's School Work Gets Barely Passing Grade."

104. "Teachers OK Plan to Quit Union Setup," *Philadelphia Tribune*, January 13, 1968, 1–2.

105. Charles Askew, "Why the Negro Teachers Are Fed Up with Union," *Philadelphia Tribune*, December 19, 1967, 1–2; John Wilder, "Negro Teachers Quitting Union; Irked by Transfer 'Sellout,'" *Philadelphia Tribune*, September 24, 1968, 1–3.

106. SDP BOE Minutes, December 1, 1967, 793. Per the SDP BOE Minutes, October 28, 1968, 777, numbers eight and nine were added to the "Policy on Disruption of Activities" almost a year after the protest on November 17, 1967.

107. John Wilder, "Heads of Some School Board Members May Be on the Chopping Block," *Philadelphia Tribune*, October 19, 1968, 1–2.

108. Per SDP BOE Minutes, December 8, 1969, 996, there were incidents at South Philly High School. A student at the Board of Education meeting said the press was spreading misinformation about the incident. Shedd said police officers were dispatched as community liaisons and that there was no evidence of violence or swinging billy clubs. He commented, "Mr. Sussman gave the impression that administration, students, parents of the community and faculty members have gone soft on their concern for safety in the schools. This is simply not so." Per SDP BOE Minutes, June 8, 1970, 489, five people at the board meeting voiced concerns about gang violence and asked for the board's support in combatting the problem. Per SDP BOE Minutes, June 22, 1970, 518, seemingly in response to concerns about gang violence, the board urged the city to give money to expand the services of the Youth Conservation Services of the City of Philadelphia. Per SDP BOE Minutes, February 8, 1971, 109, John Ryan, of the Philadelphia Federation of Teachers, blamed top administrators for violence in schools. He was joined by a rabbi from the Jewish Defense League.

109. "Art Teacher Slain; Philadelphia Police Arrest Youth, 14," *New York Times*, February 2, 1971, retrieved on January 27, 2020, from https://www.nytimes.com/1971/02/02/archives/art-teacher-slain-philadelphia-police-arrest-youth-14.html.

110. Wilder, "Mark Shedd's School Work Gets Barely Passing Grade."

111. Ray McCann, "'Building Not Worth a Dime,' Rev. Nichols Tells Parents at Kelley School Dedication," *Philadelphia Tribune*, April 4, 1967, 3.

112. "Editorials & Comment: Philadelphia School Segregation Exposed by Government Agency"; Alvarez, "There's No Such Thing as an Unqualified Teacher"; Birger, "Race, Reaction, and Reform."

113. SDP BOE Minutes, January 13, 1969, 1. According to SDP BOE Minutes, April 28, 1969, 273, "The following persons spoke in favor of a proposal for the implementation of a Shared Management Agreement for Administrators designed jointly by the Educators' Roundtable and the Association for Black Leadership in Education." John Wilder, "Negro Principals Fighting Effort to Unionize Group; Charge Collective Bargaining Rights Endangers Quality Education in City," *Philadelphia Tribune*, February 11, 1969, 1–2; John Wilder, "Black Principals, Teachers Pledge to Man Schools If There Is Strike; Union Picket Lines Will Be Crossed to Teach Children," *Philadelphia Tribune*, October 13, 1970, 1, 3. Per SDP BOE Minutes, September 29, 1969, 738–739, Black BOE members Hutt and Nichols voted against the resolution that an election be held to determine if Philadelphia Principals' Association should represent the district's principals and vice principals. The third Black board member, E. Washington Rhoads, didn't attend the meeting and didn't vote. Hutt and Nichols were the only two to vote against it.

114. SDP BOE Minutes, June 10, 1968, 348.

115. John Wilder, "20 groups Denounce Threat of School Strike" *Philadelphia Tribune*, August 24, 1968, 1. According to the SDP BOE Minutes, February 10, 1969, 96, "Mr. James Moss, representing Teachers Concerned, expressed concern of the black community for the lack of representation by the Union."

116. Ruth Wright Hayre and Alexis Moore, *Tell Them We Are Rising: A Memoir of Faith in Education* (New York: John Wiley, 1997); Theresa Perry, "Achieving in Post-Civil Rights America: The Outline of a Theory," in *Young, Gifted, and Black: Promoting High Achievement Among African-American Students*, ed. Theresa Perry, Claude Steele, and Asa Hilliard (Boston: Beacon Press, 2003), 87–108.

117. Ladson-Billings, "Landing on the Wrong Note," 9; Etheridge, "Impact of the 1954 *Brown v Topeka Board of Education* Decision on Black Educators," 217.

118. John Wilder, "Teachers Tell Why They 'Bolted' Black Community Confrontation," *Philadelphia Tribune*, October 15, 1968, 1, 3.

119. Bricklin, "Teachers Union Called 'Blatantly Biased'; Strike Threat to Block Transfers Blasted." According to SDP BOE Minutes, July 27, 1970, 647–649, citizens and community activists were concerned about contract negotiations and the potential that school wouldn't open on time. The Urban Coalition Educational Task Force presented a proposal for busing senior high school students if schools didn't open because of the financial crisis.

120. According to SDP BOE Minutes, May 13, 1968, 271–272, the board was expecting a possible shortfall of $34 million in the school district's 1968–69 operating budget, so it was starting to make cuts: reduction in central office staff by 20 percent, including supervisory positions such as associate superintendent, district superintendent, director, assistant director, and supervisor. Per SDP BOE Minutes, February 24, 1969, 107, more "financial belt-tightening taking place within The School District of Philadelphia," said Shedd. It included job freezes, which meant no hiring of new personnel unless it jeopardized the "minimal level of instruction and operation in the schools." Per SDP BOE Minutes, January 26, 1970, 57, the district took $429,000 out of the budget that had been earmarked for early childhood education. Nichols remarked, "we are taking $429,000 out of this budget that was to be spent for early childhood education. So the children are the ones who are suffering out of all of this." Per SDP BOE Minutes, January 26, 1970, 81, that day, the BOE adopted a resolution amending the general fund operating budget, reducing expenditures by $4 million. Per SDP BOE Minutes, June 22, 1970, 498, the board put forth a resolution that said if it didn't have enough money to open schools in September, the school district would operate buses to send seniors to suburban high schools so they could graduate on time. The resolution was tabled. Per SDP BOE Minutes, September 4, 1970, 703, Dilworth said "at the moment, there is no money with which to grant any salary increases; also that we could not hope to look for any more money from City Council. They having just given us an additional twenty-eight million dollars in order to just stand still." Per SDP BOE Minutes, May 24, 1971, 247–249, Dilworth said the district would have an $80 million deficit for the next school year. The city had received "a tax on over-the-bar" liquor sales, but it was thrown out by the Supreme Court of Pennsylvania. He added they were considering asking all salaried and wage earners to "accept deferred payment of their wages and salaries for this period if we are unable to arrive at any other solution with the banks but, we can assure you, and the Board of unanimous in this, that the Board itself will certainly do nothing affirmative to shut down this school system before the end of this school year." Per SDP BOE Minutes, August 16, 1971, 615, the board voted to close schools on or about May 24, 1972, because it was more than $29 million short of the money they needed to operate schools for the entire next school year.

121. Shelton, *Teacher Strike!* According to SDP BOE Minutes, June 22, 1970, 527, there were strikes across industries across the country at this time. A community member thanked the Board of Education for its support during the grape strike and brought grapes for board members to show that they were free from pesticides.

122. SDP BOE Minutes, September 4, 1970, 701, 703; John Wilder, "Community Overcame Strike," *Philadelphia Tribune*, September 15, 1970, 1, 3.

123. "School Strike Is Halted by Court Injunction," *Philadelphia Tribune*, September 12, 1970, 1; Wilder, "Community Overcame Strike"; Wilder, "Black Principals, Teachers Pledge to Man Schools If There Is Strike"; "Union Strike Fails to Close Schools in Black Areas; All Blacks Urged to Support the Schools and Educational Forum in Dispute with Union," *Philadelphia Tribune*, October 20, 1970, 1, 3.

124. Wilder, "Black Principals, Teachers Pledge to Man Schools if There Is Strike."

125. "For Whom Do Schools Exist?," *Philadelphia Tribune*, November 17, 1970, 8.

126. "Shedd Administration Counts Its (Own) Blessings; ... But Remains Cursed with Crowding, Violence, and Segregation."

127. Franklin, *The Education of Black Philadelphia*. Per SDP BOE Minutes, July 12, 1971, 518, community activist, Edward Robinson, spoke to the Board of Education regarding errors in the ways "Afro and Afro-American History" were being taught. Interview with Latifah, on July 22, 2010, described how Edward Robinson and his colleagues petitioned the district to improve how African studies and culture were addressed throughout the school system. SDP BOE Minutes, May 12, 1969, 297; SDP BOE Minutes, January 26, 1970, 81.

128. Interview with LeRoi Simmons, October 14, 2010.

129. "Editorials & Comment: Dr. Mark Shedd Is Doing a Commendable Job ss School Superintendent."

130. According to SDP BOE Minutes, June 8, 1970, 447, James Lytle was appointed to the school district on this date, though it doesn't say to what role; interview with Torch Lytle, August 18, 2010.

131. John Wilder, "Educator Says Racism Made Him Resign Key Post in School System," *Philadelphia Tribune*, May 19, 1970, 1, 3.

132. John Wilder, "Nichols Predicts Big Battle over Position Resigned by M. Foster," *Philadelphia Tribune*, May 26, 1970, 1, 3.

133. John Wilder, "2 of Top 3 Black Educators Quit; Called Irreplaceable," *Philadelphia Tribune*, April 7, 1970, 2. Per SDP BOE Minutes, April 13, 1970, 274, Shedd "expressed his regret upon loosing [sic] Dr. Bernard C. Watson and Mr. Marcus Foster."

134. Joseph R. Daughen and Peter Binzen, *The Cop Who Would Be King: Mayor Frank Rizzo* (Boston: Little, Brown, 1977).

135. Mari J. Matsuda, Charles R. Lawrence III, Richard Delgado, and Kimberle Williams Crenshaw, eds., *Words That Wound: Critical Race Theory, Assaultive Speech, and the First Amendment* (Boulder, CO: Westview, 1993).

136. Franklin, *The Education of Black Philadelphia*; Hayre and Moore, *Tell Them We Are Rising*; "Equality in Public School Education Remains Historic Goal of the Negro," *Philadelphia Tribune*, February 14, 1970, 23.

137. Wilder, "Educators Rising Rapidly but Can't Keep Up with Soaring Numbers and Hopes of Students."

138. Interview with Torch Lytle, August 18, 2010; interview with Mary, August 2, 2010.

139. Franklin, *The Education of Black Philadelphia*.

140. Wilder, "Educator Says Racism Made Him Resign Key Post in School System."

141. SDP BOE Minutes, May 25, 1970, 405.

142. Wilder, "Educator Says Racism Made Him Resign Key Post in School System."

143. SDP BOE Minutes, June 22, 1970, 528.

Chapter 2

1. J. R. Daughen and P. Binzen, *The Cop Who Would Be King: The Honorable Frank Rizzo* (Boston: Little, Brown, 1977), 174.
2. School District of Philadelphia (SDP) Board of Education (BOE) Minutes, March 28, 1974, 304–305.
3. Vernon Loeb, "Clayton and Co.: New Zest to Revitalize Schools," *Philadelphia Inquirer*, September 26, 1983, B01.
4. Nina, interview with the author, July 12, 2010; Mary, interview with the author, August 2, 2010; Jolley Christman, interview with the author, August 19, 2010.
5. "'Close Down Public School System Permanently,' Citizens' Unit Says," *Philadelphia Tribune*; September 19, 1972, 4; Deborrah Wilkinson, "Teacher Absenteeism Closed Ben Franklin," *Philadelphia Tribune*, January 26 1982, 3.
6. Matthew J. Countryman, *Up South: Civil Rights and Black Power in Philadelphia* (Philadelphia: University of Pennsylvania Press, 2006).
7. Countryman, "From Protests to Politics," *Up South.*
8. Joseph R. Daughen and Peter Binzen, *The Cop Who Would Be King: The Honorable Frank Rizzo* (Boston: Little, Brown and Company, 1977), 111.
9. Daughen and Binzen, *The Cop Who Would Be King*, 176.
10. Daughen and Binzen, *The Cop Who Would Be King*, 131, 150–151; Len Lear and Pamela Haynes, "Leading Black and White Citizens Criticize Rizzo's Handling of Black Panthers Case," *Philadelphia Tribune*, September 5, 1970, 2; C. Royal, "Reflections of Three Black Philadelphia Educators: An Oral History," paper presented at the Annual Meeting of the American Educational Research Association, Division F, History and Historiography, San Diego, CA, April 2009.
11. J. Brantley Wilder and Pamela Haynes, "Edison Hi Controversy Had 'Bad Racial Aroma,'" *Philadelphia Tribune*, August 26, 1972, 1–2.
12. Daughen and Binzen, *The Cop Who Would Be King*, 112–113.
13. Daughen and Binzen, *The Cop Who Would Be King*, 144.
14. John Wilder, "Merge All Local Schools Dilworth Urgently Asks," *Philadelphia Tribune*, January 15, 1972, 1–2.
15. Daughen and Binzen, *The Cop Who Would Be King*, 127.
16. Daughen and Binzen, *The Cop Who Would Be King*, 167.
17. Daughen and Binzen, *The Cop Who Would Be King*, 121.
18. Richard Nixon to reporters in 1968, per Daughen and Binzen, *The Cop Who Would Be King*, 140.
19. Daughen and Binzen, *The Cop Who Would Be King*, 179.
20. Daughen and Binzen, *The Cop Who Would Be King*, 120.
21. Daughen and Binzen, *The Cop Who Would Be King*, 165.
22. Daughen and Binzen, *The Cop Who Would Be King*, 173.
23. Ray Holton, "Mayor Rizzo Is Entombed in Cold Print," *Washington Post*, October 26, 1977, retrieved on May 5, 2019, from https://www.washingtonpost.com/archive/politics/1977/10/26/mayor-rizzo-is-entombed-in-cold-print/4791d7b6-cc02-4188-994a-0f025d051b19/?noredirect=on&utm_term=.436f913a1e0f.
24. Daughen and Binzen, *The Cop Who Would Be King*, 175; interview with Mary, August 2, 2010; SDP BOE Minutes, October 26, 1971, 741; Constance Clayton, interview with the author, September 30, 2010.

25. Daughen and Binzen, *The Cop Who Would Be King*, 174, 182.

26. Jon S. Birger, "Race, Reaction, and Reform: The Three Rs of Philadelphia School Politics, 1965–1971," *Pennsylvania Magazine of History and Biography* 120, no. 3 (July 1996): 163–216.

27. Daughen and Binzen, *The Cop Who Would Be King*; Birger, "Race, Reaction, and Reform"; Countryman, *Up South*; Royal, "Reflections of Three Black Philadelphia Educators."

28. During Rizzo's tenure as mayor, hundreds of unemployed Philadelphians stood in the rain waiting for federally funded summer jobs that Rizzo had already given out secretly. "Opinion: Where Is the Leadership in This Time of Crisis?," *Philadelphia Tribune*, August 31, 1990, 6A; SDP BOE Minutes, June 11, 1973, 479.

29. SDP BOE Minutes, August 16, 1971, 611–612.

30. SDP BOE Minutes, October 26, 1971, 726; SDP BOE Minutes, November 8. 1971, 742; SDP BOE Minutes, November 22, 1971, 803.

31. "Augustus 'Gus' Baxter, 88, Former Philadelphia School Board Member," *Philadelphia Inquirer*, January 31 2017, retrieved on August 15, 2020, from https://www.inquirer.com/philly/obituaries/ Augustus-Gus-Baxter-former-Philadelphia-School-Board-member-dies-at-88-.html; "Arthur Thomas Gets School Board Post," *Philadelphia Tribune*, January 11, 1972, 1. Thomas said that he and board member Davidoff had served on the Board of Trustees of Philadelphia Prisons together and that the prison board's work wasn't as obvious to the public as the Board of Education's work is. SDP BOE Minutes, January 10, 1977, 57; SDP BOE Minutes, May 27, 1980, 418.

32. Ross said that Thomas was on the Board of Education only because of Ross's efforts to get him on that board. He goes on to make a condescending statement about Black representation: SDP BOE Minutes, December 2, 1974, 950.

33. The board accepted more than $52,000 from the William Penn Foundation to research academically gifted students, "especially among minority groups and culturally disadvantaged." SDP BOE Minutes, July 22, 1974, 658.

34. Per the SDP BOE Minutes, April 10, 1972, 236, there was a school named after E. Washington Rhodes, one of the first Black board members and the former head of the *Philadelphia Tribune*. Many believed Marcus Foster should have been Philly's first Black superintendent of schools. He was a longtime district principal and administrator and central office administrator under Mark Shedd. He left Philadelphia to be superintendent of schools in Oakland, California, and he was assassinated by the Symbionese Liberation Army on November 6, 1973. For more information on Foster, read John P. Spencer, *In the Crossfire: Marcus Foster and the Troubled History of American School Reform* (Philadelphia: University of Pennsylvania, 2014). The board issued a resolution about Marcus Foster after his assassination, and they named the athletic field near Gratz High School after him. SDP BOE Minutes, November 19, 1973, 889–890; SDP BOE Minutes, February 25 1974, 202. The board passed a resolution to honor Paul Robeson's life, as well. SDP BOE Minutes, January 26, 1976, 37–38; SDP BOE Minutes, August 9, 1976, 586. The board honored Floyd Logan, saying he had devoted most of his life to the district's public school children. They named the gym at West Philly High School after him. This came a little more than forty years after he lobbied them to get rights for Black people. SDP BOE Minutes, January 8, 1979, 2. He died in 1978. SDP BOE Minutes, November 24, 1975, 879.

35. Daughen and Binzen, *The Cop Who Would Be King*.

36. Interview with Mary, August 2, 2010; Elaine Welles, "Flack over Limousines Misdirected, School Board Members Claim," *Philadelphia Tribune*, February 1, 1975, 1, 7; SDP BOE Minutes February 25, 1974, 217, 220–221.

37. Someone wrote to the board members to say this wouldn't be an issue if there weren't three Black board members. SDP BOE Minutes, February 25, 1974, 219–221. The auditor general for the

Commonwealth of Pennsylvania had audited the School District of Philadelphia for the fiscal years ending 1972 and 1973. He found that the Board of Education did not have current bylaws or a formal policy manual. SDP BOE Minutes, March 10, 1975, 177–182. Happy Fernandez (who would go on to be a City Council member) requested guidelines for the expense accounts kept by the board and Marcase. SDP BOE Minutes, February 12, 1979, 127; Vincent P. Franklin, *The Education of Black Philadelphia: The Social and Educational History of a Minority Community, 1900–1950* (Philadelphia: University of Pennsylvania Press, 1979); William L. Boyd and Jolley Bruce Christman, "A Tall Order for Philadelphia's New Approach to School Governance: Heal the Political Rifts, Close the Budget Gap, *and* Improve the Schools," in *Powerful Reforms with Shallow Roots: Improving America's Urban Schools*, ed. Larry Cuban and Michael Usdan (New York: Teachers College Press, 2003), 96–124. Eugene Bivins—a district educator active in the Philadelphia Federation of Teachers, who frequently spoke on behalf of Black educators at board meetings—expressed concern over the school district's integrity: SDP BOE Minutes, October 15, 1973, 823; SDP BOE Minutes, February 10, 1975, 114. The director of the Citizens Committee on Public Education asked the Board of Education to issue guidelines on using chauffeur-driven vehicles. SDP BOE Minutes, February 26, 1975, 156; SDP BOE Minutes, December 2, 1974, 953.

38. The food services department was known for fraud and embezzlement. SDP BOE Minutes, February 12, 1979, 127; SDP BOE Minutes, March 12, 1979, 194; SDP BOE Minutes, December 8, 1979, 887; SDP BOE Minutes, April 5, 1976, 239.

39. SDP BOE Minutes, October 29, 1973, 852; SDP BOE Minutes, December 2, 1974, 947–948.

40. SDP BOE Minutes, May 19, 1975, 337–338; SDP BOE Minutes, March 28, 1974, 302–304; SDP BOE Minutes, May 20, 1974, 468.

41. SDP BOE Minutes, April 15, 1974, 388; SDP BOE Minutes, May 20, 1974, 468; SDP BOE Minutes, August 4, 1975, 594; SDP BOE Minutes, September 8, 1975, 688. Per SDP BOE Minutes, June 12, 1978, 366, a community member asked the board to televise their meetings.; Per SDP BOE Minutes, March 12, 1979, 193, a community activist spoke to the board about the disabled needing TV broadcasting to have access to board meetings.

42. SDP BOE Minutes, February 9, 1981, 215; SDP BOE Minutes, February 23, 1981, 236; SDP BOE Minutes, March 9, 1981, 269; SDP BOE Minutes, December 7, 1981, 962. Board of Education member Davidoff had apparently suffered some illness and was resigning from the board. SDP BOE Minutes, January 10, 1977, 57–58. Board member Hutt had attended the previous meeting on May 31, but when the board met on June 30, he was dead. He died suddenly on June 19. SDP BOE Minutes, June 30, 1977, 393; "George Hutt," *New York Times*, June 20, 1977, retrieved on July 29, 2020, from https://www.nytimes.com/1977/06/20/archives/george-hutt.html.

43. SDP BOE Minutes, January 10, 1977, 57. District Superintendent Costanzo put on record that the usual procedures were not followed and that he disclaimed any part of the resolutions on the funding for the next school year that were read into the meeting. SDP BOE Minutes, March 28, 1974, 314; SDP BOE Minutes, April 1, 1974, 317–318, 320–322. Threats of court action and other consequences were based on how the board voted for the budget. Thomas threatened the board with going to jail if they violated the City Charter. SDP BOE Minutes, December 1, 1975, 885–886. Board member Davidoff told the board that the resolution they passed to pay Saga Food Service of PA was illegal and that he believed everyone who voted for it would be liable for associated costs until a contract had been negotiated and approved by the board. SDP BOE Minutes, July 12, 1976, 517; March 28, 1974, 304–305; April 1, 1974, 328–329.

44. SDP BOE Minutes, December 6, 1971, 806–808; SDP BOE Minutes, March 26, 1973, 248–249; SDP BOE Minutes, November 24, 1975, 878.

45. Ross had a problem with Arthur Thomas becoming president of the Board of Education. Ross complained that Thomas's positions were unclear even though he had been on the board for two years. SDP BOE Minutes, December 3, 1973, 929–931. Thomas tried to assert his commitment to Black people by saying, "I will work toward that end because anything we do for Black children is for the benefit of all children of Philadelphia. I need not remind you that 63% of the school population is Black." Eugene Bivins offered support for the new board president: SDP BOE Minutes, December 18, 1973, 982.

46. Ross said that board member Oberholtzer organized a caucus on the board on behalf of the mayor and that she supported the city on giving the district less money than what they said they needed, which would have been detrimental for the district. He also complained that she did not believe in integrated education. Still, Black board members Hutt and Baxter voted for Oberholtzer to be board vice president. SDP BOE Minutes, December 3, 1973, 930. Ross and Hutt got into an argument in the board meeting because Hutt criticized Ross, saying he misled the board about the site the board wanted for the new Edison High School. Ross says Hutt just wants to be a "good boy" and that he should try getting something done for the city schools. SDP BOE Minutes, January 28, 1974, 128. Ross critiqued Thomas because he did not think he had the ability to raise additional funds for the school district, but what he learned was that Thomas was trying to sabotage the board's being able to secure additional funds for the district. Ross complained that Thomas reprimanded him for contacting the governor and Costanzo for sending his own budget to City Council and circumventing Thomas. He also referred to an "evil element" on the board and said some members were harassing school district administrators, which he said led to a morale issue among administrators. He also said the way the board operated led to the public having a bad opinion of the board. SDP BOE Minutes, December 2, 1974, 947–948.

47. SDP BOE Minutes, June 2, 1976, 389–394. As an example, the BOE had a meeting to accept a draft of the desegregation plan, and Thomas said that there would be no discussion from the floor and that board members could accept it or ask questions.

48. SDP BOE Minutes, December 2, 1974, 952.

49. SDP BOE Minutes, December 2, 1974, 949.

50. SDP BOE Minutes, December 5, 1977, 901–902. On being reelected board president once again, Thomas commented, "You may consider these mere words but in New York federal money has been taken out of the school system because of their lack of effort on the part of desegregation. In Los Angeles, Proposition 13 has just about ruined the public school system. In Chicago, they voted their Superintendent over 80 thousand dollars a year and two months ago, and two weeks ago, he resigned because of pressures. This morning, I read that the President of the Board had also resigned." SDP BOE Minutes, December 3, 1979, 939.

51. SDP BOE Minutes, December 3, 1973, 931. Arthur Thomas commented, "I will work toward that end because anything we do for Black children is for the benefit of all children of Philadelphia. I need not remind you that 63% of the school population is Black." The board members were discussing the Atlanta child murders in their meetings, but they did not mention that all the children were Black. SDP BOE Minutes, March 9, 1981, 242–243. Constance Clayton read aloud a resolution regarding the Atlanta child murders. The one-day fundraising drive would be on Tuesday, April 7, 1981. The committee responsible for this fundraising effort consisted of Marcase, Arthur Thomas, Delores Oberholtzer, Constance Clayton, Mathew Knowles, Edmund Forte, and Anita Poindexter. SDP BOE Minutes, March 23, 1981, 272.

52. SDP BOE Minutes, October 14, 1980, 810.

53. The Board of Education issued a statement on Title IX (SDP BOE Minutes, April 11, 1977, 244), but then they voted on Title IX again in the next meeting, and Hutt, Oberholtzer, and Stack voted against it, whereas Hutt and Stack had voted for it the first time. Oberholtzer was not present for the first vote. It passed both times because there must be five votes in order to pass a resolution. SDP BOE Minutes, April 25, 1977, 262.

54. SDP BOE Minutes, December 1, 1975, 884–886; SDP BOE Minutes, December 6, 1976, 888–889; SDP BOE Minutes, December 5, 1977, 901–902; SDP BOE Minutes, December 1, 1975, 882–883.

55. Camika Royal, "Policies, Politics, and Protests: Black Educators and the Shifting Landscape of Philadelphia's School Reforms, 1967–2007" (PhD diss., Temple University, 2012); SDP BOE Minutes, October 29, 1973, 853–854; SDP BOE Minutes, January 13, 1975, 19; SDP BOE Minutes, February 26, 1975, 117–118. Costanzo's second in command, Poindexter, informed the board that it was not up to them to evaluate school district staff members and that it was the superintendent's job. There was a repeated issue of the board overstepping the boundaries of their role and Costanzo's. Poindexter told them it is the board's job to set policy and for the superintendent and those he appoints to assess the extent to which those hired are meeting expectations and implementing board policies. There was a resolution drawn up that described the functions of the board as distinct from the administration, but Black board member Hutt withdrew this resolution. The board interrogated Costanzo about his vacation day and why he wasn't in communication with Thomas. SDP BOE Minutes, September 23, 1974, 759.

56. "Integration Among Top Priorities, New School Head Says," *Philadelphia Tribune*, December 18, 1971, 1-2; John Wilder, "New School Head Has Worked with Blacks for Years," *Philadelphia Tribune*, January 8, 1972, 1, 3; SDP BOE Minutes, January 10, 1973, 44.

57. Loeb, "Clayton and Co."

58. Interview with Jolley Christman, August 19, 2010; Torch Lytle, interview with the author, August 18, 2010; interview with Mary, August 2, 2010; interview with Constance Clayton, September 30, 2010.

59. Interview with Mary, August 2, 2010.

60. SDP BOE Minutes, March 13, 1972, 166, 197. On the Board of Education, there was political wrangling over jobs amidst budget problems and a looming teacher strike. The resolution before them was about reduction in salaries the board approved on August 12, 1968, for people whose positions were eliminated or demoted. SDP BOE Minutes, June 26, 1972, 461–462.

61. SDP BOE Minutes, May 8, 1972, 319–320.

62. Daughen and Binzen, *The Cop Who Would Be King*, 189.

63. Hutt described what was happening as a showdown between the board, the superintendent, and the mayor. SDP BOE Minutes, March 28, 1974, 307. This issue was also being cast as a rift between Costanzo and Thomas. SDP BOE Minutes, March 28, 1974, 311.

64. SDP BOE Minutes, March 28, 1974, 302–304.

65. SDP BOE Minutes, March 28, 1974, 312.

66. SDP BOE Minutes, April 1, 1974, 327; SDP BOE Minutes, December 2, 1974, 947–948.

67. SDP BOE Minutes, March 28, 1974, 304–306. Charles Bowser, executive director of the Philadelphia Coalition spoke the quote that begins this chapter at this meeting. Sam Evans (from the *Philadelphia Tribune*) said he was there representing the American Foundation of Negro Affairs. He commented that this was the first time the board would go before City Council and ask for less than the school district actually needed. He said that if they voted against the proposal, they would be voting against community interests. He also added that he wanted to see the

board be successful since this was the first time there was a Black chair. Onah Weldon commented that some of the union members went to jail fighting for a fair contract and may have to go
back to jail. She was representing the Philadelphia Federation of Teachers and said they want the
contract financed but not on the backs of the children. She also threatened them with another
strike in 1975.

68. SDP BOE Minutes, March 28, 1974, 310–311.
69. Charles Bowser, an attorney and president of Philadelphia Urban Coalition, added, "Whether
you want to risk that on a single sheet of paper which you know and I know was typed written
at the last meeting. There is more at stake here then who we are going to please and who we're
not going to please. I also think that those who are in conflict of interest, if there be any on the
Board, should not vote. Anyone on the Board who has been offered a job recently to work with
the city administration shouldn't vote on this question.... I came back here because it's right to
be here. It's right to recognize your dignity and to believe that you will not be intimidated by the
Mayor, that you will do what you know is right. And that you will not do what you know is not
right, but also illegal. I appeal to you now for yourselves, because history will record what you
did. You have reputations. You have lives to live in this city that will exist with all of this around
us is just an unpleasant memory. And how will you be remembered? Will you be remembered
for someone who had enough courage to resist intimidation or will you be remembered as someone who caved in? I hope you don't cave in." SDP BOE Minutes, April 1, 1974, 329–330.
70. State Senator Hardy Williams said he was "shocked" that the Board of Education seemed
"bashful" to ask for the money the school district needed. He remarked that there were folks in
Harrisburg who did not want Philly to have the money they need, so they certainly can't ask for
less than what they need. SDP BOE Minutes, April 1, 1974, 326–329.
71. The clerk of the Quarter Sessions Court said people were there from different parties pleading
with the board not to "play parlimentary procedure with our children's education." SDP BOE
Minutes, April 1, 1974, 328. Community City Council member Charles Durham commented,
"I just want to say that I am very proud of Dr. Costanzo and I will stick with you as long as I can
and that is until they run us both out of Philadelphia." He also said they have to tell City Council exactly what they need, not ask for less than they need. Isadore Scott said that it was no sur-
prise that Costanzo recommended more money than what was currently available. SDP BOE
Minutes, April 1, 1974, 326, 330–331.
72. SDP BOE Minutes, April 1, 1974, 331.
73. SDP BOE Minutes, June 10, 1974, 536.
74. Christopher Cubbison, June 4, 1973. "Costanzo May Keep His Philadelphia Job," *St. Petersburg
Times*, 1B, 4B; SDP BOE Minutes, February 26, 1973, 133–135; SDP BOE Minutes, May 21,
1973, 396. Ross said there had been talk to get rid of Costanzo but the board was not planning
to do that.; "Costanzo Resigns; Poindexter Will Serve in Interim," *Philadelphia Tribune*, July 8,
1975, 1, 6.
75. Trace Gibson, "Education Groups Not at All Happy with Marcase's Contract," *Philadelphia
Tribune*, December 1, 1978, 19.
76. Interview with Torch Lytle, August 18, 2010; SDP BOE Minutes, March 27, 1972, 235; SDP
BOE Minutes, April 10, 1972, 265. Paul Bennett, "Flack over Degree Will Be Settled Soon:
Marcase," *Philadelphia Tribune*, July 19, 1975, 4.
77. SDP BOE Minutes, July 9, 1975, 514.
78. Judy, interview with the author, July 26, 2010; Betty, interview with the author, July 15, 2010;
Nina, interview with the author, July 12, 2010; Joe, interview with the author, January 5, 2011;
Marsha, interview with the author, July 2, 2010; George, interview with the author, July 15,

2010; Latifah, interview with the author, July 22, 2010; interview with Jolley Christman, August 19, 2010; SDP BOE Minutes, July 14, 1975, 515.

79. SDP BOE Minutes, July 14, 1975, 515. Kendall Wilson, "Marcase Intends to Stay in Supt. Job," *Philadelphia Tribune*, August 26, 1980, 1, 19.

80. SDP BOE Minutes, July 28, 1975, 554.

81. Bennett, "Flack over Degree Will Be Settled Soon: Marcase"; "Marcase Doesn't Fill Bill as Superintendent of Schools: Richardson," *Philadelphia Tribune*, November 1, 1975, 8.

82. Interview with Torch Lytle, August 18, 2010; interview with Mary, August 2, 2010; interview with Constance Clayton, September 30, 2010; SDP BOE Minutes, May 14, 1973, 360.

83. SDP BOE Minutes, November 22, 1976, 864.

84. SDP BOE Minutes, March 8, 1976, 182. For example, the Philadelphia Federation of Teachers president complained about the Board of Education passing policy on retirements without consulting the union, and the union opposed the "contracting out" of food services, asking the board to consider both resolutions.

85. Theresa, interview with the author, July 29, 2010; interview with Constance Clayton, September 30, 2010; SDP BOE Minutes, February 9, 1976, 68. Oberholtzer chided Marcase because Fidelity Bank and other organizations were supporting Ben Franklin's football team in their all-star football game while the Board of Education was not mentioned at all as supporting the team. SDP BOE Minutes, July 18, 1977, 562. The board accepted a gift of a 1977 Oldsmobile whose list price was $9,800 from the Northeast Philadelphia Chamber of Commerce from Henry Faulkner to be used at the Swinson Skills Center.

86. SDP BOE Minutes, July 14, 1975, 516. The board takes up the issue of parents' "right to know" and "the client's right to confidentiality." SDP BOE Minutes, September 27, 1976, 692. Marcase also said, "All of us should be very concerned about our clients, the school children of Philadelphia. They are the clients of the Board of Education, the Superintendent and of every member of the School District family." SDP BOE Minutes, May 8, 1978, 246.

87. The Board of Education eliminated several positions. SDP BOE Minutes, October 20, 1975, 776; SDP BOE Minutes, November 24, 1975, 866. Board member Boonin said that if average class sizes were increased by one child, the board would save $4.5 million. She added that, in order to address the budget deficit, the board should start eliminating "non-mandated programs," saying they may still be important but if the state mandates them, the state should pay for them. Boonin said cuts were necessary but will be made thoughtfully. SDL BOE Minutes, May 27, 1976, 373. More administrative positions were eliminated. Board members Boonin and Oberholtzer voted against these eliminations. SDL BOE Minutes, July 17, 1978, 449; D. Mezzacappa, "The School System at a Crossroads After Seven Years of Peace: A New Era of Challenges, *Philadelphia Inquirer*, January 8, 1990, A1; T. Mirga, "Foes Want Him Out, But Superintendent Defends Policies," *Education Week*, November 2, 1981, retrieved on November 11, 2021, from https://www.edweek.org/education/foes-want-him-out-but-superintendent-defends-policies/1981/11; J. Gonzalez, "Clayton's First Year: A Mid-Term Exam," *Philadelphia Daily News*, September 30, 1983, 4; Stephen Williams, "School Budget Approved; 2,500 Positions to Be Cut," *Philadelphia Tribune*, May 30 1980, 1, 16. The federal government was withholding funds from the school district because of school desegregation issues. Stephen Williams, "Marcase Refuses to Be Scapegoat," *Philadelphia Tribune*, August 11, 1981, 2. The School District of Philadelphia was audited by the state, and the state determined that the fiscal problems of the district had worsened in the last decade (during the Costanzo and Marcase administrations). Tommie Hill, "Street Says the Teacher Contract 'Is Dead,'" *Philadelphia Tribune*, January 1, 1982, 1, 5; SDP BOE Minutes, May 29, 1981, 479–481. In the months before the 1981 strike,

board member Boonin wanted the school district, the teachers' union, and others to renege on the salary increases guaranteed in their contracts and to not take the raises they had contractually agreed to. Oberholtzer was questioning how Green was spending the city's money now that he was mayor.

88. Maurice White, "Panel Named to Investigate Marcase's Use of School Workers on His House: Baxter Heads Unit Checking Up on Supt.," *Philadelphia Tribune*, December 27, 1977, 1, 5; Maurice White, "At Taxpayers' Expense: School District's Security Guards Used to Patrol Dr. Marcase's Home," *Philadelphia Tribune*, January 7, 1978, 1, 11; Maurice White, "School Committee Rules Marcase Did Not Misuse Post," *Philadelphia Tribune*; , January 24, 1978, 3; "Thomas Says Marcase Did Not Violate Board Policy on Vacation Accruals," *Philadelphia Tribune*, August 4, 1978, 16; "Dr. Marcase's New Contract," *Philadelphia Tribune*, November 21, 1978, 4; interview with Mary, August 2, 2010; interview with Torch Lytle, August 18, 2010.

89. SDL BOE Minutes, September 11, 1972, 645, notes in the minutes on a violent, racist teacher: "On September 16, 1971, you were involved in an altercation with a fellow teacher concerning your locking students in a storage room as a means of punishment. At a conference following this incident, your conduct was extremely unprofessional including such racial comments as referring to the fellow teacher as a 'black savage,'"

90. SDP BOE Minutes, February 25, 1974, 226; SDP BOE Minutes, January 26, 1976, 66: Eugene Bivins makes a comment at the Board of Education about the numbers of Black and white people hired by the district.

91. SDP BOE Minutes, February 25, 1974, 219; SDP BOE Minutes, March 9, 1981, 269. Black education activist Karen Bivins spoke to the board about protecting Black teachers in various district schools. SDP BOE Minutes, 158. Karin Bivins, representing the Black Caucus of the Philadelphia Federation of Teachers, asked the board for the racial and gender breakdown on instructional staff and coaches. SDP BOE, Minutes, April 5, 1982, 217. Eugene Bivins asked for data to demonstrate the nonwhite people appointed under the 5 percent rule/provision of the Home Rule Charter.

92. Jackie, interview with the author, June 28, 2010; interview with Betty, July 15, 2010; Lauren, interview with the author, June 17, 2010; George, interview with the author, July 15, 2010; Harold, interview with the author, July 20, 2010; Jim, interview with the author, June 24, 2010; SDP BOE Minutes, January 7, 19774, 37–38, discussion of the hiring of "temporary professional employees" en masse.

93. SDP BOE Minutes, January 4, 1973, 2.

94. J. Brantley Wilder, "Education Confrontation: Education's Lost Weekend," *Philadelphia Tribune*, September 30, 1972, 2; James Smith, "A Man Concerned," *Philadelphia Tribune*, October 17, 1972, 8.

95. J. Brantley Wilder, "Schools Opened as Court Intervenes," *Philadelphia Tribune*, September 30, 1972, 1; interview with Mary, August 2, 2010.

96. John Wilder, "School Strike Ban Lauded by Leaders," *Philadelphia Tribune*, January 13, 1973, 1, 6; interview with Nina, July 12, 2010.

97. Donald Janson, "Philadelphia Teachers Strike; Many Schools Shut," *New York Times*, January 9, 1973, retrieved on May 17, 2019, from https://www.nytimes.com/1973/01/09/archives/philadelphia-teachers-strike-many-schools-shut-strike-in-september.html; "John Ryan Endorses Working Educators," Working Educators, retrieved on February 23, 2021, from https://www.workingeducators.org/john_ryan.

98. J. Brantley Wilder, "Parents March, Council Debates, Strike Goes On," *Philadelphia Tribune*, September 16, 1972, 1, 3.

99. "Board Seeks Contempt Rap Against Union," *Philadelphia Tribune*, January 16, 1973, 6; "Keep Schools Open Now," editorial, *Philadelphia Tribune*, January 16, 1973, 8; J. Brantley Wilder, "Pact Approved, Aid Offered to Non-Strikers," *Philadelphia Tribune*, March 3, 1973, 1, 5; interview with Mary, August 2, 2010.

100. Stephen Williams, "Public Schools Opening Delayed," *Philadelphia Tribune*, September 5, 1980, 1, 17; Pamela Smith, "School Opening Delayed Again," *Philadelphia Tribune*, September 9, 1980, 1, 18.

101. Interview with Nina, July 12, 2010; interview with Theresa, July 29, 2010; SDP BOE, Minutes, September 28, 1981, 801–802. The board is engaged in a strike. The Philadelphia Federation of Teachers is out of work. The board issues a resolution saying it plans to cut $25 million in "administrative costs" from the 1981–82 budget. Board member Katz says they will find the money from other sources. Stephen Williams, "More Black Teachers Will Cross Picket Line," *Philadelphia Tribune*, October 13, 1981, 1, 13; "Children Are Back at School But for How Long, at What Cost?," *Philadelphia Tribune*, November 3, 1981, A2.

102. Hill, "Street Says the Teacher Contract 'Is Dead'"; interview with Theresa, July 29, 2010; Linda, interview with the author, June 21, 2010.

103. Interview with Jackie, June 28, 2010; interview with Joe, January 5, 2011.

104. Interview with Jackie, June 28, 2010; interview with Judy, July 26, 2010; interview with Nina, July 12, 2010; interview with Theresa, July 29, 2010; interview with George, July 15, 2010; John Wilder, "Black Principals, Teachers Pledge to Man Schools If There Is Strike; Union Picket Lines Will Be Crossed to Teach Children," *Philadelphia Tribune*, October 13, 1970, 1, 3. In this article, Frank Sullivan, president of the teachers' union, was quoted as saying, "we will not tolerate scabs breaking our strike." Interview with Nina, July 12, 2010.

105. Interview with Jackie, June 28, 2010; interview with Torch Lytle, August 18, 2010; "Board Seeks Contempt Rap Against Union," *Philadelphia Tribune*, January 16, 1973, 6. Picketing was done in shifts. The first shift was 6 a.m. to 8 a.m. to deter the maintenance people from turning the heat on in the schools. The next shift started at 8:30 a.m. to block teachers and other school workers.

106. Interview with Theresa, July 29, 2010.

107. Interview with George, July 15, 2010; interview with Theresa, July 29, 2010; "Teamsters Support the Teachers," *Philadelphia Tribune*, January 13, 1973, 23; interview with Mary, August 2, 2010.

108. Belinda, interview with the author, June 28, 2010; interview with Jackie, June 28, 2010; interview with Betty, July 15, 2010; interview with Theresa, July 29, 2010; J. Brantley Wilder, "Pact Approved, Aid Offered to Non-Strikers," *Philadelphia Tribune*; , March 3, 1973, 1, 5; "During School Strike: Alternative Schools Set to Handle 150,000 Students," *Philadelphia Tribune*, August 21, 1976, 1, 17.

109. Interview with Joe, January 5, 2011; interview with Belinda, June 28, 2010.

110. Interview with George, July 15, 2010; interview with Jackie, June 28, 2010; interview with Mary, August 2, 2010.

111. Interview with Torch Lytle, August 18, 2010; interview with George, July 15, 2010; interview with Jackie, June 28, 2010; interview with Jim, June 24, 2010; interview with Theresa, July 29, 2010.

112. Interview with Nina, July 12, 2010.

113. Franklin, "*The Education of Black Philadelphia*" 213; "Philadelphia Lags Behind Many Large Southern Cities," *Philadelphia Tribune*, June 19, 1971, 1, 4. According to this article, "The entire state of Mississippi, long called the bastion of racism in America, ranks ahead of the Philadelphia public schools in efforts to integrate."

114. SDP BOE Minutes, August 2, 1982, 516.
115. David Kushma, "Funds Hinge on Massive Teacher Transfers," *Philadelphia Evening Bulletin*, August 9, 1978, Temple University Urban Archives, box 204; David Kushma, "Phila. Schools Cut Funds for Integration," *Philadelphia Evening Bulletin*, July 8, 1978, Temple University Urban Archives, box 204; David Kushma, "Phila. Is Appealing Again for Desegregation Funds," *Philadelphia Evening Bulletin*, August 8, 1978, Temple University Urban Archives, box 204.
116. Anne E. Phillips, "A History of the Struggle for School Desegregation in Philadelphia, 1955–1967," *Philadelphia History: A Journal of Mid-Atlantic Studies* 72, no. 1 (2005): 49-76; SDP BOE Minutes, November 19, 1973, 926; December 3, 1973, 928; M. Halsey, "Public, Parochial Division of Pupils Rapped for Delaying City Integration," Temple University Urban Archives, unmarked newspaper clipping, box 204, May 29, 1973; William P. Herron, "School Desegregation, the Philadelphia Experience," paper presented at the Annual Meeting of the American Educational Research Association, 1975.
117. Herron, "School Desegregation, the Philadelphia Experience"; SDP BOE Minutes, March 26, 1979, 196; September 9, 1974, 757; October 7, 1974, 833.
118. SDP BOE Minutes, March 24, 1975, 229; SDP BOE Minutes, June 21, 1982, 455: Pairing schools for desegregation is mentioned. This meant bringing together the student populations of two racially segregated schools such that one building was newly dedicated to only grades K–2 or 3 and the other building was for grades 3–5. Some parents were opposed to the pairing of certain schools for desegregation. SDP BOE Minutes, June 7, 1982, 390. Parents attended the board meeting to protest school closures. School closures were part of the Human Relation Commission's recommendations as part of the desegregation program. Many of the schools slated to be closed due to racial isolation were located in Northeast Philly, where the highest concentration of the school district's white students lived. SDP BOE Minutes, May 8, 1978, 265; SDP BOE Minutes, June 12, 1978, 366; SDP BOE Minutes, March 24, 1980, 290; SDP BOE Minutes, March 23, 1981, 311; SDP BOE Minutes, June 8, 1981, 543; SDP BOE Minutes, August 17, 1981, 768; SDP BOE Minutes, June 22, 1981, 595; SDP BOE Minutes, August 17, 1981, 767; SDP BOE Minutes, January 18, 1982, 1; SDP BOE Minutes, April 26, 1982, 267; Herron, "School Desegregation, the Philadelphia Experience"; "Fellowship Commission on Busing," *Philadelphia Tribune*, March 7, 1972, 21; "Editorials & Comment: Black School Children Abandoned by President," *National Black News*, April 4, 1972, 8. Representative Dennis O'Brien spoke to the Board of Education about complaints he had received from parents in Northeast Philly about busing. SDP BOE Minutes, September 25, 1978, 544; SDP BOE Minutes, June 30, 1975, 507–508; J. Dubois, "1,000 in Northeast Meet to Fight Busing," *Philadelphia Evening Bulletin*, July 7, 1978, Temple University Urban Archives newspaper clipping, box 204; R. Rich, "Some Black, White Parents in Opposing School Integration," *Philadelphia Evening Bulletin*;, June 1, 1975, Temple University Urban Archives newspaper clipping, box 204. People came to the board meeting to speak about their opposition to the desegregation plan, saying they supported "neighborhood schools." SDP BOE Minutes, February 10, 1975, 116; SDP BOE Minutes, June 2, 1976, 389–394; SDP BOE Minutes, December 15, 1980, 1017; SDP BOE Minutes, April 5, 1976, 243; SDP BOE Minutes, June 12, 1978, 366; C. Rich, "Marcase Orders Desegregation Plan Prepared," *Philadelphia Evening Bulletin*, May 7, 1976, Temple University Urban Archives newspaper clipping, box 204; D. Kushma, "U.S. Balks on Phila. Integration Funds," *Philadelphia Evening Bulletin*, April 7, 1979, Temple University Urban Archives newspaper clipping, box 204. There were concerns about conditions at Carver School. SDP BOE Minutes, March 12, 1979, 193. Carver School

was being converted into the new High School for Engineering and Science as part of the voluntary desegregation program. SDP BOE Minutes, September 10, 1979, 662. A new magnet school—Germantown Motivation—would be housed in Lankenau School of Roxborough. SDP BOE Minutes, December 15, 1980, 999. Lankenau was the new magnet high school established as part of the desegregation program. SDP BOE Minutes, January 12, 1981, 60; SDP BOE Minutes, September 23, 1976, 687–691; SDP BOE Minutes, July 7, 1975, 509–510; SDP BOE Minutes, July 26, 1976, 568–569.

119. The Board of Education was advertising the voluntary desegregation program to recruit students. SDP BOE Minutes, January 8, 1979, 2. Board member Baxter showed a twenty-minute movie about desegregation in the school district, SDP BOE Minutes, September 10, 1979, 662. The board was still having desegregation materials created and disseminated, but who was the audience for this communication, and who was the district trying to invest in? SDP BOE Minutes, May 27, 1980, 453. Advertisements for the district's voluntary desegregation. SDP BOE Minutes, September 22, 1980, 801; SDP BOE Minutes, December 14, 1979, 726–727; SDP BOE Minutes, May 27, 1980, 418.

120. SDP BOE Minutes, January 28, 1974, 128. They were discussing the new site for the Edison High School. SDP BOE Minutes, September 24 1973, 769. People opposed the location of the new Edison High School. SDP BOE Minutes, January 7, 1974, 64; SDP BOE Minutes, January 28, 1974, 125–127. People came to board meetings to complain about the current Edison High School. SDL BOE Minutes, February 11, 1974, 18; SDP BOE Minutes, March 11, 1974, 249. Community members expressed an urgent need for a new high school in "district 5," which meant they were pleading for a new Edison High School. SDP BOE Minutes, September 24, 1979, 740. City Council member Augusta Clark said, "At last the new Edison High is to be built after more than a dozen years of frustration, disappointment and waiting." SDP BOE Minutes, February 22, 1982, 106; SDP BOE Minutes, June 11, 1979, 430.

121. SDP BOE Minutes, April 23, 1979, 287: Community members voiced concern over the boundary lines for Frankford High School. But the boundary lines were intentionally changed for desegregation. The Board of Education changed the boundary lines for Frankford High School to foster desegregation on April 9, 1979.

122. SDP BOE Minutes, August 27, 1979, 655–661.

123. SDP BOE Minutes, September 10, 1979, 709; SDP BOE Minutes, September 17, 1979, 710–713: Representative Robert (Bob) Borski spoke at the board meeting about the Frankford-Edison boundary lines.

124. SDP BOE Minutes, April 28, 1980, 354, 365; SDP BOE Minutes, May 27, 1980, 452.

125. SDP BOE Minutes, March 22, 1976, 183; SDP BOE Minutes, December 6, 1976, 890; SDP BOE Minutes, May 31, 1979, 328–330; "Dr. Marcase's New Contract," *Philadelphia Tribune*, November 21, 1978, 4; Jim Davis, "Council Members Get Lesson in Ethics Regarding Marcase Contract," *Philadelphia Tribune*, November 28, 1978, 4; Pamela Smith, "Angry Black Parents Oppose $4000 Raise, Demand His Resignation," *Philadelphia Tribune*, November 24, 1978, 1, 16; Sandra Featherman, "Marcase's New Pact," *Philadelphia Tribune*, December 1, 1978, 4; Jim Davis, "Council Condemns Marcase's Contract," *Philadelphia Tribune*; December 1, 1978, 15; Trace Gibson, "Education Groups Not at All Happy with Marcase's Contract," *Philadelphia Tribune*, December 1, 1978, 19; SDP BOE Minutes, January 8, 1979, 34; SDP BOE Minutes, January 22 1979, 66–67. At the Board of Education meeting on March 13, 1979, 192, the BOE decided that no one else could speak for or against Marcase's contract at BOE meetings.

126. SDP BOE Minutes, August 18, 1980, 641–642. Stephen Williams, "Marcase's Contract Is Illegal," *Philadelphia Tribune*, July 29, 1980, 1, 20; Stephen Williams, "Thomas Would Shorten Supt. Marcase's Contract," *Philadelphia Tribune*, August 8, 1980, 1; Stephen Williams, "School Board Takes Up Marcase's Contract Vote," *Philadelphia Tribune*, October 14, 1980, 1; SDP BOE Minutes, August 18, 1980, 746; SDP BOE Minutes, September 9, 1980, 792; SDP BOE Minutes, September 22, 1980, 809; SDP BOE Minutes, October 18, 1980, 832; SDP BOE Minutes, September 22, 1980, 809; SDP BOE Minutes, October 14, 1980, 810–813; SDP BOE Minutes, December 15, 1980, 1016.

127. "Our Opinion: What Happens When Mayor Green Wipes Out School Board, Marcase?," *Philadelphia Tribune*, January 30, 1981, 6.

128. Hill, "Street Says the Teacher Contract 'Is Dead'"; Helen Oakes, "Superintendent a Failure, Must Be Replaced at Once," *The Oakes Newsletter*, September/October 1980, 1–4.

129. Mirga, "Foes Want Him Out"; Loeb, "Clayton & Co."; "Children Are Back at School But for How Long, at What Cost?," *Philadelphia Tribune*, November 3, 1981, A2. Per SDP BOE Minutes, September 22, 1980, 809, the Honorable William Gray asked the Board of Education to appoint a new superintendent. SDP BOE Minutes, December 21, 1981, 1024. Citizens were continuing to implore the board to look for a new superintendent. SDP BOE Minutes, January 18, 1982, 30; Stephen Williams, "Marcase Vote Pact Delayed," *Philadelphia Tribune*, August 19, 1980, 1; Kendall Wilson, "Marcase Intends to Stay in Supt. Job," *Philadelphia Tribune*, August 26, 1980, 1; "Our Opinion: Saving Face with Marcase Deal," *Philadelphia Tribune*, January 29, 1982, 4; Tommie Hill, "Celebrating Black History: Board Approves Mayor's Price Tag on Marcase," *Philadelphia Tribune*, February 9, 1982, 1; Deborrah Wilkinson, "Search Begins in Five Cities for Marcase's Replacement," *Philadelphia Tribune*, February 12, 1982, 1; SDP BOE Minutes, February 8, 1982, 51–52. The board was looking for a superintendent to replace Marcase, as his contract was ending on June 30, 1982. By a memorandum of understanding, they outlined that on July 1, 1982, until June 30, 1984, Marcase would be paid his same salary with the title of "consultant." During that time, he would no longer have access to a car, credit cards, and leave accrual. He would retire at the end of this time and would receive his full pension. Helen Oakes, "A New Superintendent: What to Look For," *The Oakes Newsletter*, March 4, 1982, 1–4; Rhoda Houston, "Mad About Marcase," *Philadelphia Tribune*, February 12, 1982, 4.

Chapter 3

1. Nina, interview with the author, July 12, 2010. This is a reference to Booker T. Washington, who founded the Tuskegee Institute in Tuskegee, Alabama.

2. Linda, interview with the author June 21, 2010.

3. Constance Clayton, interview with the author, September 30, 2010; Pamela Smith, "Dr. Constance Clayton: Education, Children, Women Are Personal Issues for the New Supt.," *Philadelphia Tribune*, October 12, 1982, 6.

4. School District of Philadelphia (SDP) Board of Education (BOE) Minutes, February 8, 1993, 68.

5. Eduardo Bonilla-Silva, *Racism Without Racists: Color-Blind Racism and the Persistence of Racial Inequality in America*, 4th ed. (Lanham: Rowman and Littlefield, 2013), 41; Roger D. Simon and Brian Alnutt, "Philadelphia, 1982–2007: Toward the Postindustrial City," *Pennsylvania Magazine of History and Biography* 131, no. 4 (October 2007): 395–444; Liz Spikol, "A History of Violence: Philadelphia Political Brawls," *Philadelphia Magazine*, May 15, 2016, retrieved on May 2, 2019, from https://www.phillymag.com/news/2016/05/15/philadelphia-political-brawls/. Philadelphia's first Black mayor was responsible for the deadliest police event in the city's history,

which killed eleven members of the Black radical organization MOVE and destroyed sixty-one homes in a Black working-class neighborhood in 1985. Joanne Ball, "Black Journalists Question Goode on MOVE Bombing," *Boston Globe*, August 2, 1985, 12; Carline Rand Herron, Michael Wright, and Katherine Roberts, "The Nation; Philadelphia Fire Blamed on Police," *New York Times*, August 4, 1985, http://link.galegroup.com/apps/doc/A176532440/AONE?u=temple_main&sid=AONE&xid=e467c 344. Accessed 1 May 2019; William K. Stevens, "Head of Philadelphia Police Quits in Wake of Furor over Bombing," *New York Times*, November 14, 1985, http://link.galegroup.com/apps/doc/A176492095/AONE?u=temple_main&sid=AONE&xid=b02fb 230. Accessed 1 May 2019; Victoria Irwin, "Mayor Choices Frustrate Many in Philadelphia," *Christian Science Monitor*, November 2, 1987, retrieved on May 1, 2019, from https://search-proquest-com.libproxy.temple.edu/docview/1034971887?accountid=14270&rfr_id=info%3Axri%2Fsid%3 Aprimo.
6. M. J. Countryman, "From Protest to Politics: Community Control and Black Independent Politics in Philadelphia, 1965–1984," *Journal of Urban History* 32, no. 6 (2006): 813–861.
7. William W. Cutler III, "Public Education: The School District of Philadelphia," *The Encyclopedia of Greater Philadelphia*, accessed March 5, 2015, doi: http://philadelphiaencyclopedia.org/archive/public-educationthe-school-district-of-philadelphia/.
8. SDP BOE Minutes, April 14, 1986, 352–355. There were federal grand jury indictments involving the Food Services Operations of the School District of Philadelphia, perhaps corruption left over from Marcase's tenure. When senior administrators found out there was a problem, they notified Clayton, and she reported it to the FBI and the US Attorney's Office. The issue was the awarding of contracts by the Food Services division. The division had made changes to the process for 1985–86 school year, and these changes were supposed to save the district $1 million. The former director of Food Services resigned.
9. Michael J. Dumas, Adrienne D. Dixson, and Edwin Mayorga, "Educational Policy and the Cultural Politics of Race: Introduction to the Special Issue," *Educational Policy* 30, no. 1 (2016): 3–12.
10. Marc Lamont Hill, *Nobody: Casualties of America's War on the Vulnerable, from Ferguson to Flint and Beyond* (New York: Atria, 2016); SDP BOE Minutes, February 5, 1990, 73–74; SDP BOE Minutes, February 8, 1988, 137; SDP BOE Minutes, October 11, 1988, 956; SDP BOE Minutes, November 6, 1989, 961; SDP BOE Minutes, June 24, 1991, 555, 557; SDP BOE Minutes, November 6, 1989, 961; SDP BOE Minutes, February 5, 1990, 73–74; Ujju Aggarwal, "The Ideological Architecture of Whiteness as Property in Educational Policy," *Educational Policy* 30, no. 1 (2016); 128–152; .interview with Nina, July 12, 2010.
11. Countryman, "From Protest to Politics."
12. Lester K. Spence, *Knocking the Hustle: Against the Neoliberal Turn in Black Politics* (New York: Punctum Books, 2015); SDP BOE Minutes, November 6, 1989, 961; SDP BOE Minutes, December 16, 1991, 925; Simon and Alnutt, "Philadelphia, 1982–2007: Toward the Postindustrial City."
13. Spence, *Knocking the Hustle*, 20; Constance Clayton, "None of Us Did It Alone," *Philadelphia Tribune*, October 6, 1992, 11D (she wrote, "The economics and politics of the 1980s brought many cities (including Philadelphia) to the brink of bankruptcy. Across the nation school districts have been forced to confront massive budget deficits, to slash programs and salaries, and to lay off thousands of employees"); Camika Royal and Simone Gibson, "They Schools: Culturally Relevant Pedagogy Under Siege," *Teachers College Record* 119, no. 1 (2017): 1–25; Neil Brenner and Nik Theodore, *Spaces of Neoliberalism: Urban Restructuring in North America and Western Europe* (Hoboken: Wiley-Blackwell, 2002); Jason Hackworth, *The Neoliberal City: Governance, Ideology, and Development in American Urbanism* (Ithaca: Cornell University Press, 2007).

14. Larry Cuban and Michael Usdan, *Powerful Reforms with Shallow Roots: Improving America's Urban Schools* (New York: Teachers College Press, 2003); H Kantor and R. Lowe, "Reflections on History and Quality Education," *Educational Researcher* 33, no. 6 (2004): 6–10; S. Enderlin-Lampe, "Empowerment: Teacher Perceptions, Aspirations and Efficacy," *Journal of Instructional Psychology* 29, no. 3 (2002): 139–146.

15. "Our Opinion: Searching for a New Supt.," *Philadelphia Tribune*, March 5, 1982, 4; Deborrah Wilkinson, "New Superintendent Holds the Key to School's Future?," *Philadelphia Tribune*, August 24, 1982, 1; "Our Opinion: Saving Face with Marcase Deal," *Philadelphia Tribune*, January 29, 1982, 4; interview with Nina, July 12, 2010.

16. Wilkinson, "New Superintendent Holds the Key."

17. Countryman, "From Protests to Politics."

18. Jim Davis, "A Man Concerned: Mayor Has Failed Us," *Philadelphia Tribune*, September 8, 1981, 8.

19. John P. Spencer, *In the Crossfire: Marcus Foster and the Troubled History of American School Reform* (Philadelphia: University of Pennsylvania Press, 2012).

20. Camika Royal, "Policies, Politics, and Protests: Black Educators and the Shifting Landscape of Philadelphia's School Reforms, 1967–2007," unpublished doctoral dissertation, Temple University, Philadelphia, PA; Paul A. Bennett, "Costanzo Resigns: Poindexter Will Serve in Interim," *Philadelphia Tribune*, July 8, 1975, 1; Tommie St. Hill, "Board Approves Mayor's Price Tag on Marcase," *Philadelphia Tribune*, February 9, 1982, 1; Deborrah Wilkinson, "Search Begins in 5 Cities for Marcase's Replacement," *Philadelphia Tribune*, February 12, 1982, 1; SDP BOE Minutes, January 18, 1982, 50.

21. Stephen Williams, "Marcase Vote Pact Delayed," *Philadelphia Tribune*, August 19, 1980, 1; Wilkinson, "Search Begins in 5 Cities for Marcase's Replacement"; Elizabeth, interview with the author, July 27, 2010.

22. "Woman Green's Choice to Head Phila. Schools," *Reading Eagle*, September 28, 1982, 144, accessed March 5, 2015, doi: http://news.google.com/newspapers?nid=1955&dat=19820928&id=MfwxAAAAIBAJ&sjid=feQFAAAAIBAJ&pg=6020,6441558.

23. Jim Smith, "A Man Concerned: Mayor Has Failed Us," *Philadelphia Tribune*, September 8, 1981, 8; Tommie St. Hill, "Mayor Still Has Goode on His Side," *Philadelphia Tribune*, March 26, 1982, 1; Tommie St. Hill and Kendall Wilson, "Mayor May Not Seek 2nd Term After Insulting Blacks," *Philadelphia Tribune*, June 29, 1982, 1; Tommie St. Hill, "'Goode Government,' a Draft Call for Mayor," *Philadelphia Tribune*, July 23, 1982, 1; Lynette Hazelton, "Mayor Sees Some Goode in Draft Call," *Philadelphia Tribune*, July 30, 1982, 1;"Our Opinion: Mayor's Move Was Calculated," *Philadelphia Tribune*, September 7, 1982; 4; Tommie St. Hill, "ADA Bears Goode Wishes for Green," *Philadelphia Tribune*, October 1, 1982, 3.

24. Smith, "Mayor Has Failed Us"; Norris West, "Coalition of Minority Contractors Seeks to Open Doors for Members," *Philadelphia Tribune*, June 15, 1982, 23; Simon and Alnutt, "Philadelphia, 1982–2007: Toward the Postindustrial City."

25. Tommie St. Hill, " 'Goode Government'"; "Our Opinion: Public Schools Can Be Opened on Time," *Philadelphia Tribune*, August 17, 1982, 4; "Green Sees Hope for Settlement," *Philadelphia Tribune*, August 20, 1982, 1.

26. Torch Lytle, interview with the author, August 18, 2010; Jim Davis, "Dr. Clayton Promises to Upgrade 'Quality' of Schools," *Philadelphia Tribune*, October 1, 1982, 1.

27. Jim Smith, "Constance Clayton Is Best Prepared," *Philadelphia Tribune*, August 31, 1982, 4.

28. Wilkinson, "New Superintendent Holds the Key."

29. Interview with Constance Clayton, September 30, 2010; Wilkinson, "New Superintendent Holds the Key"; Deborrah Wilkinson, "Clayton Needs Time to Upgrade Schools," *Philadelphia Tribune*, October 5, 1982, 3.

30. SDP BOE Minutes, October 4, 1982, 749.

31. Helen Oakes, "The Need to Look Ahead," *Oakes Newsletter*, October 22, 1982; Vernon Loeb, "Clayton and Co.: New Zest to Revitalize Schools," *Philadelphia Inquirer*, September 26, 1983, B01; Davis, "Dr. Clayton Promises to Upgrade 'Quality' of Schools"; "Our Opinion: Dr. Clayton Is Committed to Children in the City Schools," *Philadelphia Tribune*, October 5, 1982, 4; SDP BOE Minutes, October 4, 1982, 747.

32. "Where Is the Leadership in This Time of Crisis?," editorial, *Philadelphia Tribune*, August 31, 1990, 6A.

33. James Perry, "Philadelphia, Bursting at Seams with Problems, Offers Voters Politics as Usual in Mayoral Race," *Wall Street Journal*, May 6, 1991, A18; William K. Stevens, "Goode Claims Victory over Rizzo in the Philadelphia Mayoral," *New York Times*, November 4, 1987, http://link.galegroup.com/apps/doc/A176043367/AONE?u=temple_main&sid=AONE&xid=a9182e09. Accessed 1 May 2019.

34. "A City Flounders," *Wall Street Journal*, September 20, 1990, A14; "Philadelphia Gets Aid from Swiss on Loans," *New York Times*, September 12, 1990, A28; Simon and Alnutt, "Philadelphia, 1982–2007: Toward the Postindustrial City."

35. Constance Clayton said, "This administration has stated publicly and frequently its position that teachers need and deserve a salary increase. We have gone on record urging the Mayor and the City Council to provide increased revenues to the School District to fund such a salary increase. We have been successful in obtaining the support of advocacy groups and of the business community. The business community has taken the unprecedented step to endorse a tax increase so that the School District can pay its teachers more." SDP BOE Minutes, August 26, 1985, 877; SDP BOE Minutes, May 31, 1988, 368–369; SDP BOE Minutes, May 8, 1989, 321.

36. Kendall Wilson and Wayne Browne, "Hayre Won't Seek Another Term as Board President," *Philadelphia Tribune,* November 24, 1992, 1A. Ruth Hayre was the first Black woman principal of a senior high school in the School District of Philadelphia. Mayor Wilson Goode appointed Hayre to the Board of Education in 1985. The board voted her in as president in 1990.

37. Camika Royal, "Reflections of Three Black Philadelphia Educators: An Oral History," paper presented at the annual meeting of the American Educational Research Association, San Diego, California, April 13–17, 2009; LeRoi Simmons, interview with the author, October 14, 2010; interview with Torch Lytle, August 18, 2010; Wilkinson, "Clayton Needs Time."

38. Interview with Nina, July 12, 2010; interview with Torch Lytle, August 18, 2010; interview with LeRoi Simmons, October 14, 2010.

39. Marsha, interview with the author July 2, 2010; Joe, interview with the author, January 5, 2011; interview with Nina, July 12, 2010; Latifah, interview with the author, July 22, 2010; Belinda, interview with the author, June 28, 2010; "Clayton's Tenure Restored Confidence in School System," editorial, *Philadelphia Tribune*, August 20, 1993, 6A.

40. Interview with Nina, July 12, 2010; Jackie, interview with the author, June 28, 2010; Lauren, interview with the author, June 17, 2010; Betty, interview with the author, July 15, 2010; Mark, interview with the author, June 21, 2010; interview with Joe, January 5, 2011; interview with Torch Lytle, August 18, 2010; Jolley Christman, interview with the author, August 19, 2010; June, interview with the author, October 25, 2010.

41. Terri, interview with the author, June 24, 2010; interview with LeRoi Simmons, October 14, 2010.

42. Mark, interview with the author, June 21, 2010; Jim, interview with the author, June 24, 2010; interview with June, October 25, 2010; interview with Marsha, July 2, 2010.

43. Interview with Constance Clayton, September 30, 2010; interview with Torch Lytle, August 18, 2010.

44. Interview with Constance Clayton, September 30, 2010; August 19, 2010; October 14, 2010; Merritt Wilson, "Clayton Plans to 'Improve' Schools," *Philadelphia Tribune*, October 12, 1982, 15; "Businesses Form Support Partnership for Schools," *Philadelphia Tribune*, September 23, 1983, 13. Greater Philadelphia First Corporation was formed to address the financial, managerial, and education requirements of the school district. This committee provided an opportunity for the private sector to do its share in contributing to society through public education. Stephen Williams, "Schools' Budget Balanced," *Philadelphia Tribune*, May 8, 1984, 1; "Dr. Constance Clayton ... 'The partnership grows ...,'" *Philadelphia Tribune*, June 3, 1986, 7C; Stanley Bailey, "Millions Donated to Revamp Schools," *Philadelphia Tribune*, April 21, 1989, 1A. Pew Charitable Trusts donated $8.3 million to improve twenty-one neighborhood/comprehensive high schools. At that time, it was the single largest grant ever given to the School District of Philadelphia. "Clayton Continues Standard of Excellence," editorial, *Philadelphia Tribune*, November 28, 1989, 8A; "Clayton, Business Leaders Join to Aid Schools," *Philadelphia Tribune*, July 3, 1990, 5A.

45. Interview with Torch Lytle, August 18, 2010.

46. Interview with Jackie, June 28, 2010; interview with June, October 25, 2010; interview with Jim, June 24, 2010; Jolley Christman, interview with the author, August 19, 2010; Robin White, "Clayton Rejects NY Offer; Issues New Plans for 1988," *Philadelphia Tribune*, January 12, 1988, 1A; Kendall Wilson, "Superintendent Bids Farewell," *Philadelphia Tribune*, July 23, 1993, 3D.

47. " Clayton Continues Standard of Excellence."

48. Interview with Torch Lytle, August 18, 2010.

49. Interview with Constance Clayton, September 30, 2010; "Clayton's Tenure Restored Confidence."

50. SDP BOE Minutes, November 12, 1991, p. 831.

51. Jacqueline Jordan Irvine, "Beyond Role Models: An Examination of Cultural Influences on the Pedagogical Perspectives of Black Teachers," *Peabody Journal of Education* 66 (1989): 51–63; interview with Nina, July 12, 2010; interview with Latifah, July 22, 2010; interview with Constance Clayton, September 30, 2010; Smith, "Dr. Constance Clayton: Education, Children, Women Are Personal Issues for the New Supt."

52. Interview with Nina, July 12, 2010; interview with Latifah, July 22, 2010.

53. Interview with Latifah, July 22, 2010; interview with Jackie, June 28, 2010; Judy, interview with the author, July 26, 2010; interview with Joe, January 5, 2011; interview with Jim, June 24, 2010; interview with Belinda, June 28, 2010; Harold, interview with the author, July 20, 2010.

54. Interview with Joe, January 5, 2011.

55. Interview with Terri, June 24, 2010.

56. Interview with LeRoi Simmons, October 14, 2010.

57. Mary, interview with the author, August 2, 2010; interview with Constance Clayton, September 30, 2010; Yvonne Reynolds, "ADL Claims 'Ethnic Patronage' Blocks Jewish Promotions," *Philadelphia Tribune*, January 4, 1983, 7; SDP BOE Minutes, December 3, 1984, 1035.

58. Interview with Jim, June 24, 2010; interview with Constance Clayton, September 30, 2010.

59. Lori Cornish, "Clayton Toughens Graduation Requirements," *Philadelphia Tribune*, September 10, 1985, 1; "School District's First Balanced Budget in 18 Years Pays Off," *Philadelphia Tribune*, August 14, 1984, 2; Onah Weldon, "Letter to the Editor: Don't Blame Dr. Clayton," *Philadelphia Tribune*, September 16, 1988, 6A; " Clayton Continues Standard of Excellence"; "Clayton's Tenure Restored Confidence"; Jim Smith, "A Man Concerned: Did Clayton Really Have to Retire?," *Philadelphia Tribune*, July 23, 1993, 5A; William Boyd and Jolley Christman, "A Tall Order for Philadelphia's New Approach to School Governance: Heal the Political Rifts, Close the Budget Gap, *and* Improve the Schools," in *Powerful Reforms with Shallow Roots: Improving*

America's Urban Schools, ed. Larry Cuban and Michael Usdan (New York: Teachers College Press, 2003); Kendall Wilson, "School District Marked Triple B in Fund Management," *Philadelphia Tribune,* March 15, 1991, 2A; interview with Constance Clayton, September 30, 2010; Lori Cornish, "Fattah Urges School Talks," *Philadelphia Tribune,* August 20, 1985, 1A; Lori Cornish, "Teachers, Board Must Be Committed to Kids," *Philadelphia Tribune,* August 27, 1985, 1A; Tommie St. Hill and Kendall Wilson, "School's Open, But Were Students Biggest Victors?," *Philadelphia Tribune,* September 6, 1985, 1A; Frank Wilson, "The PFT-School District Settlement: Who Really Won?," *Philadelphia Tribune,* October 8, 1985, 16A; Lori Cornish, "Clayton Unfazed by Teamster Vote," *Philadelphia Tribune,* October 14, 1986, 1A; Kendall Wilson, "Teachers Strike in September?," *Philadelphia Tribune,* June 30, 1992, 3A (the Philadelphia Federation of Teachers contract would expire August 31, 1992); Vincent Thompson, "What If the Teachers Walk Out? Some Suggestions," *Philadelphia Tribune,* September 8, 1992, 5A; "Teachers Set Good Example for City, Unions to Follow," editorial, *Philadelphia Tribune,* September 11, 1992, 6A; Wilson, "Superintendent Bids Farewell" (according to this article, prior to her, the system had been "fraught with teacher strikes and student underachievement").

60. Interview with LeRoi Simmons, October 14, 2010; interview with Torch Lytle, August 18, 2010; "Clayton to Address Teachers," *Philadelphia Tribune,* September 5, 1986, 3B; Lori Cornish, "Teachers Give High Grades to Clayton's Learning Reforms," *Philadelphia Tribune,* September 5, 1986, 1A; Tommie St. Hill, "School District Plans Ambitious Improvement in Student Performance," *Philadelphia Tribune,* April 23, 1991, 1A.

61. Interview with Constance Clayton, September 30, 2010; Constance Clayton, "None of Us Did It Alone," *Philadelphia Tribune,* October 6, 1992, 11D; "Clayton's Tenure Restored Confidence."

62. Loeb, "Clayton and Co."; " Clayton's Tenure Restored Confidence"; Wilson, "Superintendent Bids Farewell."

63. SDP BOE Minutes, November 18, 1985, 1354; SDP BOE Minutes, May 30, 1986, 618.

64. Interview with Elizabeth, July 27, 2010; interview with Jim, June 24, 2010; interview with Latifah, July 22, 2010; interview with Betty, July 15, 2010; Ernestine, interview with the author, July 6, 2010; Harold, interview with the author, July 20, 2010; interview with Jolley Christman, August 19, 2010.

65. John, interview with the author, August 5, 2016.

66. Interview with Nina, July 12, 2010.

67. Interview with Jackie, June 28, 2010; interview with Jolley Christman, August 19, 2010; interview with Nina, July 12, 2010; Cornish, "Clayton Toughens Graduation Requirements in Public Schools."

68. Interview with Nina, July 12, 2010; interview with Elizabeth, July 27, 2010; interview with LeRoi Simmons, October 14, 2010.

69. SDP BOE Minutes, September 12, 1983, 646; SDP BOE Minutes, September 26, 1983, 683–684; SDP BOE Minutes, October 11, 1983, 716.

70. SDP BOE Minutes, June 10, 1991, 472.

71. SDP BOE Minutes, October 12, 1970, 842.

72. SDP BOE Minutes, April 10, 1989, 275–276; SDP BOE Minutes, June 24, 1991, 552–555.

73. SDP BOE Minutes, June 24, 1991, 552–555, 557, 559–564.

74. SDP BOE Minutes, March 18, 1991, 149; SDP BOE Minutes, August 20, 1991, 678; SDP BOE Minutes, September 16, 1991, 723.

75. SDP BOE Minutes, June 30, 1982, 464; SDP BOE Minutes, January 10, 1983, 45; SDP BOE Minutes, April 26, 1982, 268; SDP BOE Minutes, November 8, 1982, 887; SDP BOE Minutes, November 22, 1982, 917–918; SDP BOE Minutes, February 22, 1983, 139.

76. SDP BOE Minutes, October 3, 1983, 686–692.

77. SDP BOE Minutes, October 24, 1983, 753.

78. SDP BOE Minutes, March 23, 1987, 351; SDP BOE Minutes, March 12, 1984, 275.

79. SDP BOE Minutes, January 27, 1986; 167; SDP BOE March 7, 1988, 200.

80. SDP BOE Minutes, December 19, 1983, 909.

81. SDP BOE Minutes, May, 30, 1985, 448; May 30, 1986, 525; May 11, 1987, 510–511.

82. William F. Tate, Gloria Ladson-Billings, and Carl A. Grant, "The *Brown* Decision Revisited: Mathematizing Social Problems," *Educational Policy* 7, no. 3 (1993): 255–275.

83. Dale Mezzacappa, "Board Would Appeal Busing Order, Lee Says," *Philadelphia Inquirer*, February 9, 1993, A1, 11, retrieved on May 4, 2019, from https://www.newspapers.com/clip/8537842/the_philadelphia_inquirer/.

84. "Forced Busing Rejected in Philadelphia Schools Suit," *Orlando Sentinel*, April 16, 1993, retrieved on May 4, 2019, from (https://www.orlandosentinel.com/news/os-xpm-1993-04-16-9304160669-story.html.

85. SDP BOE Minutes, November 23, 1987, 1542.

86. SDP BOE Minutes, November 23, 1987, 1583; SDP BOE Minutes, January 22, 1990, 67.

87. Aggarwal, "The Ideological Architecture of Whiteness as Property in Educational Policy."

88. SDP BOE Minutes, July 21, 1987, 1043. The president of the School Nurses Association (Mrs. Mary Brewster) protested that an outside consultant would work on the school district's modified school health program. Brewster offered the expertise of her organization as an alternative. SDP BOE Minutes, June 28, 1993, 586. Parents from Carnell School did not want their maintenance services to be privatized.

89. David B. Tyack and Larry Cuban, *Tinkering Toward Utopia: A Century of Public School Reform* (Cambridge: Harvard University Press, 1995); David B. Tyack, *The Ones Best System: A History of American Urban Education* (Cambridge: Harvard University Press, 1974); Royal and Gibson, "They Schools".

90. SDP BOE Minutes June 25, 1984, 630; SDP BOE Minutes, June 24, 1985, 700–701.

91. SDP BOE Minutes, September 9, 1985, 884–888.

92. SDP BOE Minutes, August 26, 1985, 877.

93. Simon and Alnutt, "Philadelphia, 1982–2007: Toward the Postindustrial City."

94. SDP BOE Minutes, May 31, 1988, 368–369.

95. SDP BOE Minutes, June 10, 1991, 471.

96. SDP BOE Minutes, August 20, 1991, 679.

97. SDP BOE Minutes, June 24, 1991, 565.

98. SDP BOE Minutes, August 20, 1991, 678.

99. SDP BOE Minutes, June 24, 1991, 564–565.

100. SDP BOE Minutes, June 10, 1991, 472.

101. SDP BOE Minutes, January 7, 1991, 2; interview with Torch Lytle, August 18, 2010.

102. SDP BOE Minutes, October 4, 1982, 747; SDP BOE Minutes, October 9, 1984, 883; SDP BOE Minutes, July 21, 1987, 981–983.

103. White, "Clayton Rejects NY Offer"; SDP BOE Minutes, January 11, 1988, 1–7.

104. Lester K. Spence, *Knocking the Hustle: Against the Neoliberal Turn in Black Politics* (Brooklyn: Punctum Books, 2015).

105. Royal, "Policies, Politics, and Protests."

106. Interview with Linda, June 21, 2010.

107. Weldon, "Don't Blame Dr. Clayton"; interview with Marsha, July 2, 2010.

108. " Don't Blame Clayton for Service Cuts," editorial, *Philadelphia Tribune*, July 22, 1988, 6A.

109. Constance Clayton, "Guest Opinion: Public Schools Need Long-Term Financing, Commitment to Kids," *Philadelphia Tribune*, August 26, 1988, 6A.

110. "Who's Historically Privileged?," editorial, *Philadelphia Inquirer*, August 26, 1988, A18.

111. Royal, "Reflections of Three Black Philadelphia Educators"; interview with Marsha, July 2, 2010; Stanley Bailey, "School District Asks for Money," *Philadelphia Tribune*, January 20, 1989, 2A.

112. Bill Miller, "Salvatore Calls for Clayton to Resign," *Philadelphia Inquirer*, September 4, 1988, N09.

113. June Smith, interview with the author, October 25, 2010. A 2012 article from the *Northeast Times* celebrates the retirement of former City Council member Jack Kelly: "While representing the 7th district, he battled the administration of Mayor Wilson Goode. He opposed Goode's reappointment of School District of Philadelphia Superintendent Constance Clayton, who infamously called Northeast residents 'historically privileged.'" This article goes on to say, "Overall, he's hopeful that local Council members fight for the Northeast. 'I'd like to see the Northeast get its fair share,' he said." "Citizen Kelly," *Northeast Times*, January 4, 2012, retrieved on May 4, 2019, from https://northeasttimes.com/2012/01/04/citizen-kelly/.

114. Sam Evans, "Readers' Viewpoints: Clayton Speaks Profound Truths," *Philadelphia Tribune*, September 13, 1988, 6A;" Who's Historically Privileged?"; Lini S. Kadaba, "Parents Take a Stand Against Clayton," *Philadelphia Inquirer*, September 8, 1988, N03; Dan Meyers, "Northeast Residents Are Angered by Clayton's Comment on Privilege," *Philadelphia Inquirer*, August 25, 1988, B03; Bill Miller, "Salvatore Calls for Clayton to Resign," *Philadelphia Inquirer*, September 4, 1988, N09; Martha Woodall and Robert J. Terry, "Phone Calls to Clayton Bring Police Protection," *Philadelphia Inquirer*, August 31, 1988, B05.

115. Miller, "Salvatore Calls for Clayton to Resign."

116. "Who's Historically Privileged?"

117. Subini Ancy Annamma, Darrell D. Jackson, and Deb Morrison, "Conceptualizing Color-Evasiveness: Using Dis/Ability Critical Race Theory to Expand a Color-Blind Racial Ideology in Education and Society," *Race Ethnicity and Education* 20, no. 2 (2017): 147–162.

118. SDP BOE Minutes May 30, 1984, 497.

119. SDP BOE Minutes, December 3, 1984, 1032.

120. SDP BOE Minutes, August 8, 1985, 811; Christman and Boyd, "A Tall Order."

121. SDP BOE Minutes, June 24, 1985, 579; SDP BOE Minutes, September 26, 1988, 868; SDP BOE Minutes, April 24, 1989, 283; Christman and Boyd, "A Tall Order."

122. SDP BOE Minutes, February 8, 1988, 107; SDP BOE Minutes, January 7, 1991, 2, 16.

123. Dale Mezzacappa, "The School System at a Crossroads After Seven Years of Peace, a New Era of Challenges," *Philadelphia Inquirer*, January 8, 1990, A01; SDP BOE Minutes, September 25, 1989, 837; interview with Torch Lytle, August 18, 2010.

124. Boyd and Christman, "A Tall Order"; interview with Betty, July 15, 2010; interview with LeRoi Simmons, October 14, 2010; interview with Jackie, June 28, 2010.

125. Simon and Alnutt, "Philadelphia, 1982–2007: Toward the Postindustrial City."

126. SDP BOE Minutes, December 3, 1984, 1033: Mattleman commends Clayton for the balanced budget of 1984. SDP BOE Minutes, June 24, 1985, 579: Mattleman celebrates Clayton for receiving the grant from the William Penn Foundation. SDP BOE Minutes, December 2, 1985, 1364: Mattleman declares, "Dr. Clayton came to the Superintendent's office at a time when we were in educational and fiscal disarray. She proclaimed that 'the children come first' and moved rapidly to gain control over a budget that in June 30, 1982, had swollen to a $78.7 million deficit. We have achieved budget surpluses every year since that time, which is the more remarkable because in the period from 1968 to 1982, there were fiscal year-end deficits in 11 of those 15 years!" https://www.philadelphiaaward.org/winners/herman-mattleman/.

127. Ruth Wright Hayre and Alexis Moore, *Tell Them We Are Rising: A Memoir of Faith in Education* (Hoboken: Wiley and Sons, 1998), 81.

128. Hayre and Moore, *Tell Them We Are Rising*, 81.

129. SDP BOE Minutes, December 3, 1990, 884.

130. Wilson and Brown, "Hayre Won't Seek Another Term as Board President."

131. SDP BOE Minutes, June 25, 1984, 632.

132. SDP BOE Minutes, March 27, 1989, 201.

133. SDP BOE Minutes, May 28, 1991, 430.

134. SDP BOE Minutes, May 28, 1991, 431.

135. Sherry Stone, "Key School District Officials Responsible for Settlement," *Philadelphia Tribune*, September 15, 1992, 1A.

136. Sam Evans, "Having Your Say: Clayton, Lee Are on the Same Team," *Philadelphia Tribune*, May 25, 1993, 6A.

137. Jim Smith, "A Man Concerned: Don't Move Over, Dr. Clayton," *Philadelphia Tribune*, May 7, 1993, 4A.

138. Interview with Torch Lytle, August 18, 2010.

139. Smith, "Did Clayton Really Have to Retire?"

140. Interview with LeRoi Simmons, October 14, 2010.

141. Smith, "Did Clayton Really Have to Retire?"; Wilson, "Superintendent Bids Farewell."

Chapter 4

1. School District of Philadelphia (SDP) Board of Education (BOE) Minutes, July 20, 1994, 554.

2. SDP BOE Minutes, September 4, 1996, 563.

3. SDP BOE Minutes, May 30, 1997, 311.

4. William Boyd and Jolley Christman, "A Tall Order for Philadelphia's New Approach to School Governance: Heal the Political Rifts, Close the Budget Gap, *and* Improve the Schools," in *Powerful Reforms with Shallow Roots: Improving America's Urban Schools*, ed. Larry Cuban and Michael Usdan (New York: Teachers College Press, 2003); Jon S. Birger, "Race, Reaction, and Reform: The Three Rs of Philadelphia School Politics, 1965–1971," *Pennsylvania Magazine of History and Biography* 120, no. 3 (July 1996): 163–216.

5. "David M. Hornbeck, Ph.D.," State Superintendent of Schools, State Department of Education, Maryland Manual On-Line: A Guide to Maryland & Its Government, retrieved on February 1, 2021, from https://msa.maryland.gov/msa/mdmanual/13sdoe/former/html/msa15113.html.

6. Carole Feldman, "Needy Schools Are Shortchanged by Regs," *Philadelphia Tribune*, January 28, 1984, 5D; Kendall Wilson, "Walton Exits Race for Superintendent," *Philadelphia Tribune*, June 28, 1994, 3A, 5B; James Sutton, "Having Your Say: Hornbeck Doesn't Understand," *Philadelphia Tribune*, June 28, 1994, 6A; David W. Hornbeck and Katherine Conner, *Choosing Excellence in Public Schools: Where There's a Will, There's a Way* (Lanham: Rowman & Littlefield Education, 2009).

7. Buzz Bissinger, *A Prayer for the City* (New York: Vintage Books, 1999), 312.

8. "Let's See What Hornbeck Can Do for Our Schools," editorial, *Philadelphia Tribune*, August 19, 1994, 6A.

9. Dave, interview with the author, August 6, 2016. Dave referred to Hornbeck as a "missionary" and "the savior."

10. Cherese D. Childers-McKee and Kathy Hytten, "Critical Race Feminism and the Complex Challenges of Educational Reform," *Urban Review* (2015): 393–412.

11. Kalman R. Heitleman, "The Trial and Other Tribulations of David Hornbeck," *Baltimore Sun*, July 19, 1995, retrieved on February 17, 2021, from https://www.baltimoresun.com/news/bs-xpm-1995-07-19-1995200046-story.html.

12. SDP BOE Minutes, April 25, 1994, 275–276.

13. SDP BOE Minutes, March 29, 1993, 262; SDP BOE Minutes, April 12, 1993, 301–302; SDP BOE Minutes, April 26, 1993, 331.

14. SDP BOE Minutes, April 25, 1994, 275–276; Bissinger, *A Prayer for the City*, 298.

15. SDP BOE Minutes, July 26, 1993, 588.

16. SDP BOE Minutes, December 13, 1993, 876.

17. SDP BOE Minutes, October 12, 1993, 747; SDP BOE Minutes April 11, 1994, 245.

18. SDP BOE Minutes November 8, 1993, 814–815; SDP BOE Minutes, November 22, 1993, 842; SDP BOE Minutes, February 7, 1994, 75; SDP BOE Minutes, March 24, 1994, 167.

19. SDP BOE Minutes, May 26, 1995, 334; SDP BOE Minutes, June 12, 1995, 377; SDP BOE Minutes, August 14, 1995, 509.

20. SDP BOE Minutes, November 8, 1993, 815: Neighborhood violence was rampant every day after school in the McDonald's parking lot near Broad and Girard. SDP BOE Minutes, November 22, 1993, 820: Community violence plagued the school district throughout every era since the 1960s. Rotan Lee announced a partnership with the Urban League and Cheyney University and State Representative Dwight Evans regarding conflict resolution and crisis interventions. SDP BOE Minutes, December 13, 1993, 876; SDP BOE Minutes, January 10, 1994, 4: Violence-prevention and conflict resolution efforts were led by the Philadelphia Anti-Drug/Anti-Violence Network for work at King High School. SDP BOE Minutes January 24, 1994, 57; SDP BOE Minutes, April 11, 1994, 247: The school district paid the Urban League to help with violence prevention in schools. SDP BOE Minutes, November 21, 1994, 822: A school nurse practitioner commented that, per her interpretation of the Elementary and Secondary Education Act (ESEA), because students caught with firearms would be prohibited from attending school for at least one year, it would increase the number of students on the streets with guns, especially since alternative school placements were limited. She wanted to know what Hornbeck would do about this. SDP BOE Minutes, September 12, 1994, 685. Lee said he was OK with video cameras in classrooms as long as the cameras passed the "test of intrusiveness."

21. SDP BOE Minutes, January 10, 1994, 32; SDP BOE Minutes, January 24, 1994, 34; SDP BOE Minutes, February 7, 1994, 73–74: There was a lot of testimony from community members regarding the multicultural-multiracial-gender education policy of the Board of Education, mostly for, though some against. Board president Lee described this process as a good way to engage community stakeholders. SDP BOE Minutes, March 7, 1994, 130: The Citizens Committee for Public Education supported the multicultural-multiracial-gender education policy. SDP BOE Minutes March 24, 1994, 131.

22. SDP BOE Minutes, May 23, 1994, 334; SDP BOE Minutes, June 27, 1994, 525: The board reinstated the Asian American studies curriculum specialist position. SDP BOE Minutes, March 24, 1994, 167: The School District of Philadelphia was the only school district in the state with an Office of Education of Latino students.

23. SDP BOE Minutes, May 9, 1994, 331; SDP BOE Minutes June 27, 1994, 525: A representative from the Asian American Youth Associated requested that the board be considerate of Asian American young people whose families were in transition. He requested more English to Speakers of Other Languages (ESOL) programs or that access to those programs move as the students moved throughout the city. He also requested Southeast Asian bilingual teachers.

24. LeRoi Simmons, interview with the author, October 14, 2010; Bissinger, *A Prayer for the City*, 320, 325. Eighteen Black ministers from across Philadelphia pressed Rendell about the next superintendent of schools, saying they wanted it to be a Black man. Rendell was proud that he had appointed Philadelphia's first Black fire commissioner in 1992.

25. Wilson, "Walton Exits Race for Superintendent."

26. Kalman R. Heitleman, "The Trial and Other Tribulations of David Hornbeck," *Baltimore Sun*, July 19, 1995, retrieved on February 17, 2021, from https://www.baltimoresun.com/news/bs-xpm-1995-07-19-1995200046-story.html.

27. Wilson, "Walton Exits Race for Superintendent"; James Sutton, "Having Your Say: Hornbeck Doesn't Understand," *Philadelphia Tribune*, June 28, 1994, 3A; Bissinger, *A Prayer for the City*, 294: "the search for a new school superintendent, which continued to be mired in the misery of racial politics."

28. Bissinger, *A Prayer for the City*, 342–343; SDP BOE Minutes, May 23, 1994, 334.

29. Richard L. Berke, "The 1994 Elections: The Overview; GOP Wins Control of the Senate and Makes Big Gains in House; Pataki Denies Cuomo 4th Term," *New York Times*, November 9, 1994, retrieved on February 17, 2021, from https://www.nytimes.com/1994/11/09/us/1994-elections-overview-gop-wins-control-senate-makes-big-gains-house-pataki.html; Lesley Kennedy, "The 1994 Midterms: When Newt Gingrich Helped Republicans Win Big," History, October 9, 2018, retrieved on February 17, 2021, from https://www.history.com/news/midterm-elections-1994-republican-revolution-gingrich-contract-with-america.

30. SDP BOE Minutes, April 25, 1994, 275–276; Carole Feldman, "Needy Schools Are Shortchanged by Regs," *Philadelphia Tribune*, January 28, 1994, 5D.

31. David E. Rosenbaum, "Republicans Offer Voters a Deal for Takeover of House," *New York Times*, September 28, 1994, retrieved on February 17, 2021, from https://www.nytimes.com/1994/09/28/us/republicans-offer-voters-a-deal-for-takeover-of-house.html.

32. Berke, "The 1994 Elections: The Overview; GOP Wins Control of the Senate and Makes Big Gains in House; Pataki Denies Cuomo 4th Term"; Michael Janofsky, "The 1994 Campaign: Pennsylvania; Crime and Echoes of 'Willie Horton' in Campaign," *New York Times*, October 10, 1994, retrieved on February 17, 2021, from https://www.nytimes.com/1994/10/10/us/the-1994-campaign-pennsylvania-crime-and-echoes-of-willie-horton-in-campaign.html; Mario F. Cattabiani, "Ridge Next PA. Governor GOP Hopeful Beats Singel in Tough Race," *Morning Call*, retrieved on February 17, 2021, from https://www.mcall.com/news/mc-xpm-1994-11-09-3006883-story,amp.html.

33. SDP BOE Minutes, April 11, 1994, 272; SDP BOE Minutes, November 8, 1993, 815; SDP BOE Minutes, January 22, 1996, 34.

34. SDP BOE Minutes, April 11, 1994, 272; SDP BOE Minutes November 21, 1994, 824.

35. SDP BOE Minutes, September 12, 1994, 685.

36. SDP BOE Minutes, May 23, 1994, 334–336.

37. SDP BOE Minutes, May 27, 1994, 338.

38. SDP BOE Minutes, May 27, 1994, 339; SDP BOE Minutes, June 13, 1994, 423–424.

39. SDP BOE Minutes, July 20, 1994, 554.

40. SDP BOE Minutes, October 24, 1994, 733.

41. Hornbeck and Conner, *Choosing Excellence in Public Schools*.

42. Judy, interview with the author, July 26, 2010.

43. SDP BOE Minutes, October 24, 1994, 764; SDP BOE Minutes, August 22, 1994, 572; Michael Dabney, "Broad School Reforms Planned," *Philadelphia Tribune*, February 7, 1995, 1A, 4A; Hornbeck and Conner *Choosing Excellence in Public Schools*. Hornbeck wrote, "I was convinced that there is a parsimonious set of ten components that, if faithfully implemented, would result in all children learning to high standards. I began to look for the opportunity to serve as a superintendent in a big city that wanted to implement this aggressive and comprehensive agenda. Baltimore, Cleveland, and Pittsburgh said thanks but no thanks. Philadelphia at least seemed to say yes to the ten-part agenda."

44. SDP BOE Minutes, January 9, 1995, 33; SDP BOE Minutes, March 6, 1995, 129: Schools added twenty-three minutes to the school day so Philly's teachers would be in compliance with state law. This had been negotiated in the contract.

45. "Let's See What Hornbeck Can Do for Our Schools"; June, interview with the author, October 25, 2010; Jolley Christman, interview with the author, August 19, 2010.

46. SDP BOE Minutes, April 3, 1995, 174; Vincent Thompson, "Teachers and School District Reach Agreement," *Philadelphia Tribune*, August 26, 1994, 5A; SDP BOE Minutes, March 20, 1995, 153. Per SDP BOE Minutes, April 3, 1995, 177: Parents and community members had questions and concerns about "quest" and "keystone" schools.

47. Boyd and Christman, "A Tall Order for Philadelphia's New Approach to School Governance," 97; Hornbeck and Conner, *Choosing Excellence in Public Schools*; David Hornbeck, "Our City's Children Can—and Will—Achieve," *Philadelphia Tribune*, November 11, 1994, 7A.

48. Hornbeck, "Our City's Children Can—and Will—Achieve."

49. SDP BOE Minutes, December 16, 1996, 746, 775.

50. SDP BOE Minutes, November 21, 1994, 821.

51. SDP BOE Minutes, March 6, 1995, 129; SDP BOE Minutes, October 11, 1994, 708, 729.

52. SDP BOE Minutes, March 6, 1995, 130.

53. SDP BOE Minutes, May 26, 1995, 335.

54. Elizabeth, interview with the author, July 27, 2010; interview with Judy, July 26, 2010; Latifah, interview with the author, July 22, 2010; Joe, interview with the author, January 5, 2011; Theresa, interview with the author, July 29, 2010; interview with June, October 25, 2010.

55. Interview with LeRoi Simmons, October 14, 2010; interview with Elizabeth, July 27, 2010; interview with Judy, July 26, 2010; Linda, interview with the author, June 21, 2010; interview with Theresa, July 29, 2010; Belinda, interview with the author, June 28, 2010; Dabney, "Broad Reforms Planned."

56. Dabney, "Broad Reforms Planned."

57. Kia Morgan, "District Plans National Search for Superintendent," *Philadelphia Tribune*, June 13, 2000, 1A, 4A.

58. Nina, interview with the author, July 12, 2010; interview with Judy, July 26, 2010; interview with Elizabeth, July 27, 2010, Betty, interview with the author, July 15, 2010, Linda, interview with the author, June 21, 2010; Joe, interview with the author, January 5, 2011; Jolley Christman, interview with the author, August 19, 2010; "Public School Children Lose Out to State Politics," editorial, *Philadelphia Tribune*, April 28, 1998, 6A; Michael Dabney, "Board to Vote on Hornbeck's Contract," *Philadelphia Tribune*, January 29, 1999, 1A, 4A; Chad Glover, "Hornbeck Calls State Funding for Schools Bias," *Philadelphia Tribune*, February 19, 1999, 1A, 4A; Chad Glover, "Hornbeck's Relationship with State Worries Council," *Philadelphia Tribune*, March 2, 1999, 2A; "A Fine Legacy from Hornbeck," *Philadelphia Tribune*, August 15, 2000, 6A.

59. Interview with Theresa, July 29, 2010.

60. Jim, interview with the author, June 24, 2010; George, interview with the author, July 15, 2010; Harold, interview with the author, July 20, 2010; interview with Elizabeth, July 27, 2010; interview with Judy, July 26, 2010; interview with Linda, June 21, 2010; interview with Joe, January 5, 2011.

61. Interview with Joe, January 5, 2011.

62. Missy, interview with the author, July 19, 2010.

63. Betty, interview with the author, July 15, 2010; interview with Harold, July 20, 2010; Torch Lytle, interview with the author, August 18, 2010; Jolley Christman, interview with the author, August 19, 2010.

64. Interview with Belinda, June 28, 2010; Marsha, interview with the author, July 2, 2010; interview with Harold, July 20, 2010; Michael Dabney, "Hornbeck Aide Clarifies Speech on School Reform," *Philadelphia Tribune.*, April 2, 1996, 1A, 4-A. According to Warren Simmons, head of the Philadelphia Education Fund, Black people were not supporting Hornbeck's plan. "Hornbeck's Reform Plan Is Being Unfairly Attacked," editorial, *Philadelphia Tribune*, April 26, 1996, 6_A.

65. Interview with Marsha, July 2, 2010.

66. Interview with Elizabeth, July 27, 2010.

67. Interview with Betty, July 15, 2010; interview with LeRoi Simmons, October 14, 2010.

68. SDP BOE Minutes, March 6, 1995, 129.

69. Interview with Betty, July 15, 2010.

70. Boyd and Christman, "A Tall Order for Philadelphia's New Approach to School Governance," 97.

71. Interview with Jim, June 24, 2010.

72. SDP BOE Minutes, January 9, 1995, 35.

73. SDP BOE Minutes, May 8, 1995, 235.

74. SDP BOE Minutes, January 9, 1995, 34.

75. SDP BOE Minutes, March 6, 1995, 130.

76. SDP BOE Minutes, October 11, 1994, 708, 729; SDP BOE Minutes, May 26, 1995, 335; Kalman R. Heitleman, "The Trial and Other Tribulations of David Hornbeck," *Baltimore Sun*, July 19, 1995, retrieved on February 17, 2021, from https://www.baltimoresun.com/news/bs-xpm-1995-07-19-1995200046-story.html; SDP BOE Minutes, June 26, 1995, 438.

77. SDP BOE Minutes, April 3, 1995, 174.

78. SDP BOE Minutes, June 26, 1995, 439.

79. SDP BOE Minutes, January 22, 1996, 35; SDP BOE Minutes, March 11, 1996, 113.

80. SDP BOE Minutes, January 22, 1996, 35; SDP BOE Minutes, March 25 1996, 146: Community member asks the board to repair buildings and bring security to schools for teachers and students; SDP BOE Minutes, March 11, 1996, 113: More concern about conditions of West Philly schools, seen as unsafe; SDP BOE Minutes, September 24, 1996, 601.

81. SDP BOE Minutes, January 22, 1996, 35; SDP BOE Minutes, October 7, 1996, 628.

82. SDP BOE Minutes, January 22, 1996, 35.

83. SDP BOE Minutes, June 24, 1996, 435–436.

84. Interview with Jim, June 24, 2010; SDP BOE Minutes, May 8, 1995, 235.

85. Boyd and Christman, "A Tall Order for Philadelphia's New Approach to School Governance"; Wellford W. Wilms, "Altering the Structure and Culture of American Public Schools," *Phi Delta Kappan*, 84 no. 8 (2003): 606–615; interview with Marsha, July 2, 2010; interview with Betty, July 15, 2010; interview with Harold, July 20, 2010; interview with Belinda, June 28, 2010.

86. Boyd and Christman, "A Tall Order for Philadelphia's New Approach to School Governance"; Camika Royal, "Reflections of Three Black Philadelphia Educators: An Oral History," paper presented at the Annual Meeting of the American Educational Research Association, Division F, History and Historiography, San Diego, CA, April 2009; interview with Judy, July 26, 2010; interview with Betty, July 15, 2010; interview with Theresa, July 29, 2010.

87. Hornbeck and Conner, *Choosing Excellence in Public Schools*, 10–12.

88. SDP BOE Minutes, April 24, 1995, 203; interview with Judy, July 26, 2010; interview with Theresa, July 29, 2010.

89. SDP BOE Minutes, January 22, 1995, 35.

90. SDP BOE Minutes, January 23, 1995, 37.

91. SDP BOE Minutes, January 23, 1995, 60.

92. SDP BOE Minutes, October 23, 1995, 819.

93. SDP BOE Minutes, March 11, 1996, 113.

94. State Senator Vince Fumo congratulated the Board of Education on choosing Hornbeck. SDP BOE Minutes, October 24, 1994, 732.

95. Interview with June Smith, October 25, 2010. According to Hornbeck, "Ironically, within a year, the racial alignment of the board had reversed itself, with all the African Americans supporting the agenda and all but one of the white board members in opposition on the most controversial issues." Hornbeck and Conner, *Choosing Excellence in Public Schools*, xx–xxi. SDP BOE Minutes, July 26, 1993, 588: Board member Jacques Lurie voted against Constance Clayton staying on until November 1993.

96. Hornbeck and Conner, *Choosing Excellence in Public Schools*.

97. SDP BOE Minutes, December 5, 1994, 826.

98. SDP BOE Minutes, December 4, 1995, 885.

99. SDP BOE Minutes, December 5, 1994, 828, 829.

100. SDP BOE Minutes, December 4, 199512, 884. Ramos's appointment was seen as a nod to Latinx representation to the board.

101. SDP BOE Minutes, December 4, 1995, 887.

102. SDP BOE Minutes, December 4, 1995, 890–891.

103. SDP BOE Minutes, December 2, 1996, 742–743.

104. Bissinger, *A Prayer for the City*.

105. Bissinger, *A Prayer for the City*; Boyd and Christman, "A Tall Order for Philadelphia's New Approach to School Governance"; Hornbeck and Conner, *Choosing Excellence in Public Schools*.

106. SDP BOE Minutes, April 3, 1995, 155.

107. SDP BOE Minutes, May 8, 1995, 234.

108. SDP BOE Minutes, May 8, 1995, 235.

109. Desegregation funds paid for Northeast High School's Aerospace Magnet School Program, but they had been cut. SDP BOE Minutes, June 12, 1995, 376.

110. SDP BOE Minutes, November 4, 1996, 691; SDP BOE Minutes, December 16, 1996, 775.

111. SDP BOE Minutes, December 18, 1995, 930.

112. SDP BOE Minutes, May 8, 1995, 207.

113. SDP BOE Minutes, May 8, 1995, 235–236.

114. SDP BOE Minutes, September 18, 1995, 604; SDP BOE, Minutes, April 29, 1996, 206.

115. SDP BOE Minutes, April 29, 1996, 205–208; SDP BOE Minutes, May 13, 1995, 238–239; SDP BOE, Minutes April 3, 1995, 173: Board president Alston said that the board had to make hard decisions with limited funds and that everything can't be funded.

116. "Pew Grants Will Help 'Children Achieving' Program," *Philadelphia Tribune*, November 3, 1995, 8A. Pew Charitable Trusts gave $9.8 million for Philadelphia school reform, specifically, Children Achieving. Most of the money would go toward creating new academic standards for students. William Penn Foundation gave $13.8 million to Children Achieving. Michael Dabney, "Foundation Gives $13 Million for 'Children Achieving,'" *Philadelphia Tribune*, March 15, 1996, 1A, 2A; Michael Dabney, "Gov's Proposed Budget Will Come as Heavy Blow to Philadelphia Schools," *Philadelphia Tribune*, February 9, 1996, 1A, 4-A. Governor Ridge proposed freezing basic education funding for all 501 school districts in the state. The School District of Philadelphia is the largest district in the state. The district was expecting to get $606 million in basic funding but instead would get only $594 million. The district was also expecting $85 million for special education but would receive only $83 million.

117. SDP BOE Minutes, November 7, 1994, 793; SDP BOE Minutes, March 20, 1995, 153.

118. Robin Leary, "State Unfazed by Phila. Schools' Budget Gap," *Philadelphia Tribune*, February 27, 1998, 2A; "State Might Take Over City Schools, Hornbeck Predicts," *Philadelphia Tribune*, November 17, 1998, 2A. A parent suggested schools open in the fall with full funds until funds run out, even if it is before the end of the school year. SDP BOE Minutes, April 15, 1996, 173.

119. SDP BOE Minutes, May 31, 1996, 348–349.

120. SDP BOE Minutes April 3, 1995, 173; SDP BOE Minutes, April 24, 1995, 204. A student representative to the Board of Education implored other students to petition the city and state for "equality in funding." SDP BOE Minutes, November 20, 1995, 883; SDP BOE Minutes, Aril 15 1996, 170–171.

121. SDP BOE Minutes, March 25, 1996, 148; SDP BOE Minutes, April 15, 1996, 171; SDP BOE Minutes, April 3, 1995, 173; SDP BOE Minutes, November 18, 1996, 738; David Hornbeck, "Superintendent Hornbeck's Plea: Schools Between 'Rock, Hard Place,'" *Philadelphia Tribune*, May 14, 1996, 7A; Robin Leary, "School District Faced with Drastic Cuts," *Philadelphia Tribune*, March 8 1996, 1A, 2A; Michael Dabney, "City and State Squabble in Court over Funds," *Philadelphia Tribune*, May 31, 1996, 1A, 3A.

122. SDP BOE Minutes, April 29, 1996, 204.

123. Dabney, "City and State Squabble in Court over Funds."

124. SDP BOE Minutes, February 24, 1997, 91; SDP BOE Minutes, May 12, 1997, 268.

125. Dale Mezzacappa, "A History Lesson on Historic Day for School Reform Commission," Chalkbeat Philadelphia, November 16, 2017, retrieved on February 1, 2021 from https://philadelphia.chalkbeat.org/2017/11/16/22184825/a-history-lesson-on-historic-day-for-school-reform-commission; Fred Siegel and Kay S. Hymowitz, "Why Did Ed Rendell Fizzle Out?," City Journal, Autumn 1999, retrieved on February 1, 2021, from https://www.city-journal.org/html/why-did-ed-rendell-fizzle-out-11907.html; interview with Joe, January 5, 2011.

126. Interview with Judy, July 26, 2010; interview with Torch Lytle, August 18, 2010; Glover, "Hornbeck Calls State Funding for Schools Bias"; Glover, "Hornbeck's Relationship with State Worries Council"; Kia Morgan, "District Plans National Search for Superintendent," *Philadelphia Tribune*; , June 13, 2000, 1A, 4A; Boyd and Christman, "A Tall Order for Philadelphia's New Approach to School Governance".

127. Robert C. Johnston, "Hornbeck Quits as Power Shifts in Philadelphia," *Education Week*, June 14, 2000, retrieved on February 1, 2021, from https://www.edweek.org/leadership/hornbeck-quits-as-power-shifts-in-philadelphia/2000/06.

128. "Our Opinion: What Happens After Mayor Green Wipes Out School Board, Marcase?," *Philadelphia Tribune*, January 30, 1981, 6.

129. "Our Opinion: What Happens After Mayor Green Wipes Out School Board, Marcase?"

130. SDP BOE Minutes, August 21, 1997, 511: The Commonwealth of Pennsylvania's Act 22 of 1997 on June 19, 1997 was regarding charter schools.

131. SDP BOE Minutes, September 4, 1996, 559–563.

132. Interview with Theresa, July 29, 2010, interview with Torch Lytle, August 18, 2010; interview with Nina, July 12, 2010; interview with Latifah, July 22, 2010; interview with Linda, June 21, 2010; interview with Jim, June 24, 2010.

133. Leary, "State Unfazed by Phila. Schools' Budget Gap"; "State Might Take Over City Schools, Hornbeck Predicts"; Richardson Dilworth, "Lack of Funds Could Slice Nine Weeks from the School Year," *Philadelphia Tribune*, November 29, 1969; SDP BOE Minutes, April 14, 1996, 173.

134. "Public School Children Lose Out to State Politics"; Kendall Wilson, "Officials Expected Takeover Proposal," *Philadelphia Tribune*, April 14, 2000, 1A.

135. Chad Glover, "Hornbeck Calls State Funding for Schools Bias," *Philadelphia Tribune*, February 19, 1999, 1A; Glover, "Hornbeck's Relationship with State Worries Council."

136. Garland Thompson, "Grim Reality for the City's Public Schools," *Philadelphia Tribune*, May 19, 2000, 1A, 8A.

137. E. Useem, J. B. Christman, and W. L. Boyd, *The Role of District Leadership in Radical Reform: Philadelphia's Experience Under the State Takeover, 2001–2006* (Philadelphia: Research for Action, 2006); Boyd and Christman, "A Tall Order for Philadelphia's New Approach to School Governance"; Kia Morgan, "District Plans National Search for Superintendent," *Philadelphia Tribune*, June 13, 2000, 1A; "A Fine Legacy from Hornbeck," *Philadelphia Tribune*, August 15, 2000, 6A.

138. Michael Dabney, "Tempers Flare over Proposed District Break Up," *Philadelphia Tribune*, January 31, 1997, 2A.

139. "State Might Take Over City Schools, Hornbeck Predicts"; Torch Lytle, interview with the author, August 18, 2010.

140. "Public School Children Lose Out to State Politics."

141. Ayana Jones, "School District Options Limited," *Philadelphia Tribune*, July 24, 2001, 1A.

142. David I. Backer, "A Democrat Against Democracy," Jacobin, May 4, 2017, retrieved on February 1, 2021, from https://www.jacobinmag.com/2017/05/corporate-education-reform-dwight-evans; Chrystal Dyer LaRoche, "Pennsylvania's Act 46: Aimed at Improving Education or Punishing Educators?," *University of Pennsylvania Journal of Labor and Employment Law* 5, no. 3 (2003): 611–628.

143. Johnston, "Hornbeck Quits as Power Shifts in Philadelphia."

144. Useem, Christman, and Boyd, *The Role of District Leadership in Radical Reform*; interview with Torch Lytle, August 18, 2010.

145. Kenneth K. Wong and Francis X. Shen, "Measuring the Effectiveness of City and State Takeover as a School Reform Strategy," *Peabody Journal of Education* 78, no. 4 (2003): 89-119.

146. "State Might Take Over City Schools, Hornbeck Predicts."

147. Boyd and Christman, "A Tall Order for Philadelphia's New Approach to School Governance".

148. Boyd and Christman, "A Tall Order for Philadelphia's New Approach to School Governance"; Useem, Christman, and Boyd, *The Role of District Leadership in Radical Reform*.

149. Regan Toomer, "Vallas Waits on $10M from City," *Philadelphia Tribune*, July 14, 2006, 8A; Boyd and Christman, "A Tall Order for Philadelphia's New Approach to School Governance"; Scott Goss, "Takeover Tonight? Investment Advisor Targeted to Run Philadelphia Schools," *Philadelphia Tribune*, November 30, 2001, 1A; Mignon Brooks, "Nevels Optimistic on Schools' Future, Rendell Relations," *Philadelphia Tribune*, December 13, 2002, 5A.

150. Kia Morgan, "School Board Names District's New Chief," *Philadelphia Tribune*, August 15, 2000, 1A; Michael Dabney, "School CEO Accepts Challenge," *Philadelphia Tribune*, October 17, 2000, 1A; "Commitment to Our Schools: Mayor John F. Street Says That Paul Vallas Is the Right Man to Run Philadelphia Public Schools," *Philadelphia Tribune*, July 19, 2002, 1A. Mayor John Street was an advocate for the new governance structure in which a CEO was running the district.

151. SDP BOE Minutes, December 5, 1994, 829 Floyd Alston quoted Horace Mann, referring to him as the Massachusetts Secretary of Education in 1848, saying, "Education then, beyond all other devices of human origin, is a great equalizer of the condition of men, the balance wheel of social machinery."

152. Saviorism is the combination of racism and classism that manifests as oppression in schools. In an interview, a Black veteran Philly educator referred to David Hornbeck as "a missionary" and "the savior." Interview with Dave, August 6, 2016.

Chapter 5

1. Mignon Brooks, "Education Secretary Pleased with Contracts," *Philadelphia Tribune*, August 2, 2002, 3A.
2. Mignon Brooks, "Nevels Optimistic on Schools' Future, Rendell Relations," *Philadelphia Tribune*, December 13, 2002, 5A.
3. Torch Lytle, interview with the author, August 18, 2010.
4. Regan Toomer, "Trying to Erase $73M Deficit," *Philadelphia Tribune*, October 27, 2006, 5A.
5. School Reform Commission (SRC) Minutes, October 18, 2006, 20. The ten-year tax abatement was an issue. P. D. Brown asked that it be rescinded, that the commission pressure the mayor and City Council to rescind it because "middle class and lower class citizens cannot afford to pay this tax."
6. Nancy Leong, "Racial Capitalism," *Harvard Law Review* 126, no. 8 (2013): 2151–2226; Cedric Robinson, *Black Marxism: The Making of the Black Radical Tradition* (London: University of North Carolina Press, 2000); Bree Picower and Edwin Mayorga, *What's Race Got to Do with It? How Current School Reform Policy Maintains Racial and Economic Inequality* (New York: Peter Lang, 2015); Lauren Anderson, "Private Interests in a Public Profession: Teacher Education and Racial Capitalism," *Teachers College Record* 121, no. 4 (2019): 1–38; Robin D. G. Kelley, "What Did Cedric Robinson Mean by Racial Capitalism?," *Boston Review* (January 12, 2017), retrieved from https://bostonreview.net/race/robin-d-g-kelley-what-did-cedric-robinson-mean-racial-capitalism.
7. Picower and Mayorga, "What's Race Got to Do with It?," 9.
8. SRC Minutes, May 28, 2005, 9. Commissioner James P. Gallagher stated, "The School Reform Commission inherited a School District that was failing its students. Great successes have been made, but the District is still battling a culture of failure. How can [we] begin not to continue to chase additional EMOs, Charters, and additional new ideas? The Commission inherited a monopoly that did not work and is in many ways not working."
9. Camika Royal and Vanessa Dodo Seriki, "Overkill: Black Lives and the Spectacle of the Atlanta Cheating Scandal," *Urban Education* 53, no. 2 (2018): 196–211; Cory Turner, "No Child Left Behind: What Worked, What Didn't," October 27, 2015, NPR, retrieved on March 27, 2021, from https://www.npr.org/sections/ed/2015/10/27/443110755/no-child-left-behind-what-worked-what-didnt; Larry Cuban and Michael Usdan, eds., *Powerful Reforms with Shallow Roots: Improving America's Urban Schools* (New York: Teachers College Press, 2003); Pedro Noguera, *City Schools and the American Dream* (New York: Teachers College Press, 2003); John L. Rury, *Urban Education in the United States: A Historical Reader* (New York: PalgraveMacmillan, 2005); Camika Royal and Simone Gibson, "They School: Culturally Relevant Pedagogy Under Siege," *Teachers College Record* 119, no. 1 (2017): 1-25; Adrienne Dixson, Camika Royal, and Kevin Lawrence Henry, "School Reform and School Choice," in *Handbook of Urban Education*, ed. H. Richard Milner and Kofi Lomotey (New York: Routledge, 2014), 474–503; Camika Royal and James Earl Davis, "Leaders of the New School: Exploring Teacher Leadership and the Future of School Reform," *New Perspectives in Educational Leadership: Exploring Social, Political, and Community Contexts and Meaning* (New York: Peter Lang, 2010), 239–259; Jack Schenider, *Excellence for All: How a New Breed of Reformers Is Transforming America's Public Schools* (Nashville, TN: Vanderbilt University Press. 2011).
10. Pauline Lipman, *High Stakes Education: Inequality, Globalization and Urban School Reform* (New York: Taylor & Francis, 2004); S. Vergari, "Federalism and Market-Based Education Policy: The Supplemental Educational Services Mandate," *American Journal of Education* 113 (2007): 311–339; Cuban and Usdan, *Powerful Reforms with Shallow Roots*.

11. Royal and Dodo Seriki, "Overkill"; L. Darling-Hammond, "Race, Inequality and Educational Accountability: The Irony of "No Child Left Behind," *Race Ethnicity and Education 10* (2007): 245–260; SRC Minutes, May 10, 2006, 11.

12. William Boyd and Jolley Christman, "A Tall Order for Philadelphia's New Approach to School Governance: Heal the Political Rifts, Close the Budget Gap, *and* Improve the Schools," in *Powerful Reforms with Shallow Roots: Improving America's Urban Schools*, ed. Larry Cuban and Michael Usdan (New York: Teachers College Press, 2003); Dixson, Royal, and Henry, "School Reform and School Choice"; Kenneth J. Saltman, *The Edison Schools: Corporate Schooling and the Assault on Public Education* (New York: Routledge, 2005); Elizabeth Useem, Jolley Bruce Christman, and William L. Boyd, "The Role of District Leadership in Radical Reform: Philadelphia's Experience Under the State Takeover, 2001–2006," *Philadelphia: Research for Action* (2006); Elizabeth Useem, "Learning from Philadelphia's School Reform: What Do the Research Findings Show So Far?," *Philadelphia: Research for Action* (2005).

13. Brooks, "Education Secretary Pleased with Contracts."

14. Brooks, "Nevels Optimistic on Schools' Future, Rendell Relations"; Regan Toomer, "Vallas Waits on $10M from City," *Philadelphia Tribune*, July 14, 2006, 8A; SRC Minutes, May 18, 2005, 3; Eva Travers, "Philadelphia School Reform: Historical Roots and Reflections on the 2002–2003 School Year Under State Takeover," *Urban Journal* 2, no. 2 (Fall 2003), retrieved on March 27, 2021, from https://urbanedjournal.gse.upenn.edu/archive/volume-2-issue-2-fall-2003/philadelphia-school-reform-historical-roots-and-reflections-2002-.

15. SRC Minutes, January 17, 2007, 1; SRC Minutes, March 14, 2007, 1.

16. "Money Maven Goes to School," *Penn Today*, February 21, 2002, retrieved on March 27, 2021, from https://penntoday.upenn.edu/2002-02-21/latest-news/money-maven-goes-school; Mensah Dean,"Nutter to Replace SRC Chair Sandra Dungee Glenn, Sources Say," *Philadelphia Inquirer*, March 24, 2009, retrieved on March 27, 2021, from https://www.inquirer.com/philly/news/homepage/20090324_Nutter_to_dump_SRC_chair_Sandra_Dungee_Glenn__sources_say.html#loaded.

17. Brooks, "Nevels Optimistic on Schools' Future, Rendell Relations."

18. "Glenn, Bednarnek Sworn in to 2nd Four Year Terms on SRC," The Philadelphia Public Record, January 2005, retrieved on March 27, 2021, from http://www.phillyrecord.com/2005/0120/0-article-07.html.

19. Bryton, interview with the author, August 25, 2016; "Commitment to Our Schools: Mayor John F. Street Says That Paul Vallas Is the Right Man to Run Philadelphia Public Schools," *Philadelphia Tribune*, July 19, 2002, 1A; SRC Minutes, July 14, 2004, 1; SRC Minutes, August 18, 2004, 1; SRC Minutes, August 24, 2004, 1. Gregory Thornton was the school district's new chief academic officer, and LaVonne Sheffield was the district's chief accountability officer. The district's chief operating officer, Karen Burke, was leaving. She had been appointed in August 2002.

20. Mignon Brooks, "Vallas to Be School's CEO," *Philadelphia Tribune*, July 9, 2002, 1A; Useem, Christman, and Boyd, "The Role of District Leadership in Radical Reform"; Jolley Christman, interview with the author, August 19, 2010.

21. "Vallas Named as a Top Leader in U.S.," *Philadelphia Tribune*, October 24, 2006, 1A.

22. Mignon Brooks, "School District CEO Finalist Well Regarded: Paul Vallas Gets Praise from Former Peers and Colleagues," *Philadelphia Tribune*, July 5, 2002, 1A.

23. LeRoi Simmons, interview with the author, October 14, 2010; Theresa, interview with the author, July 29, 2010; Regan Toomer, "Schools Facing $21M Deficit," *Philadelphia Tribune*, October 13, 2006, 1A; Regan Toomer, "Teachers' Union May Face Layoffs," *Philadelphia*

Tribune, October 20, 2006, 4A. By October 2006, what was thought to be a $21 million deficit for the school district's budget was found to be a $70 million budget deficit. Toomer, "Trying to Erase $73 Million Deficit," *Philadelphia Tribune*, October 27, 2006, 5A. By the end of October 2006, the deficit was $73 million.

24. "A New Beginning for Philadelphia Schools," *Philadelphia Tribune*, September 3, 2002, 6A; Nina, interview with the author, July 12, 2010; Judy, interview with the author, July 26, 2010; Joe, interview with the author, January 5, 2011; Marsha, interview with the author, July 2, 2010.

25. Useem, Christman, and Boyd, "The Role of District Leadership in Radical Reform"; Mary, interview with the author, August 2, 2010, interview with Nina, July 12, 2010, interview with Marsha, July 2, 2010; interview with Jolley Christman, August 19, 2010.

26. Elizabeth, interview with the author, July 27, 2010; Torch Lytle, interview with the author, August 18, 2010; interview with Nina, July 12, 2010; Latifah, interview with the author, July 22, 2010; interview with Mary, August 2, 2010; Belinda, interview with the author, June 28, 2010; Harold, interview with the author, July 20, 2010; Terri, interview with the author, June 24, 2010; interview with Judy, July 26, 2010, Betty, interview with the author, July 15, 2010; interview with Joe, January 5, 2011; interview with Marsha, July 2, 2010; Theresa, interview with the author, July 29, 2010; Ernestine, interview with the author, July 6, 2010; interview with LeRoi Simmons, October 14, 2010.

27. Interview with Judy, July 26, 2010; interview with Betty, July 15, 2010; interview with Theresa, July 29, 2010.

28. SRC Minutes, May 11, 2005, 8.

29. SRC Minutes, October 19, 2005, 9.

30. Interview with Judy, July 26, 2010.

31. Elizabeth Useem, "Big City Superintendent as Powerful CEO: Paul Vallas in Philadelphia," *Peabody Journal of Education* 84, no. 3 (2009): 300–317.

32. Interview with Torch Lytle, August 18, 2010; Regan Toomer, "Vallas Grateful: Contract Support," *Philadelphia Tribune*, July 11, 2006, 1A; Toomer, "Vallas Waits on $10M from City." Speaker of the Pennsylvania House of Representatives John Perzel, State Senator Vincent Fumo, and State Representative Dwight Evans worked together to get $12 million additional funds from the state. SRC Minutes, May 10, 2006, 10; SRC Minutes, March 14, 2007, 16. Community members and parents were concerned about student safety as they traveled to and from Edison High. They requested additional school police officers, the installation of outside surveillance cameras, and updated metal detectors. Vallas wanted state money to go to "community based organizations who can supplement school safety and security." Hamilton School was seen as out of control, with a parent saying her child had been harassed all year and another parent saying a white teacher was using racist comments against students and that school police were berating, threatening, and cursing at students. Thornton rejected the idea that the school was out of control, based on his visiting every classroom and having met with staff and students. Community member wanted the school district to do something other than locking kids up for being violent.

33. SRC Minutes, August 18, 2004, 2. SRC Minutes, September 15, 2004, 3.

34. SRC Minutes, May 25, 2005, 2–3. Commissioner Dungee Glenn said that twenty-seven high schools did not have librarians. Vallas said they had gotten that number down to twelve. He said that all schools received library funds but not all schools were using those funds for libraries. She was also concerned with the high counselor-to-student ratio in comprehensive high schools.

35. SRC Minutes, October 13, 2004, 10; SRC Minutes, November 10, 2004, 24. A parent complained that she had to rent a violin for her daughter and she only received one day a week of gifted instruction. A community member said they needed to have plenty of reference, fiction,

and nonfiction texts chosen by library professionals and that Scholastic sets of materials were insufficient and should not replace a school's library.

36. SRC Minutes, March 9, 2005, 10; SRC Minutes, August 10, 2005, 19; SRC Minutes, May 9, 2007, 8. Community Education Partners was running an alternative high school program for 150 students at 12th Street and Allegheny Avenue for $500,000. A parent of a Community Education Partners student told the School Reform Commission that the school does not have an academic program and that her child does not get homework. Novaturience, interview with the author, August 26, 2016.

37. SRC Minutes, August 24, 2004, 1–2; SRC Minutes, November 10, 2004, 12, 24; SRC Minutes, September 29, 2005, 1; Elaine Welles, "Schools State Development Plans, Goals," *Philadelphia Tribune*, May 25, 2004, . 1A; SRC Minutes, March 8, 2006, 1.

38. June, interview with the author, October 25, 2010.

39. Dave, interview with the author, August 6, 2016.

40. Don McAdams had worked on school reform efforts in Houston, Texas, with Rod Paige, who became President George W. Bush's secretary of education. Ellen R. Delisio, "Inside Track on Houston School Reform Effort (an Education World e-interview with Donald R. McAdams), Education World, retrieved on March 20, 2021, from https://www.educationworld.com/a_issues/chat/chat035.shtml; Welles, "Schools State Development Plans, Goals"; SRC Minutes, February 8, 2006, 8–9.

41. Laura Jones, "Minding the Gap: A Rhetorical History of the Achievement Gap" (PhD dissertation, Louisiana State University and Agricultural and Mechanical College, August 2013); Camika Royal, "Please Stop Using the Phrase 'Achievement Gap,'" Good, November 8, 2012, retrieved August 19, 2021, from https://www.good.is/articles/please-stop-using-the-phrase-achievement-gap; Gloria Ladson-Billings, "From the Achievement Gap to the Education Debt: Understanding Achievement in U.S. Schools," *Educational Researcher* 35, no. 7 (2006): 3–12; Asa Hilliard, "No Mystery," *Young, Gifted, and Black: Promoting High Achievement among African-American Students*, authors: Theresa Perry, Claude Steele, and Asa Hilliard III; Beacon Press 2003; SRC Minutes, March 8, 2006, 1.

42. SRC Minutes, March 8, 2006, 1.

43. SRC Minutes, August 11, 2004, 3; SRC Minutes, August 10, 2005, 9; SRC Minutes, February 9, 2005, 11; Elaine Welles, "Black Studies to Hit Schools; Courses Enter All Schools by 2005," *Philadelphia Tribune*, 1A; Ngina Nia Meeks, "Battle Ensues over School Lessons; Activists Dissatisfied with Vallas' Efforts to Better Curriculums," *Philadelphia Tribune*, March 21, 2003, 8A; Useem, Christman, and Boyd, "The Role of District Leadership in Radical Reform."

44. Jim, interview with the author, June 24, 2010; Nina, interview with the author, July 12, 2010; Judy, interview with the author, July 26, 2010; Betty, interview with the author, July 15, 2010.

45. Dean, "Nutter to Replace SRC Chair, Sources Say"; SRC Minutes, August 24, 2004, 10; SRC Minutes, June 15, 2005, 27. Robert Gray, chair of the African American Free and Reconstruction League, challenged the School Reform Commission on not including African history in classrooms. Dungee Glenn shared that the school district would do a pilot program in four schools beginning January 2005 for African and African American studies in K–12. They would do a full rollout in school year 2005–06. The Philadelphia NAACP supported mandating African American studies in Philadelphia schools as of fall 2005. SRC Minutes, February 16, 2005, 2; SRC Minutes, March 14, 2007, 1. Vallas and the School Reform Commission celebrated Edward Robinson and Charles Blockson, who had been integral in making Black studies a reality for the district. Robinson was part of the original ad hoc committee after the student uprising early in Shedd's tenure on November 17, 1967. Blockson was an eminent local historian, and his work had informed the new high school curriculum on Black history.

46. SRC Minutes, September 21, 2005, 16; SRC Minutes, February16, 2005, 34; interview with Dave, August 6, 2016; personal communication with LeRoi Simmons; personal communication with Kyla; SRC Minutes, February 9, 2005, 10–11; SRC Minutes, June 8, 2005, 15; SRC Minutes, June 15, 2005, 24. Bartram School of Business became Philadelphia High School for Business and Technology. Bartram School of Communications became Communications Technology High School. Bartram School of Human Services became Paul Robeson High School for Human Services. Bartram Motivation became Motivation High School. SRC Minutes, February 16, 2005, 34; SRC Minutes, February 16, 2005, 33.

47. SRC Minutes, August 17, 2005, 33.

48. Interview with Jim, June 24, 2010.

49. SRC Minutes, October 13, 2004, 1. Vallas requested a moment of silence for slain Philadelphians in the military.

50. SRC Minutes, February 9, 2005, 10–11; interview with Dave, August 6, 2016.

51. SRC Minutes, April 20, 2005, 32–33; Useem, "Big City Superintendent as Powerful CEO: Paul Vallas in Philadelphia"; SRC Minutes, June 29, 2005, 6; SRC Minutes, September 14, 2005, 4.

52. SRC Minutes, February 15, 2006, 1; SRC Minutes, October 11, 2006, 6. At the new School of the Future (also previously referred to in the SRC Minutes as the "Microsoft School"), the student body was slated to be 150 to 170 students, and the district's plan was that 75 percent of the students would come from West Philly. Rev. Arthur White told the commission that, of that 75 percent, he wanted to ensure that 25 percent came from the East Parkside neighborhood, where the School of the Future was located. Further, a parent complained about not being able to enroll his child in Penn Alexander Elementary School because he does not live in the catchment area. He wanted the district to redo the catchment area.

53. Camika Royal and Adell Cothorne, "School Closures and Urban Education," in *Handbook of Urban Education*, 2nd ed., ed. Rich Milner and Kofi Lomotey (New York: Routledge, 2021); see also Jon N. Hale's *The Choice We Face: How Segregation, Race, and Power Have Shaped America's Most Controversial Education Reform Movement* Beacon Press: Boston. 2021.

54. SRC Minutes, February 15, 2006, 2; SRC Minutes, April 12, 2006, 2; SRC Minutes, April 19, 2006, 1.

55. SRC Minutes, May 25, 2005, 2–3; SRC Minutes, March 8, 2006, 1: The school district's chief academic officer, Gregory Thornton, eventually recognized this discord, as he put forth a resolution that "speaks to the issue of equalization versus equity. It is an attempt to provided [*sic*] a focused change in organization."

56. SRC Minutes, September 15, 2004, 2.

57. SRC Minutes, October 15, 2004, 1–2. The School Reform Commission ratified its contract with the Philadelphia Federal of Teachers from September 1, 2004, through August 31, 2008. Nevels said, "The agreement sets forth a new standard for public education in Philadelphia by clearly putting children first. ... The new site selection process all but replaces the system of using seniority as a basis to fill vacancies." Meeks, "Battle Ensues over School Lessons; Activists Dissatisfied with Vallas' Efforts to Better Curriculums"; Elaine Welles, "District Staffs New Leadership for Fall," *Philadelphia Tribune*, August 8, 2003, 3A; interview with Judy, July 26, 2010; interview with Betty, July 15, 2010.

58. Welles, "District Staffs New Leadership for Fall." According to the Vallas administration, principals were being moved between schools based on their experiences and the needs of the schools. Interview with Jim, June 24, 2010; Elizabeth, interview with the author, July 27, 2010; interview with Nina, July 12, 2010; Joe, interview with the author, January 5, 2011; Belinda, interview with the author, June 28, 2010; Regan Toomer, "District Moves to Fill Firings," *Philadelphia*

Tribune., August 22, 2006, 1A. According to the Vallas administration, people were removed because of No Child Left Behind requirements.

59. Interview with Joe, January 5, 2011; Mignon Brooks, "Vallas Transition Team Led by Two Chicago Educators," *Philadelphia Tribune*, July 16, 2002, 1A.

60. Marsha, interview with the author, July 2, 2010.

61. Interview with Nina, July 12, 2010.

62. Menah M. Dean, "Black Teachers in Phila. Schools: A Vanaishing Breed," *Philadelphia Inquirer*, September 10, 2008, retrieved on March 30, 2021, from https://www.inquirer.com/philly/hp/news_update/20080910_Black_teachers_in_Phila__schools__A_vanishing_breed.html.

63. Interview with June, October 25, 2010.

64. Interview with Jim, June 24, 2010; Latifah, interview with the author, July 22, 2010; Torch Lytle, interview with the author, August 18, 2010; Regan Toomer, "Vallas Plans to Take Action," *Philadelphia Tribune*, June 18, 2006, 1A; Regan Toomer, "Do Black Officials Want Vallas to Stay?," *Philadelphia Tribune*, June 30, 2006, 1A; Toomer, "Vallas Grateful: Contract Support." Each of these articles describes how two of Vallas's top administrators took a no-bid contract with Plato Learning Inc. after the company sponsored their trip to South Africa.

65. Interview with Latifah, July 22, 2010.

66. Missy, interview with the author, July 19, 2010.

67. Interview with Marsha, July 2, 2010; Toomer, "Teachers Union May Face Layoffs." According to Nevels, there was a large increase in the number of educator retirements from the district at this time.

68. Interview with Elizabeth, July 27, 2010.

69. LeRoi Simmons, interview with the author, October 14, 2010; interview with Latifah, July 22, 2010; interview with Missy, July 19, 2010. Vallas was seen as oppositional to community groups because he would not engage them for their input. Useem, Christman, and Boyd, "The Role of District Leadership in Radical Reform"; interview with Belinda, June 28, 2010; interview with June, October 14, 2010.

70. Interview with Belinda, June 28, 2010.

71. SRC Minutes, August 15, 2007, 2, 33. Commissioner Bednarek: "no schools will be closed between now and next September 2008." A parent wanted an update on what the School Reform Commission would do with Ada Lewis School, which had recently been closed. She also questioned the proposed closure of twenty-two additional schools and wanted to know if the school district had considered the ways charters were impacting the district. She said commissioners did not attend community meetings. SRC Minutes, July 14, 2004, 11; SRC Minutes, May 11, 2005, 7; SRC Minutes, May 18, 2005, 2; SRC Minutes, May 25, 2005, 7; SRC Minutes, May 31, 2005, 3–4.

72. Welles, "Schools State Development Plans, Goals"; Mensah H. Dean, "School District Mulling $20M Offer for 3 Sites," *Philadelphia Daily News*, June 12, 2003, 8.

73. Dean, "School District Mulling $20M Offer for 3 Sites," *Philadelphia Daily News*, June 12, 2003, 8; Valeria M. Russ, "Beep! Beep! District's Moving In," *Philadelphia Daily News*, September 21, 2005, 9; Ron Goldwyn, "Schools Moving Headquarters to Broad Street," *Philadelphia Daily News*, June 19, 2003, 10; Mensah M. Dean, "Move to District's New Digs Moving Along," *Philadelphia Daily News*, July 29, 2005, 16; Mark McDonald, "A Flood of Work? Pipe Burst Damages Auditors' Basement Office," *Philadelphia Daily News*, January 18, 1997, 8. This article describes district headquarters at 21st Street and the Parkway as "an opulent palace for overpaid bureaucrats." Terri, interview with the author, June 24, 2010; interview with Nina, July 12, 2010; interview with Elizabeth, July 27, 2010; interview with Latifah, July 22, 2010; interview

with Marsha, July 2, 2010; Ernestine, interview with the author, July 6, 2010; Theresa, interview with the author, July 29, 2010; interview with June, October 14, 2010; Constance Clayton, interview with the author, September 30, 2010; correspondence dated May 1, 1956 on school district letter head and signed by Allen Wetter (the heading of this attachment reads "Negro Personnel—Administrative Offices").

74. Pablo Vila, "Appendix: Categories, Interpellations, Metaphors and Narratives. A Brief Theoretical Discussion," in *Crossing Borders. Reinforcing Borders. Social Categories, Metaphors and Narrative Identities on the U.S.-Mexico Frontier* (Austin: University of Texas Press, 2000), 227–249.

75. Dean, "Move to District's New Digs Moving Along"; interview with June, October 25, 2010.

76. Goldwyn, "Schools Moving Headquarters to Broad Street."

77. Interview with LeRoi Simmons, October 14, 2010; "Whelan's Last Words Criticized by School Board," *Philadelphia Tribune*, January 19, 2007, 1A. Outgoing SRC member Daniel Whelan recommended that the district sell portions of its art collection to supplement money in the budget crisis. His idea was supported by commission members Sandra Dungee Glenn and James Gallagher. Commission member Martin Bednarek opposed this suggestion, arguing that much of the artwork was precious and included pieces by famous artists, such as Henry Ossawa Turner.

78. SRC Minutes, September 21, 2005, 10.

79. SRC Minutes, September 14, 2005, 1. They had a moment of silence for Hurricane Katrina. Twenty-two children impacted by Katrina were enrolled in Philadelphia public schools. SRC Minutes, October 19, 2005, 3. Hurricane Katrina survivors relocated to Philly had been staying in the Wanamaker Middle School building since September 2, 2005.

80. SRC Minutes, August 10, 2005, 8, 22; SRC Minutes, March 8, 2006, 3; SRC Minutes, March 15, 2006, 7–8; SRC Minutes, March 14, 2007, 16.

81. SRC Minutes, June 7, 2006, 5; SRC Minutes, June 14, 2006, 5. Stoddart-Fleisher would reopen as Philadelphia High School for Business and Technology. For fall 2007, Rush would reopen as Creative and Performing Arts High.

82. SRC Minutes, April 18, 2007, 23.

83. SRC Minutes, June 13, 2007, 1; SRC Minutes, April 11, 2007, 8; SRC Minutes, April 18, 2007, 22; SRC Minutes, May 16, 2007, 22.

84. Brooks, "Education Secretary Pleased with Contracts"; "A New Beginning for Philadelphia Schools"; SRC Minutes, August 10, 2005, 1; August 17, 2005, 1. As of April 17, 2002, memorandums of understanding (MOUs) were established with University of Pennsylvania to manage a small number of schools in West Philly and with Temple University to manage a small number of schools in North Philly. SRC Minutes, July 21, 2004, 2.

85. Useem, "Big City Superintendent as Powerful CEO: Paul Vallas in Philadelphia"; SRC Minutes, May 28, 2005, 9.

86. SRC Minutes, February 16, 2005, 3–8.

87. SRC Minutes, September 15, 2004, 1; Dave Davies, "Feds to Retry Philly Charter School Founder After Jury Deadlocks on Most Charges," Whyy, PBS, January 9, 2014, retrieved on March 29, 2021, from https://whyy.org/articles/verdicts-in-charter-school-fraud-case-june-brown/.

88. Interview with Dave, August 6, 2016.

89. SRC Minutes, August 17, 2005, 45.

90. SRC Minutes, April 19, 2006, 21.

91. SRC Minutes, February 16, 2005, 9.

92. SRC Minutes, February 16, 2005, 1; SRC Minutes, February 16, 2005, 8–9; SRC Minutes, April 20, 2005, 3–4; SRC Minutes, February 15, 2006, 11, 21; SRC Minutes, March 1, 2007, 3–4.

93. SRC Minutes, August 10, 2005, 9, 18; SRC Minutes, October 11, 2006, 5. The School Reform Commission was considering $28 million for supplemental educational service providers under No Child Left Behind for October 1, 2005, through June 30, 2005. SRC was accepting a $9,677,016 grant from the US Department of Education's Reading First program, with $526,430 going to the Archdiocese of Philadelphia. This purpose of this grant was "to ensure that every child becomes a proficient reader by the end of third grade." This would pay for Reading First coaches in the Catholic schools, but those coaches would be trained by district personnel. The commission was paying almost $14 million for "Contracts with Supplemental Educational Service Providers to provide Title 1 Supplemental Educational Services" from October 19, 2006, through June 30, 2007.

94. SRC Minutes, August 15, 2007, 1, 32; SRC Minutes, August 10, 2005, 16; SRC Minutes, August 17, 2005, 17, 36.

95. SRC Minutes, August 24, 2004, 1.

96. SRC Minutes, May 11, 2005, 8.

97. Brooks, "Education Secretary Pleased with Contracts"; "A New Beginning for Philadelphia Schools"; SRC Minutes, August 10, 2005, 1; SRC Minutes, August 17, 2005, 1; Scott Goss, "SRC Discontinues Contract with Private Company," *Philadelphia Tribune*, April 18, 2003, 8A.

98. SRC Minutes, August 18, 2004, 23. The commission was hoping to get a $3.65 million grant from the US Department of Education through the Pennsylvania Department of Education for comprehensive school reform. It would bring five providers to eight high schools in its first year for six neighborhood schools and two vocational schools. In the second year of the grant, it would bring six providers to eleven schools.

99. SRC Minutes, October 19, 2005, 6–7; SRC Minutes, August 11, 2004, 5; SRC Minutes, September 15, 2004, 12; SRC Minutes, September 21, 2005, 18–19. The commission contracted with Delta-T Group to provide consulting and youth service assistants at Victory Schools for $400,000 for the 2005–06 school year. Edison-managed schools were also having their school, family, and community services paid for by the school district. It contracted with We Overcome for $270,000 to work at Gillespie Middle, McMichael Elementary, Shaw Middle, Stoddart-Fleisher Middle, Tilden Middle, Anderson Middle, and Comegys Elementary. The commission approved a $600,000 memo of understanding with Drexel University "to provide services and resources and support in areas of leadership training, business practices and operations, professional development, IT enhancement and support, classroom-based assistance and co-curricular assistance" from September 1, 2004, through August 31, 2005. Over time, the commission debated the usefulness of contracts with Drexel University and other entities that provided professional development. They wanted to see a guarantee of specific, quantitative outcomes, such as graduation rates and PSSA scores. The commission was concerned about justifying this money spent without seeing outcomes. Whelan did not think the district was doing a good job of being data-driven. SRC Minutes, May 11, 2005, 2; SRC Minutes, June 8, 2005, 18; SRC Minutes, May 25, 2005, 1.

100. SRC Minutes, May 9, 2007, 9.

101. SRC Minutes, July 21, 2004, 25–26; SRC Minutes, August 10, 2005, 20. The commission's agreement with Camelot Schools of Pennsylvania to manage Daniel Boone was for four hundred students from July 22, 2004, until June 30, 2009, for $4 million. The school district could terminate contract. Camelot also managed Shallcross School (three hundred students) for $3,196,665 for school year 2005–06 and would be adjusted each following school year. The agreement would be in effect from August 18, 2005, through June 30, 2010, but could be terminated by the district "for convenience."

102. SRC Minutes, July 21, 2004, 25. The $2 million was for the first year, and the cost could go up. The agreement was from July 22, 2004, to June 30, 2009, but could be terminated by the district. The program would cover up to 165 students. This company was already operating in Harrisburg School District.
103. SRC Minutes, May 10, 2006, 9–10; SRC Minutes, May 17, 2006, 22.
104. SRC Minutes, August 9, 2006, 7; SRC Minutes, August 16, 2006, 7.
105. SRC Minutes, June 8, 2005, 6; SRC Minutes, June 15, 2005, 3. This memorandum of understanding began April 17, 2002, and was being extended through June 30, 2007.
106. SRC Minutes, August 17, 2005, 42
107. SRC Minutes, August 10, 2005, 1; SRC Minutes, August 17, 2005, 1.
108. SRC Minutes, September 21, 2005, 18–19; SRC Minutes, August 11, 2004, 5; SRC Minutes, September 8, 2004, 4.
109. SRC Minutes, September 15, 2004, 12.
110. Executive Order No. 1-94, Payments in Lieu of Taxes, June 30, 1994, retrieved on March 22, 2021, from https://www.phila.gov/phils/docs/inventor/textonly/execorders/94-01.htm.
111. Alissa Falcone, "Q&A: PILOTs and SILOTs—What Is Drexel's Responsibility?," Drexel Now, November 13, 2020, retrieved on March 22, 2021, from https://drexel.edu/now/archive/2020/November/Q-and-A-PILOTs-and-SILOTs/; Ernest Owens, "Now Is the Time for Penn and Philly's Other Big-Money Nonprofits to Pay PILOTs," Philadelphia, May 20, 2020, retrieved on March 22, 2021, from https://www.phillymag.com/news/2020/05/20/penn-pilots-corona-virus/; Chase Sutton and Celia Kreth, "Penn's History of Refusing to Pay PILOTs, Explained," Daily Pennsylvanian, July 11, 2020, retrieved on March 22, 2021, from https://www.thedp.com/article/2020/07/penn-pilots-taxes-exempt-nonprofit-protest-defund-police-philly-schools.
112. SRC Minutes, July 21, 2004, 25.
113. SRC Minutes, July 21, 2004, 25.
114. SRC Minutes, September 15, 2004, 26–27.
115. Royal and Gibson, "They Schools"; Dixson, Royal, and Henry, "School Reform and School Choice"; Royal and Davis, "Leaders of the New School"; Jack Schneider, *Excellence for All: How a New Breed of Reformers Is Transforming America's Public Schools* (Nashville, TN: Vanderbilt University Press, 2011).
116. SRC Minutes, July 21, 2004, 28.
117. SRC Minutes, August 10, 2005, 3; SRC Minutes, August 17, 2005, 13.
118. SRC Minutes, August 11, 2004, 5; SRC Minutes, October 19, 2005, 9.
119. "Bennet Under Fire for Remarks on Blacks, Crime," September 30, 2005, CNN, https://www.cnn.com/2005/POLITICS/09/30/bennett.comments/.
120. SRC Minutes, October 19, 2005, 8–9; SRC Minutes, November 9, 2005, 2.
121. SRC Minutes, October 19, 2005, 9. The African American Chamber of Commerce requested in writing that Vallas and the commission terminate its contract with the school district. SRC Minutes, November 9, 2005, 2–3. It's a Family Affair lodged a formal complaint with the district, insisting the contract with K12 be terminated because of Bennett's comments. SRC Minutes, November 9, 2005, 1. "The African American Freedom and Reconstruction League and its supporters reject the racist genocidal remarks made by William Bennett. ... Mr. Nevels, as an African American male, has taken a very weak and unacceptable position in this matter. ... Mr. Vallas has given the allusion of being a fair and understanding proponent of African American students and their plight, but on the matter of William Bennett has come up short and his position is equally disturbing. ... The African American Freedom and Reconstruction

League applauds Ms. Dungee Glenn and Mr. Bednarek for their principled position in reject-ing the K12 program." SRC Minutes, December 7, 2005, 6.

122. SRC Minutes, November 9, 2005, 3.

123. SRC Minutes, January 12, 2005, 7; SRC Minutes, June 15, 2005, 22. The school district would "analyze the relative performance of students taught by teachers from Teach for America and assess the value of the program in terms of student outcomes." Vallas said this was a three-year grant and that they would need to make a decision the next year about whether to extend this program.

124. SRC Minutes, August 10, 2005, 3; SRC Minutes, August 17, 2005, 12; SRC Minutes, June 7, 2006, 10; SRC Minutes, June 14, 2006, 27; SRC Minutes, September 14, 2005, 1.

125. SRC Minutes, August 17, 2005, 14.

126. SRC Minutes, September 8, 2004, 4; SRC Minutes, September 15, 2004, 12.

127. Kerry Kretchmar, Beth Sondel, and Joseph J. Ferrare, "Mapping the Terrain: Teach for America, Charter School Reform, and Corporate Sponsorship," *Journal of Education Policy* 29, no. 6 (2014): 742–759; Mercedes K. Schneider, *A Chronicle of Echoes: Who's Who in the Implo-sion of American Public Education* (Charlotte, NC: Information Age Publishing, 2014).

128. E. Washington Rhodes, "Give Vallas Time to Finish the Job," *Philadelphia Tribune*, July 7, 2006, 6A; Regan Toomer, "Vallas May Have Contract by Aug.," *Philadelphia Tribune*, July 30, 2006, 4A.

129. Toomer, "Vallas Grateful: Contract Support"; Toomer, "Do Black Officials Want Vallas to Stay?"

130. Rhodes, "Give Vallas Time to Finish the Job"; Toomer, "Vallas Grateful: Contract Support."

131. Toomer, "Vallas May Have Contract by Aug."; Regan Toomer, "Vallas Likely to Get Contract Extension," *Philadelphia Tribune*, August 15, 2006, 6A; Kyla, interview with the author, August 3, 2016.

132. Regan Toomer, "SRC Likely to Offer CEO Vallas a Raise," *Philadelphia Tribune*, August 22, 2006, 6A; Regan Toomer, "Vallas Is Content with Vote, His New Contract," *Philadelphia Tribune*, August 26, 2006, 1A.

133. SRC Minutes, March 15, 2006, 2; SRC Minutes, April 19, 2006, 21.

134. SRC Minutes, May 24, 2006, 1–2.

135. SRC Minutes, June 14, 2006, 49; SRC Minutes, November 15, 2006, 6. There was concern about the financial accountability of the School Reform Commission. Nevels, as chair of the commission, was recommending a Financial Accountability Unit comprised of the chief finan-cial officer, the budget officer, the commission chief of staff, representatives of public financial management, two commission commissioners or designees of the commission chair, and the commission internal auditor. They would create two funds: the Designated Fund Balance and the Special Reserve Fund, the second of which would need a supermajority of four votes to access funds. The goal was to send a message that the commission was serious about financial accountability. Dungee Glenn agreed this was necessary to have credibility and the confidence of stakeholders.

136. Toomer, "Do Black Officials Want Vallas to Stay?"

137. Interview with Theresa, July 29, 2010; interview with Kyla, August 3, 2016; Brooks, "School District CEO Finalist Well Regarded." This article stated, "He would find sources of money to do things that were miraculous." According to this narrator (who worked closely with Vallas), he would use money inappropriately according to what it had been earmarked for.

138. Toomer, "Schools Facing $21M Deficit"; Toomer, "Teachers' Union May Face Layoffs"; Toomer, "Trying to Erase $73M Deficit."

139. SRC Minutes, January 10, 2007, 1.

140. SRC Minutes, January 17, 2007, 4.

141. Toomer, "Trying to Erase $73M Deficit."

142. SRC Minutes, November 15, 2006, 6; SRC Minutes, January 10, 2007, 1.

143. SRC Minutes, December 6, 2006, 8; SRC Minutes, December 13, 2006, 8–9. The commission authorized the sale of these four district buildings: Randolph Walton (2601 North 28th Street 19132; the name is really "Rudolph Walton, and it was built in 1902 and added to historical registry in 1986); Hunter (144 West Dauphin Street 19133); Beeber Alternative (53rd and Euclid Street 19131); and deBurgos (810 West Lehigh Avenue 19133).

144. SRC Minutes, January 10, 2007, 8; SRC Minutes, November 15, 2006, 23; SRC Minutes, January 17, 2007, 3–4; SRC Minutes, February 7, 2007, 9; SRC Minutes, January 17, 2007, 4; SRC Minutes, February 21, 2007, 15. An art collection had been removed from Wilson Middle in 2003. The collection was started by the school's first principal and purchased with funds from the school. Whelan and Bednarek said it could not and should not be sold. The district's former assistant general counsel was concerned that the commission was selling its assets. Vallas wanted to expedite the sales since the school district's population was declining and additional funds were not coming from the state. The commission tabled a motion about selling the district's valuable art. Bednarek was opposed to selling the artwork that benefactors had donated to the district. Vallas said he did not want to sell the artwork. Community member asked the commission to reconsider (not) selling the artwork. Another community member suggested making prints of the originals and selling the originals. Dungee Glenn was fine with selling the artwork because she would prefer to have reduced class sizes, libraries, books, and equity than art, based on her priorities. Community member requested a committee for community oversight on what the district did with the artwork.

145. SRC Minutes, January 10, 2007, 8; January 17, 2007, 18–19.

146. SRC Minutes, March 1, 2007, 2; SRC Minutes, May 16, 2007, 1; interview with Nina, July 12, 2010; interview with June, October 14, 2010; Regan Tooner, "Parting Words," *Philadelphia Tribune*, June 17, 2007, 1A; Regan Tooner, "Parents Concerned over CEO Severance," *Philadelphia Tribune*, July 15, 2007, 3C.

Chapter 6

1. William K. Marimow and Martha Woodall, "Ackerman Acknowledges Directing Surveillance Work to Minority Firm IBS," *Philadelphia Inquirer*, December 2, 2010, retrieved on June 27, 2021, from https://www.inquirer.com/philly/news/homepage/20101202_Ackerman_acknowledges_directing_surveillance_work_to_minority_firm_IBS.html.

2. Comment at School Reform Commission (SRC) Meeting, September 17, 2015.

3. Comments at the SRC Meeting, October 15, 2015, 4. The transcript reads, "Dr. Hite stated that it is very important to talk about minority children and ask that why, at the schools that are serving minority children, we have not been able to determine or figure out how to teach them to read and do math. He stated that these children were not performing even when we had the resources. Dr. Hite stated that his recommendations also included expanding access to quality neighborhood schools."

4. Eric Rauchway, "The 2008 Crash: What Happened to All That Money?," History, September 14, 2018, retrieved on July 5, 2021, from https://www.history.com/news/2008-financial-crisis-causes; Colin McArthur and Sarah Edelman, "The 2008 Housing Crisis: Don't Blame Federal Housing Programs for Wall Street's Recklessness," Center for American Progress, April 13 2017, retrieved on July 5, 2021, from https://www.americanprogress.org/issues/economy/reports/2017/04/13/430424/2008-housing-crisis/.

5. Valerie Russ, "Nevels to Quit School-Reform Post," *Philadelphia Inquirer*, August 11, 2007, retrieved on June 25, 2021, from https://www.inquirer.com/philly/hp/news_update/20070811_ Nevels_to_quit_school-reform_post.html.

6. SRC Meeting Minutes, September 12, 2007, 1.

7. Shanee Garner, interview with the author, August 27, 2016.

8. SRC Minutes, December 12, 2007, 7; SRC Minutes, December 19, 2007, 18. The commission paid $350,000 to Education Resource Strategies for research on the feasibility of weighted student funding for the School District of Philadelphia. SRC Minutes, June 11, 2008, 12; SRC Minutes, June 18, 2008, 31; SRC Minutes, September 19, 2007, 22.

9. SRC Minutes, March 19, 2008, 2; Ibrahaim, interview with the author, February 27, 2018; "Ackerman Announces Decision," press release, May 17, 2000, retrieved on May 30, 2021, from http://www.dcwatch.com/schools/ps000517.htm; Matt Schudel, "Arlene C. Ackerman, Former D.C. Schools Chief, Dies at 66," *Washington Post*, February 2, 2013, retrieved on May 30, 2021, from https://www.washingtonpost.com/local/obituaries/arlene-c-ackerman-former-dc-schools-chief-dies-at-66/2013/02/02/ef1d5fa6-6d64-11e2-bd36-c0fe61a205f6_story.html; Lesli A. Maxwell, "Arlene Ackerman Veteran Superintendent, Dies at 66," *Education Week*, February 4, 2013, retrieved on May 30, 2021, from https://www.edweek.org/leadership/arlene-ackerman-veteran-superintendent-dies-at-66/2013/02; Jill Anderson, "HGSE Remembers Arlene Ackerman," Harvard University, February 5, 2013, retrieved on May 30, 2021, from https://www.gse.harvard.edu/news/13/02/hgse-remembers-arlene-ackerman; SRC Minutes, March 19, 2008, 2; Douglas Martin, "Arlene C. Ackerman, Superintendent, Dies at 66," *New York Times*, February 4, 2013, retrieved on May 30, 2021, from https://www.nytimes.com/2013/02/05/education/arlene-c-ackerman-superintendent-dies-at-66.html.

10. SRC Minutes, June 11, 2008, 26; SRC Minutes, August 13, 2008, 1; Heather Knight, "San Francisco/Schools Chief Is Considering Retirement/ Conflicts with Some Board Members Worsening, She Says," SF Gate, July 27, 2005, retrieved on July 2, 2021, from https://www.sfgate.com/education/article/SAN-FRANCISCO-Schools-chief-is-considering-2620330.php; Catherine Gewertz, "Interim S.F. Chief Selected to Take Over Next Spring." *Education Week*, November 15, 2005, retrieved on July 2, 2021, from https://www.edweek.org/education/interim-s-f-chief-selected-to-take-over-next-spring/2005/11.

11. SRC Minutes, June 18, 2008, 8; Kristen A. Graham, "Phila. Schools Chief Hires 14 Staffers," *Philadelphia Inquirer*, October 7, 2008, retrieved on April 24, 2021, from https://www.inquirer.com/philly/education/20081007_Phila__schools_chief_hires_14_staffers.html; SRC Minutes, June 16, 2010, 1–2; SRC Minutes, January 16, 2014, 3–4. Hite introduced a presentation on testing integrity, since early in 2012 the issue of cheating and suspicious results on the PSSA came up in nineteen schools. In the fall of 2011, both district schools and charter schools in Philadelphia were identified by the Pennsylvania Department of Education as having multiple statistic irregularities on tests, which made the department suspect cheating. The issue was wrong-to-right erasures. After the investigation, three schools were cleared of wrongdoing. Evidence was inconclusive at three other schools. Evidence of cheating was found at thirteen schools, where they believe sixty-nine people were found to have violated testing integrity and ethical and moral standards of the profession. Twenty-nine of these employees resigned, retired, or were laid off. Forty of these employees remain with the school district. The district was considering decertifying these educators. The Philadelphia Federation of Teachers was involved in this investigation to ensure due process for educators. The four types of action the district took were termination, suspension, barred from being testing coordinators, and no action.

12. SRC Minutes, June 11, 2008, 11; SRC Minutes, August 13, 2008, 6; SRC Minutes, November 12, 2008, 4; SRC Minutes, November 19 2008, 13. A $937,312 contract with TNTP for the

Philadelphia Teaching Fellows Program was for July 1, 2008, to June 30, 2009, for 175 new teachers. TNTP was getting a $259,000 contract with the district called "Strategic Recruitment Planning Partnership" beginning November 20, 2008, through January 31, 2009. TNTP would work with the district to examine teacher quality and recruitment issues. SRC Minutes, August 13, 2008, 6; SRC Minutes, February 11, 2009, 7. Teach For America had 126 second-year teachers and 150 new teachers. The school district was paying TFA $1,500 per teacher, for a total of $189,000. Another contract with TNTP for a new cohort of 105 to 135 teachers who would begin September 2009. This contract would start February 19, 2009, and go through June 30, 2009, for $313,899.Another contract with TFA was a multiyear one for $2,397,500 at $1,500 per teacher for 150 second-year TFA teachers in the 2009–10 school year and 170 new TFA teachers for the 2009–10 school year, but this cohort would be $2,750 per teacher per year (no more than $467,500). TNTP would hire another 150 TFA teachers for 2010–11 at the $2,750 per teacher rate for each year through the 2011–12 school year. The chief talent and development officer said the district was contracting with TFA because it had a national network to recruit teachers and fill these positions. SRC Minutes, February 18, 2009, 17; SRC Minutes, June 24, 2009, 26–27; SRC Minutes, February 17, 2010, 9; SRC Minutes, February 24, 2010, 18–19; SRC Minutes, September 15, 2010, 8; SRC Minutes, September 22, 2010, 17; SRC Minutes, April 14, 2010, 11; SRC Minutes, April 21, 2010, 15. Contracts with TNTP and TFA were resubmitted on March 11, 2009, and approved on March 18. SRC Minutes, March 11, 2009, 6–7; SRC Minutes, March 18, 2009, 15. Another contract required TNTP to pay for stipends for 210 fellows for $1,500 each, for a max of $315,000. A contract with TNTP for $359,454, of which $112,500 would be for stipends for TNTP teaching fellows. The school district would pay up to seventy-five fellows $1,500 each for their preservice training. The expressed purpose of this initiative was to get math and science teachers. It was more money to TNTP for stipends for Philadelphia Teaching Fellows and still $1,500 per fellow. This was for forty new teachers who would begin February 2011 and would receive training from September 23, 2010, through June 30, 2011. A $412,500 contract with TFA was for 150 second-year corps members (what TFA calls their teachers) and 150 new corps members. They were paying TFA $2,750 per teacher. SRC Minutes, September 23, 2009, 5; SRC Minutes, September 30, 2009, 13; SRC Minutes, November 18, 2009, 14; SRC Minutes, December 8, 2010, 14; SRC Minutes, December 15, 2010, 21; SRC Minutes, April 13, 2011, 12; SRC Minutes, April 27, 2011, 30. SDP would accept $135,000 from the Broad Center for the Management of School Systems to support the Broad Residency in Urban Education for the salaries of Damien Burke and Doresah Ford-Bey from August 1, 2009, to July 31, 2011. The district accepted $75,000 from the Bill and Melinda Gates Foundation for the Renaissance Schools Initiative. The William Penn Foundation gave $1 million to the Renaissance Schools Initiative. The William Penn Foundation was giving the school district $1.3 million for the Philadelphia Leadership Institute. For more on the perils of corporate, neoliberal school reform, see also Kenneth J. Saltman, *The Failure of Corporate School Reform* (New York: Taylor & Francis, 2012); Samuel E. Abrams, *Education and the Commercial Mindset* (Cambridge, MA: Harvard University Press, 2016); Mercedes K. Schneider, *A Chronicle of Echoes: Who's Who in the Implosion of American Public Education* (Charlotte: Information Age Publishing, 2014).

13. Martin, "Arlene C. Ackerman, Superintendent, Dies at 66."
14. Interview with Shanee Garner, August 27, 2016.
15. "Ackerman Announces Decision"; Schudel, "Arlene C. Ackerman, Former D.C. Schools Chief, Dies at 66."
16. Maxwell, "Arlene Ackerman Veteran Superintendent, Dies at 66"; Anderson, "HGSE Remembers Arlene Ackerman"; SRC Meeting Minutes, March 19, 2008, 2; Martin, "Arlene C. Ackerman, Superintendent, Dies at 66."

17. SRC Meeting Minutes, June 11, 2008, 26; SRC Meeting Minutes, August 13, 2008, 1; Knight, "San Francisco/Schools Chief Is Considering Retirement/Conflicts with Some Board Members Worsening, She Says"; Gewertz, "Interim S.F. Chief Selected to Take Over Next Spring."

18. SDO BOE Minutes, March 17, 2010, 1; "Ackerman Announces Decision." Ackerman had done the weighted student funding formula in DC. Maxwell, "Arlene Ackerman Veteran Superintendent, Dies at 66"; SRC Minutes, March 17, 2010, 23. SRC Minutes, September 10, 2008, 1.

19. SRC Minutes, June 24, 2009, 28. The commission had a contract with Gans, Gans and Associates "to recruit up to 50 qualified African American teachers who will begin teaching in SY 09–10." Mensah M. Dean, "Black Teachers in Phila. Schools: A Vanishing Breed," *Philadelphia Inquirer*, September 10, 2008, retrieved on July 2, 2021, from https://www.inquirer.com/philly/hp/news_ update/20080910_Black_teachers_in_Phila__schools__A_vanishing_breed.html; SRC Minutes, August 13, 2008, 12; SRC Minutes June 24, 2009, 33; SRC Minutes, April 21, 2010, 1.

20. Interview with Ibrahaim, February 27, 2018; Kyla, interview with the author, August 3, 2016.

21. Interview with Ibrahaim, February 27, 2018.

22. SRC Minutes, January 19, 2012, 5–6; SRC Minutes, May 26, 2010, 31. Critics also cited these gaps: the corrective reading and math programs would not promote comprehension across genres or vocabulary development through context clues and would not help students be successful in grade level math or on standardized tests.

23. SRC Minutes, August 13, 2008, 17; Latifah, interview with the author, July 22, 2010; SRC Minutes, December 10, 2008, 6; SRC Minutes, February 11, 2009, 11.

24. SRC Minutes, October 8, 2008, 10. Three charter school educators told the commission they were unable to negotiate for a lease, acquire financing, enter into contracts, or apply for grants due to the commission granting them conditional status. One requested that status be removed within a week of their meeting.

25. SRC Minutes, May 13, 2009, 2.

26. SRC Minutes, April 22, 2009, 1; SRC Minutes, February 11, 2009, 5; SRC Minutes, June 16, 2010, 31.

27. SRC Minutes, April 15, 2009, 3.

28. SRC Minutes, April 15, 2009, 15; "Imagine 2014: Building a System of Great Schools," Philadelphia School District, September 2017, retrieved on June 25, 2021, from https:// www.philasd.org/budget/wp-content/uploads/sites/96/2017/09/Imagine2014.pdf; SRC Minutes, April 22, 2009, 1; Kristen A. Graham, "Phila. Schools Agree to Settle 1970 Desegregation Suit," *Philadelphia Inquirer*, July 9, 2009, retrieved on June 25, 2021, from https://www.inquirer.com/ philly/education/20090709_Phila__schools_agree_to_settle_1970_desgregation_suit.html; Valerie Russ, "Judge OKs Agreement Ending Deseg Case," *Philadelphia Inquirer*, July 14, 2009, retrieved on June 25, 2021, from https://www.inquirer.com/philly/hp/news_update/20090714_ Judge_OKs_agreement_ending_deseg_case.html; SRC Minutes, July 8, 2009, 1. Mayor Nutter's chief education officer, Lori Shorr, celebrated this victory, joined by Brian Armstead, the director of civic engagement at the Philadelphia Education Fund, Michael Churchill of the Public Interest Law Center of Philadelphia, Lola Oladapo of ACORN, and Sheila Simmons of Public Citizens for Children and Youth, among others throughout the city.

29. SRC Minutes, September 10, 2008, 1; Benjamin Herold, "The Audacity of Hope Moffett," Chalkbeat Philadelphia, February 20, 2011, retrieved on May 27, 2021, from https://philadelphia. chalkbeat.org/2011/2/20/22181880/the-audacity-of-hope-moffett.

30. SRC Minutes, April 15, 2009, 15; "Imagine 2014: Building a System of Great Schools"; Kristen A. Graham, "Phila Students Challenge 'Imagine 2014' Plan," *Philadelphia Inquirer*, February 26, 2009, retrieved on June 25, 2021, from https://www.inquirer.com/philly/news/local/20090226_ Phila_students_challenge__Imagine_2014__plan.html; SRC Minutes, January 27, 2010, 1, 10,

22–26; SRC Minutes, May 12, 2010, 2; SRC Minutes, May 12, 2010, 7–8; SRC Minutes, February 16, 2011, 1; SRC Minutes, March 16, 2011, 1–2; SRC Minutes, April 27, 2011, 14–19; SRC Minutes, April 27, 2011, 21–24.

31. SRC Minutes, November 19, 2008, 2; SRC Minutes, September 23, 2009, 2; SRC September 30, 2009, 1; SRC Minutes, October 21, 2009, 3; SRC Minutes, December 9, 2009, 6–7; SRC Minutes, December 16, 2009, 8–9; SRC Minutes, April 12, 2010, 1; SRC Minutes, April 21, 2010, 11; SRC Minutes, January 27, 2010, 10; SRC Minutes, February 24, 2010, 10; SRC Minutes, January 27, 2010, 1–2, 10.

32. SRC Minutes, March 19, 2008, 18; SRC Minutes, August 25, 2010, 13; SRC Minutes, January 14, 2009, 2; SRC Special Meeting Minutes, April 22, 2009, 1; SRC Minutes, June 24, 2009, 32–33; SRC Minutes, June 17, 2009, 16–17 SRC Minutes, June 24, 2009, 32–33. School district officials said William Penn was closing because of declining enrollment and that the capacity of the building complex exceeded future projected enrollment. Further, the school's "critical heating and air conditioning piping system has failed and has been decommissioned. Replacement of the piping is estimated to cost $5 million."

33. SRC Minutes, January 19, 2011, 1–2. Commissioner Girard-diCarlo said master planning would "allow the District to deliver a product more efficiently and affectively for our students and families."Commissioner Dwortzsky said he wanted to see plans for how the school district would reuse its facilities, and he was shocked that it had been fifteen to twenty years since a facilities master plan was created.

34. SRC Minutes, April 15, 2009, 3; SRC Minutes, April 22, 2009, 4. The commission's Rightsizing Policy stated that "the School Reform Commission recognizes that the School District of Philadelphia has significant excess space, which is a drain on District resources that could better be used to directly support academic improvement for all students. ... committed to holding public hearings and community meetings to solicit the views of parents, students, teachers, and community stakeholders prior to making decisions on the disposition and use of excess space."

35. SRC Minutes, June 24, 2009, 9; SRC Minutes, June 19, 2014, 14–15; SRC Minutes, May 13, 2009, 19; SRC Minutes, May 18, 2011, 11; SRC Minutes, June 13, 2011, 4.

36. Valerie Strauss, "Ed School Dean: Urban School Reform Is Really About Land Development (Not Kids)," *Washington Post*, May 28, 2013, retrieved on July 2, 2021, from https://www.washingtonpost.com/news/answer-sheet/wp/2013/05/28/ed-school-dean-urban-school-reform-is-really-about-land-development-not-kids/; Camika Royal and Adell Cothorne, "School Closures and Urban Education," in *Handbook of Urban Education*, 2nd ed., ed. H. Richard Milner and Kofi Lomotey (New York: Routledge, 2021); SRC Minutes, November 23, 2011, 16.

37. SRC Minutes, March 11, 2009, 1; SRC Minutes, June 17, 2009, 2. Michael Masch, chief financial officer, said options for William Penn High School were to renovate the gym and buildings on Broad Street for $29 million, to renovate the whole school for $80 million, or to demolish it and construct a new school for $54 million.

38. SRC Minutes, December 16, 2009, 22. Samuel Foley, general counsel for the National Association of Minority Contractors, said the building trades partnership with the school district has been disastrous. It was established under Vallas in June 2006. Paul Socolar, "Outpouring of Support for Supt. Ackerman," Chalkbeat Philadelphia, December 8, 2010, retrieved on June 27, 2021, from https://philadelphia.chalkbeat.org/2010/12/8/22184580/outpouring-of-support-for-supt-ackerman.

39. SRC Minutes, December 8, 2010, 1.

40. Adminphilaun, "PLBC Members Support Philly Schools Superintendent Dr. Arlene Ackerman," *Philadelphia Sun*, December 12, 2010, retrieved on June 27, 2021, from https://www.philasun.com/local/plbc-members-support-philly-schools-superintendent-dr-arlene-ackerman/.

41. "Former School District Official's Lawsuit Claims Ackerman Was Behind No-Bid Contract," Whyy, PBS, January 17, 2012, retrieved on June 8, 2021, from https://whyy.org/articles/former-school-district-officials-lawsuit-claims-ackerman-was-behind-no-bid-contract/; Martha Woodall, "Secrecy and Mistrust in Philadelphia Schools Under Arlene Ackerman," Governing, March 23, 2015, retrieved on June 8, 2021, https://www.governing.com/archive/secrecy-mistrust-philly-ackerman.html; Claire Sasko, "Philly Schools Ordered to Pay $2.3 Million in Discrimination Suit by White Firm," *Philadelphia*, June 28, 2016, retrieved on June 8, 2021, from https://www.phillymag.com/news/2016/06/28/school-district-2-million-discrimination-lawsuit/.

42. SRC Minutes, October 13, 2010, 6.

43. SRC Minutes, December 15, 2010, 2.

44. SRC Minutes, December 8, 2010, 1–2; SRC Minutes, March 17, 2016, 19. Francis Dougherty had been deputy chief financial officer for operations for the school district, and he was fired for violating employee ethics when he sent "confidential School District documents to himself and to his personal email accounts. Mr. Dougherty claimed that he was terminated in retaliation for the exercise of his First Amendment right and in retaliation for whistle-blowing after he reported to *The Philadelphia Inquirer*, the Federal Bureau of Investigation, State Representatives and the U.S. Department of Education, his allegation that former Superintendent, Dr. Arlene Ackerman, steered the award of a contract for the purchase and installation of security cameras from a white-owned vendor to a minority-owned vendor. Mr. Dougherty sought front and back pay, pain and suffering and punitive damages from the individual defendants and attorneys' fees." The case went to trial in 2015, and Dougherty won an award of $3. Dougherty said he wanted back pay and attorneys fees, and ultimately, the district settled with him for $725,000.

45. SRC Minutes, December 8, 2010, 2.

46. SRC Minutes, January 19, 2011, 1; SRC Minutes, March 9, 2011, 12. Carol Heinsdorf, president of the Association of Philadelphia School Librarians, said there were sixty-five certified librarians in the district. Three-quarters of the district's schools didn't have librarians at this point. She recommended that, in Promise Academies moving forward, there be targeted funding, flexible scheduling, cotaught library instruction, thirty library computers, and thirty library books per student. SRC Minutes, February 9, 2011, 9; Novaturience, interview with the author, August 26, 2016; interview with Ibrahim, February 27, 2018.

47. SRC Minutes, March 16, 2011, 2. The exact statement from the School Reform Commission Meeting reads, "State Representative Dwight Evans expressed the importance of everyone being included in any process, i.e., universities, political figures, faith based organizations and business people. He presented a plan for the Northwest Education Corridor—cradle to college. He urged the School Reform Commission to consider the Northwest Education Corridor – Promise Neighborhood Partnership, which Foundations, Inc. has been a part. Representative Evan [*sic*] stated that he wants to be a part of it, and if he does not feel a part of it, it will be difficult for him."

48. Dafney Tales, "Evans 'Did Not Use Power Wisely': He Lied About Role in School-Operator Selection," *Philadelphia Inquirer*, March 24, 2011, retrieved on July 2, 2021, from https://www.inquirer.com/philly/hp/news_update/20110324_Evans__did_not_use_power_wisely___He_lied_about_role_in_school-operator_selection.html.

49. Bill Hangley Jr., "King SAC Chair: Archie Pressured Us," Chalkbeat Philadelphia, April 22, 2011, retrieved on May 30, 2021, from https://philadelphia.chalkbeat.org/2011/4/22/22182271/king-sac-chair-archie-pressured-us; Martha Woodall and Susan Snyder, "Nutter Orders an Investigation of the King Charter School Flap," *Philadelphia Inquirer*, April 26, 2011, retrieved on May 30, 2021, from https://www.inquirer.com/philly/news/homepage/20110426_Nutter_

orders_an_investigation_of_the_King_charter_school_flap.html; Benjamin Herold, "Scathing Report Blasts Archie, Evans on King Charter Deal," Chalkbeat Philadelphia, September 22, 2011, retrieved on May 30, 2021, from https://philadelphia.chalkbeat.org/2011/9/22/22180761/scathing-report-blasts-archie-evans-on-king-charter-deal.

50. Bill Hangley Jr., "SRC Chair Faces Conflict-of-Interest Questions," Chalkbeat Philadelphia, April 19, 2011, retrieved on May 30, 2021, from https://philadelphia.chalkbeat.org/2011/4/19/22181379/src-chair-faces-conflict-of-interest-questions. King High School's School Advisory Council had considered both Foundations, Inc. and Mosaica and chose Mosaica as the turnaround partner for King High School.

51. Susan Snyder and Martha Woodall, "MLK High Charter Plan Falling Apart," *Philadelphia Inquirer*, April 21, 2011, retrieved on May 30, 2021, from https://www.inquirer.com/philly/news/breaking/120372524.html.

52. Hangley, "King SAC Chair: Archie Pressured Us"; Woodall and Snyder, "Nutter Orders an Investigation of the King Charter School Flap"; Herold, "Scathing Report Blasts Archie, Evans on King Charter Deal."

53. Susan Snyder and Martha Woodall, "Ackerman Says She Was Pressured to Get King Charter Pact for Nonprofit Tied to State Rep. Evans," *Philadelphia Inquirer*, September 23, 2011, retrieved on May 30, 2021, from https://www.inquirer.com/philly/news/homepage/20110923_Ackerman_says_she_was_pressured_to_get_King_charter_pact_for_nonprofit_tied_to_State_Rep__Evans.html; Bill Hangley Jr., "Ackerman Details Pressures to Change Her Mind About King HS," Chalkbeat Philadelphia, September 16, 2011, retrieved on July 2, 2021, from https://philadelphia.chalkbeat.org/2011/9/16/22183463/ackerman-details-pressures-to-change-her-mind-about-king-hs.

54. SRC Minutes, April 27, 2011, 20; SRC Minutes, May 31, 2011, 1.

55. Jake Blumgart, "Pennsylvania Governor Tom Corbett, Stealth Tea Partier," Vice, April 8, 2013, retrieved on June 27, 2021, from https://www.vice.com/amp/en/article/8gvppz/pennsylvania-governor-tom-corbett.

56. SRC Minutes, February 16, 2011, 1. For the 2011–12 school year, as federal stimulus funds dried up, Ackerman and executive management took a furlough, implemented a hiring freeze, and put a freeze on nonpersonnel expenditures. SRC Minutes, May 31, 2011, 1. Corbett's budget had massive, unprecedented cuts to education across the state, totaling more than $1.1 billion, with 25 percent of those cuts impacting the school district. Kristen A. Graham, "Teachers Fight Layoffs; Ackerman Apologizes," *Philadelphia Inquirer*, June 6, 2011, retrieved on July 2, 2021, from https://www.inquirer.com/philly/news/breaking/20110606_Teachers_fight_layoffs__Ackerman_apologizes.html; Susan Snyder, "Budget Cuts Pose a Threat to Safety in Philadelphia Schools," *Philadelphia Inquirer*, June 19, 2011, retrieved on May 30, 2021, from https://www.inquirer.com/philly/education/20110619_Budget_cuts_pose_a_threat_to_safety_in_Philadelphia_schools_1.html; SRC Minutes, May 11, 2011, 1; Adrienne D. Dixson, Camika Royal, and Kevin Lawrence Henry Jr., "School Reform and School Choice," in *Handbook of Urban Education*, 2nd ed., ed. H. Richard Milner IV and Kofi Lomotey (New York: Routledge, 2021); SRC Minutes, May 31, 2011, 1.

57. SRC Minutes, June 27, 2011, 3; SRC Minutes, July 1, 2011, 10; SRC Minutes, August 3, 2011, 10; SRC Minutes, August 10, 2011, 1, 24.

58. "Arlene Ackerman Out as Philadelphia School District Superintendent," 6abc, August 22, 2011, retrieved on May 30, 2021, from https://6abc.com/archive/8319809/; John F. Morrison, "Arlene Ackerman: Loved, Vilified, Remembered," *Philadelphia Inquirer*, February 4, 2013, retrieved on May 30, 2021, from https://www.inquirer.com/philly/obituaries/20130204_Arlene_Ackerman__loved__vilified__remembered.html.

59. SRC Minutes, August 24, 2011, 1, 17; John N. Mitchell, "Ackerman: 'It Was Always About the Money," *Philadelphia Tribune*, August 26, 2011, retrieved on June 8, 2021, from https://www. phillytrib.com/news/ackerman-it-was-always-about-the-money/article_ae0f3a08-dc24-5a85-a360-47320fd11335.html.

60. Morrison, "Arlene Ackerman: Loved, Vilified, Remembered"; SRC Minutes, August 24, 2011, 1, 17; SRC Minutes, August 24, 2011, 41.

61. Kristen A. Graham, "School Reform Commission Member Denise McGregor Armbrister Resigns," *Philadelphia Inquirer*, October 20, 2011, retrieved on June 27, 2021, from https://www. inquirer.com/philly/education/20111020_School_Reform_Commission_member_Denise_ McGregor_Armbrister_resigns.html; Eric Mayes, "Archie, Irizarry Exit School Commission," *Philadelphia Tribune*, September 19, 2011, retrieved on May 30, 2021, from https://www. phillytrib.com/news/archie-irizarry-exit-school-commission/article_05a93daa-ed0b-56e5-99fe-4bb84b92ffdb.html; Jeff Blumenthal, "Philadelphia School Reform Commission Chair Archie Resigns," Biz Journals, September 19, 2011, retrieved on May 30, 2021, from https://www.bizjournals.com/philadelphia/news/2011/09/19/philadelphia-school-reform-commission.html; "Archie to Resign from School Reform Commission: Nutter to Announce New Appointees," Whyy, PBS, September 19, 2011, retrieved on May 30, 2021, from https:// whyy.org/articles/archie-to-resign-from-school-reform-commission/; SRC Minutes, February 21, 2013, 1; SRC Minutes, October 5, 2011, 1.

62. SRC Minutes, November 2, 2011, 4; SRC Minutes, November 16, 2011, 4; SRC Minutes, December 12, 2011, 5; SRC Minutes, December 21, 2011, 8. The facilities Master Plan created with URS Corporation was approved on September 22, 2010, for $1,394,500. That corporation was hired to be the Facilities Master Plan Program manager. It added on $53 million so URS would "provide Program Management Services for the Capital Improvement Program that include continuing to provide professional staffing as an extension of existing Office of Capital Programs staff, to enable the Office of Capital Programs to meet scheduled time deadlines for existing Capital Improvement Program projects. SRC Minutes, February 16, 2012, 9, 11. The commission approved a contract with Boston Consulting Group for $1,447,941 "for professional and managerial and financial consulting services and expenses for Phase I of the project." William Penn Foundation was giving the school district $1.5 million to pay the Boston Consulting Group. SRC Minutes, February 16, 2012, 5; SRC Minutes, March 29, 2012, 2–5; SRC Minutes, February 16, 2012, 2; SRC Minutes, November 2, 2011, 7; SRC Minutes, July 2, 2012, 7–8. KIPP was looking to lease the FitzSimons building. KIPP West would use Turner Middle. In both instances, they would pay the district for their use of these spaces. KIPP was already using Turner's building. SRC Minutes, July 9, 2012, 2. The Memphis Street Academy Charter School would operate at the JP Jones building (previously closed by the district) from July 9, 2012, through June 30, 2017. Same for Philadelphia Charter School for Arts and Sciences, which would operate at HR Edmunds, which had also been previously closed. SRC Minutes, November 15, 2012, 11–13; SRC Minutes, December 20, 2012, 3–4, 11–12; SRC Minutes, December 20, 2012, 10. The SRC planned to sell Rudolph Walton Elementary School to KIPP Philadelphia Charter School and MIS Capital LLC for $320,000.

63. SRC Minutes, November 23, 2011, 16–17.

64. SRC Minutes, July 13, 2012, 1. Boys Latin sought to add 320 seats. They were renewed and seats added. SRC was considering paying $6.7 million over the course of two years for 317 additional seats at charters due to expansion. SRC Minutes, April 19, 2012, 4–5; SRC Minutes, June 22, 2012, 1; SRC Minutes, June 8, 2012, 1–3; SRC Minutes, June 15, 2012, 1; SRC Minutes, June 22, 2012, 1, 3–4.

65. SRC Minutes, June 21, 2012, 1, 20; SRC Minutes, January 19, 2012, 3; SRC Minutes, February 16, 2012, 1. The cost of outside counsel in special education litigation was $1.3 million, whereas when it was handled by in house counsel, it cost $200,000 to $250,000. SRC was also paying for several investigations and audits, such as the cheating scandal that arose shortly after Ackerman departed the school district.

66. SRC Minutes, December 21, 2011, 6; SRC Minutes, February 16, 2012, 2; SRC Minutes, December 16, 2011, 1; SRC Meeting Minutes, December 21, 2011, 2; SRC Minutes, January 19, 2012, 6. A nurse spoke to the commission about the continued need for certified school nurses in all schools. Three community members asked the commission for school nurses to be reinstated. SRC Minutes, December 20, 2012, 3. Eighty-three percent of schools in the school district did not have certified libraries or sufficient library resources, per the Legislative Committee of the Pennsylvania School Librarians Association.

67. SRC Minutes, December 21, 2011, 2.

68. editor@pr, "A Steady Hand Takes Over at PGW," *Philadelphia Record*, December 31, 2020, retrieved on June 27, 2021, from http://www.phillyrecord.com/2010/12/a-steady-hand-takes-over-at-pgw/.

69. SRC Minutes, January 19, 2012, 3–5.

70. SRC Minutes, September 10, 2012, 1–2; SRC Minutes, July 25, 2012, 1–2; George Barnette, "Hite to Head to Philly Schools," Afro News, July 4, 2012, retrieved on June 27, 2021, from https://afro.com/hite-to-head-philly-schools/.

71. SRC, November 15, 2012, 10. The contract with TNTP was for $71,193 to provide training and support for fifty teaching fellow intern teachers from October 18, 2012, through November 15, 2013. TNTP donated $55,000 to the school district for consulting services on school leadership teams from November 2012 through February 2013. SRC Minutes, December 20, 2012, 5, 8. Helen Gym also questioned the contract with TNTP for $805,419 for forty-five to fifty-five "hard to fill [teaching] positions." The district's human resources officer said it had a good track record of retaining teachers from TNTP and that the contract included mentoring and coaches. Kristen A. Graham, "Meet William Hite, Philadelphia's New School Chief," *Philadelphia Inquirer*, July 1, 2012, retrieved on June 27, 2021, from https://www.inquirer.com/philly/education/20120701_Meet_William_Hite__Philadelphia_s_new_school_chief____.html?outputType=amp.

72. LeRoi Simmons, interview with the author, August 26, 2016; SRC Minutes, May 30, 2013, 2. A school nurse said Broad Foundation was calling this education reform but it was ripping the country apart.

73. Bryton, interview with the author, August 25, 2016.

74. Interview with Novaturience, August 26, 2016.

75. Dave, interview with the author, August 6, 2016.

76. SRC Minutes, December 20, 2012, 1; SRC Minutes, February 21, 2013, 1.

77. SRC Minutes, March 28, 2013, 1.

78. SRC Minutes, May 30, 2013, 3.

79. SRC Minutes, May 30, 2013, 3.

80. SRC Minutes, May 30, 2013, 3–4.

81. SRC Minutes, April 18, 2013, 2.

82. SRC Minutes, September 10, 2008, 7; SRC Minutes, December 20, 2012, 2–3; SRC Minutes, March 7, 2013, 3–12. Students opposed closures of multiple schools. Ramos said delaying school closures would result in fewer services being available. SRC Minutes, January 17, 2013, 4–6; SRC Minutes, March 7, 2013, 1–3; SRC Minutes, March 21, 2013, 2; SRC Minutes, April 18, 2013, 1; SRC Minutes, April 18, 2013, 4–5; SRC Minutes, March 21, 2013, 2; SRC Minutes, April 18,

2013, 3; SRC Minutes, June 19, 2013, 31; Camika Royal, "The Philly Flop: Examine Yourself," keynote speech, Teach For America summer institute, June 2013, https://www.youtube.com/watch?v=7LDpSzr7meA.

83. Julia A. McWilliams and Erika M. Kitzmiller, "Mass School Closures and the Politics of Race, Value, and Disposability in Philadelphia," *Teachers College Record* (2019): 121; Ryan M. Good, "Invoking Landscapes of Spacialized Inequality: Race, Class, and Place in Philadelphia's School Closure Debate," *Journal of Urban Affairs* 39, no. (2017): 358–350.

84. Interview with Bryton, August 25, 2016.

85. Interview with Bryton, August 25, 2016; interview with Novaturience, August 26, 2016; interview with LeRoi Simmons, August 26, 2016.

86. Ceage, interview with the author, August 25, 2016; SRC Minutes, April 24, 2014, 5. Community members were concerned about the validity and uses of students' test scores as rationale for converting public schools to charter schools. SRC Minutes, May 21, 2015, 2; SRC Minutes, January 21, 2016, 2. Parent and community organizer Tomika Anglin said educators were punished for giving information on opting out of state testing, and students who opted out at Kensington CAPA were threatened. Shannon Ludwig, "Keystones No Longer a Graduation Requirement," Bashcub, January 8, 2019, retrieved on August 19, 2021, from https://bashcub.com/news/2019/01/08/keystones-no-longer-a-graduation-requirement/; SRC Minutes, February 20, 2014, 2. Parents and other community member were also concerned about testing, to what extent it was taking away from actual learning.

87. SRC Minutes, July 2, 2013, 6.

88. Traci Lee, "Philadelphia Mayor Defends School Closures, Layoffs," MSNBC, June 11, 2013, retrieved on June 27, 2021, from https://www.msnbc.com/all-in/philadelphia-mayor-defends-school-closures-l-msna60275.

89. SRC Minutes, April 18, 2013, 3, 4.

90. SRC Minutes, August 15, 2013, 2.

91. SRC Minutes, May 31, 2011, 1, 6; SRC Minutes, July 1, 2011, 1. The school district was looking at voiding collective bargaining agreements to meet the budget gap if they couldn't agree on union concessions.

92. SRC Minutes, August 15, 2013, 1–2.

93. SRC Minutes, August 22, 2013, 1–2; SRC Minutes, August 15, 2013, 2–4. The commission put forth a resolution to bring back "professional employees, including school counselors, without regard to length-of-service, for the period commencing September 1, 2013 through August 31, 2014, with consideration of the need for continued suspension in future school years." The commission suspended pay increases by seniority when they suspended the Pennsylvania School Code beginning September 1, 2013, through August 31, 2014. SRC Minutes, October 6, 2014, 1; SRC Minutes, October 16, 2014, 2; SRC Minutes, November 20, 2014, 3; SRC Minutes, August 20, 2015, 3; SRC Minutes, February 18, 2016, 1. On Tuesday, February 16, the Supreme Court of Pennsylvania ruled that it was unconstitutional for the General Assembly to grant the School Reform Commission the power to suspend school code requirements.

94. SRC Minutes, August 15, 2013, 1.

95. SRC Minutes, August 22, 2013, 1–2.

96. Interview with Shanee Garner, August 27, 2016.

97. SRC Minutes, April 24, 2014, 5.

98. SRC Minutes, September 23, 2013, 1–2; SRC Minutes, October 17, 2013, 4. One counselor spoke of being assigned to eight schools, half of which were high schools, two K–8 schools, and two K–5 schools, with a total of 3,700 students on her caseload. Fifty-three of her students had individual education plans that required school-based counseling, which she was being asked to

do this itinerant work without a cell phone or laptop computer. The year before, she had 187 students on her caseload. SRC Minutes, November 21, 2013, 2. The ratio was one counselor for every 595 students. Seventeen schools had more than one counselor. Forty elementary and middle schools were paired, and each pair shared a counselor with a counselor ratio of 1:850.

99. SRC Minutes, October 17, 2013, 1, 15. The school district was receiving $720,000 to pay for recess programs at twelve elementary schools from October 18, 2013, through June 30, 2014. This money came from Playworks, Kynett, Berwind, UPenn-Netter, Wharton Street Lofts, L.P., Drexel University, and Home and School Associations. SRC Minutes, November 21, 2013, 21. ANet donated a pilot program in ten schools valued at $150,000. SRC Minutes, November 21, 2013, 23. William Penn Foundation gave $1,926,000 to the school district from November 25, 2013, through November 25, 2015, for college counseling and academic supports in schools and would use City Year to provide the academic supports and interventions and help with establishing positive climates in schools. SRC Minutes, August 22, 2013, 18–19. The Philadelphia School Partnership facilitated a gift of $576,250 to the district for four schools, with the most going to SLA Beeber. SRC Minutes, January 15, 2015, 1. Lingelbach Elementary received $100,000 in donations from across the country to buy Chromebooks for its students and $17,000 for other supplies. Kristen A. Graham, "Running a School on $160," *Philadelphia Inquirer*, November 8 2014, retrieved on June 18, 2021, from https://www.inquirer.com/education/inq/school-with-160-budget-20141108.html; Benjamin Herold, "Cancellation of Phila. Teachers' Contract Ignites Firestorm," *Education Week*, October 27, 2014, retrieved on June 18, 2021, from https://www.edweek.org/leadership/cancellation-of-phila-teachers-contract-ignites-firestorm/2014/10#promo; Samaria Bailey, "GrassROOTS Foundation Raises Funds for Lingelbach Elementary School," *Philadelphia Tribune*, June 3, 2015, retrieved on June 18, 2021, from https://www.phillytrib.com/metros/grassroots-foundation-raises-funds-for-lingelbach-elementary-school/article_b55fea32-78d5-5edb-bd79-a1885eaff75d.html.

100. SRC Minutes, November 21, 2013, 24. The Philadelphia Education Supplies Fund donated $477,263.35 to the district for consumable supplemental classroom supplies, such as workbooks, paper, pens, and pencils.

101. SRC Minutes, May 30, 2013, 2. As there were cuts to music programs, Cecilia Thompson asked if GAMP (Girard Academic Music Program) and CAPA (High School for Creative and Performing Arts) were being considered for closure.

102. SRC Minutes, August 10, 2011, 20.

103. SRC Minutes, May 11, 2011, 14; SRC Minutes, May 18, 2011, 22. The original agreement was dated November 23, 1999. The Board of Education had agreed to it on October 25, 1999. SRC Minutes, April 19, 2012, 18.

104. SRC Minutes, October 17, 2013, 13–14.

105. SRC Minutes, March 20, 2014, 22.

106. SRC Minutes, February 20, 2014, 1.

107. SRC Minutes, March 27, 2014, 2; Kristen A. Graham, "Ramos Resigns from SRC," *Philadelphia Inquirer*, October 21, 2013, retrieved on June 9, 2021, from https://www.inquirer.com/philly/education/20131022_Ramos_resigns_from_SRC.html.

108. SRC Minutes, May 29, 2014, 2–5; SRC Minutes, June 19, 2014, 1.

109. SRC Minutes April 18, 2013, 1–2; SRC Minutes, February 20, 2014, 9–10; SRC Minutes, June 19, 2014, 39; SRC Minutes, September 18, 2014, 1; SRC Minutes, January 21, 2016, 22. The school district was launching its first ever cyber school in an attempt to bring cyber charter students back to the district, and this was one of its money-saving efforts.SRC Minutes, April 18, 2013, 5; SRC Minutes, March 17, 2016, 5; SRC Minutes, October 13,

2016, 4–5; SRC Minutes, June 16, 2016, 14; SRC Minutes, June 15, 2017, 28; SRC Minutes, December 17, 2005, 14. The district continued its contracts with TFA and TNTP. The commission was paying $6 million to outsource janitorial and custodial services at eighteen comprehensive high schools. This work had been outsourced since 2006. SRC Minutes, May 21, 2015, 9–10. The commission contracted with Relay Graduate School of Education to send twelve principals to their National Principals Academy Fellowship from May 30, 2015, through June 30, 2016, for $60,000. The contract with Education Pioneers was for $35,000. SRC Minutes, August 20, 2015, 3; SRC Minutes, October 15, 2015, 3, 6; SRC Minutes, March 16, 2017, 7; SRC Minutes, May 18, 2017, 8; SRC Minutes, May 8, 2017, 8; SRC Minutes, June 15, 2017, 27; SRC Minutes, June 15, 2017, 34; SRC Minutes, August 17, 2017, 18–20. Transportation mechanics were outsourced. The commission issued a $150,000 contract with Relay GSE for twenty teacher residents. The Philadelphia School Partnership donated $181,500 for the salary and benefits of the program support person overseeing Relay GSE's teacher residency program. A contract with New Venture Fund was for $356,000 for its Philadelphia Academy of School Leaders, which the district had participated in since 2015. This new contract would be for eighteen district leaders. The Broad Center granted $128,700 to partially fund two resident positions from July 1, 2017, through July 31, 2019. They would work in the Charter Schools Office and the Operations Division. New Leaders, Inc. would donate $350,000 "for an intensive professional development program for assistant superintendents" from August 18, 2017, through June 30, 2018. SRC Minutes, June 18, 2015, 2; SRC Minutes, June 30, 2015, 2; SRC Minutes, September 17, 2015, 3; SRC Minutes, October 15, 2015, 3;. SRC Minutes, October 13, 2016, 15. SRC was outsourcing nurses. SRC contracted with EBS Healthcare, Invo Healthcare, Mediscan, Progressus, SHC Cservices, and Staffing Plus – Private Duty Nurses for $7.26 million "to provide registered nurses, certified school nurses and school nurse practitioners to fill nurse vacancies." Hite outsourced two assistant superintendent jobs to Foundations, Inc., the organization with ties to then State Representative Dwight Evans. "Hite, Nothing Political About New Foundations Contract," Chalkbeat Philadelphia, December 18, 2015, retrieved on July 5, 2021, from https://philadelphia.chalkbeat.org/2015/12/18/22185730/hite-nothing-political-about-new-foundations-contract.

110. SRC Minutes, January 16, 2014, 3; SRC Minutes, March 20, 2014, 2. The Philadelphia School Partnership was leading Universal Enrollment, and many parents and community members were concerned about the process and the leadership of the process.
111. SRC Minutes, November 21, 2013, 23–24.
112. SRC Minutes, August 20, 2015, 2.
113. SRC Minutes, October 15, 2015, 3, 5.
114. SRC Minutes, September 17, 2015, 4. Parents were concerned about bus service that was poor quality, children who were not picked up for school or picked up late, and a lack of substitutes in schools via Durham Bus Service and Source 4 Teachers. SRC Minutes, April 16, 2015, 3–4; SRC Minutes, June 18, 2005, 41; SRC Minutes, September 17, 2015, 1–2; SRC Minutes, September 17, 2015, 3; SRC Minutes, October 15, 2015, 1–2; SRC Minutes, May 19, 2016, 2, 37. The commission approved a $34 million contract with Source 4 Teachers to provide substitute teachers. Jerry Jordan and other community members said the district needed to end its contract with Source 4 Teachers, so Source 4 Teachers was replaced with Kelly Services Substitute Staffing and Management. The commission approved a $42 million contract with Kelly Services.
115. SRC Minutes, January 21, 2016, 22.
116. SRC Minutes, February 18, 2016, 4, 6–7; SRC Minutes, March 17, 2016, 18.
117. SRC Minutes, October 13, 2016, 6–7; SRC Minutes, January 19, 2017, 13.

118. SRC Minutes, March 20, 2014, 1.

119. SRC Minutes, March 20, 2014, 2.

120. Erika M. Kitzmiller, *The Roots of Educational Inequality: Philadelphia's Germantown High School, 1907–2014* (Philadelphia: University of Pennsylvania Press, 2022).

121. SRC Minutes, March 16, 2017, 4. Green insinuated developers were in the ears of these city councillors.

122. SRC Minutes, March 20, 2014, 1.

123. SRC Minutes, October 15, 2015, 3.

124. SRC Minutes, November 20, 2014, 2.

125. SRC Minutes, December 18, 2014, 2; SRC Minutes, February 18, 2015, 2–3; SRC Minutes, August 18, 2016, 11.

126. SRC Minutes, January 16, 2014, 2.

127. SRC Minutes, October 15, 2015, 4.

128. SRC Minutes, May 26, 2016, 1; SRC Minutes, June 16, 2016, 33. The commission paid $128,000 for asbestos removal to TheSafetyHouse.com. SRC Minutes, August 18, 2016, 10. The district was installing 120 hydration stations in more than forty schools before the beginning of the school year. The rest would be installed throughout the school year. It would cost about $1 million. Interview with Shanee Garner, August 27, 2016.

129. SRC Minutes, October 15, 2015, 3; SRC Minutes, January 21, 2016, 4–5, 7, 12–14; SRC Minutes, April 28, 2016, 29–31; SRC Minutes, April 24, 2014, 5; Bill Hangley Jr., "Mastery Drops Out; Steel to Stay in District," Chalkbeat Philadelphia, May 8, 2014, retrieved on June 28, 2021, from https://philadelphia.chalkbeat.org/2014/5/8/22181205/mastery-drops-out-steel-to-stay-in-district.

130. SRC Minutes, March 27, 2014, 2–3.

131. SRC Minutes, October 19, 2017, 7.

132. SRC Minutes, October 17, 2013, 1; SRC Minutes, November 20, 2014, 2; SRC Minutes, January 15, 2015, 1; SRC Minutes, November 20, 2014, 5–6.

133. SRC Minutes, December 18, 2014, 7–8; SRC Minutes, August 18, 2010, 25; SRC Minutes, April 24, 2014, 2; SRC Minutes, April 24, 2014, 3–4, 6, 17–19; SRC Minutes, November 20, 2014, 1; SRC Minutes, January 15, 2015, 4.

134. SRC Minutes, June 15, 2017, 21–26; SRC Minutes, August 17, 2017, 15; Maddie Hanna, "Philly's Khepera Charter School Loses Appeal, Plans to Close Next Year," *Philadelphia Inquirer*, November 9, 2018, retrieved on June 28, 2021, from https://www.inquirer.com/philly/education/khepera-charter-school-philadelphia-closing-20181109.html.

135. Kristen A. Graham, "Philly's Black-Led Charter Schools Have Alleged Bias by the District. Now the Claims Will Be Investigated," *Philadelphia Inquirer*, May 11, 2011, retrieved on June 29, 2021, from https://www.inquirer.com/education/philadelphia-school-district-black-charters-reopen-20210511.html.

The Epilogue

1. Samuel Etheridge, "Impact of the 1954 *Brown v Topeka Board of Education* Decision on Black Educators," Negro Educational Review 30, no. October (1979): 217–232.

2. Patricia Hill Collins, "Mammies, Matriarchs, and Other Controlling Images," in *Black Feminist Thought: Knowledge, Consciousness, and the Politics of Empowerment*, 2nd. ed. (New York: Routledge, 2000).

3. Bill Hangley Jr., "Hite Says There's Nothing Political About New Foundations Contract," Chalkbeat Philadelphia, December 18, 2015, retrieved on July 8, 2021, from https://philadelphia.chalkbeat.org/2015/12/18/22185730/hite-nothing-political-about-new-foundations-contract.

Appendix

1. J. A. Maxwell *Qualitative Research Design: An Interactive Approach* (Thousand Oaks, CA: Sage, 1996).

2. Valerie Yow, *Oral History: A Guide for the Humanities and the Social Sciences*, 2nd ed. (Walnut Creek: Rowman Altamira, 2005).

3. Yow, *Oral History* ; Maxwell, *Qualitative Research Design*.

4. H. Richard Milner IV, "Race, Culture, and Researcher Positionality: Working Through Dangers Seen, Unseen, and Unforseen," *Educational Researcher* 36, no. 7 (2007): 388–400; Gloria Ladson-Billings and William F. Tate, "Toward a Critical Race Theory of Education," *Teachers College Record* 97, no. 1 (1995): 47–68; Richard Delgado, "When a Story Is Just a Story: Does Voice Really Matter?," *Virginia Law Review* 76, no. 1 (1990): 95–111; Derrick Bell, "*Brown v. Board of Education* and the Interest-Convergence Dilemma," *Harvard Law Review* 93, no. 3 (1980): 518–533; Derrick Bell, "Learning from Our Losses: Is School Desegregation Still Feasible in the 1980s?," *Phi Delta Kappan* 64, no. 8 (1983): 572–575; Derrick Bell, "The Politics of Desegregation," *Change* 11, no. 7 1979): 50–53; M. Matsuda, C. Lawrence, R. Delgado, and K. Crenshaw, eds., *Words That Wound: Critical Race Theory, Assaultive Speech, and the First Amendment* (Boulder, CO: Westview, 1993).

5. Ladson-Billings and Tate, "Toward a Critical Race Theory of Education," 48, 50.

6. Ladson-Billings and Tate, "Toward a Critical Race Theory of Education"; Marvin Lynn, "Race, Culture, and the Education of African Americans," *Educational Theory* 56, no. 1 (2006): 107–119.

7. Bell, "*Brown v. Board of Education* and the Interest-Convergence Dilemma"; Bell, "Learning from Our Losses"; Bell, "The Politics of Desegregation."

8. Lynn, "Race, Culture, and the Education of African Americans"; Edward Taylor, "A Critical Race Analysis of the Achievement Gap in the United States: Politics, Reality, and Hope," *Leadership and Policy in Schools* 5, no. 1 (2006): 144–154; Gloria Ladson-Billings, "Landing on the Wrong Note: The Price We Paid for *Brown*," *Educational Researcher* 33, no. 7 (2004): 3–13.

9. Jerome Bruner, "Life as Narrative," *Social Research* 71, no. 3 (2004): 691–710; Richard Delgado, "When a Story Is Just a Story"; Laurence Parker and Marvin Lynn, "What's Race Got to Do with It? Critical Race Theory's Conflicts with and Connections to Qualitative Research Methodology and Epistemology," *Qualitative Inquiry* 8, no. 3 (2002): 7–22; Jerome Bruner, "The Narrative Construction of Reality," *Critical Inquiry* 18, no. 1 (1991): 1–21; Jerome Bruner, "What Is Narrative Fact?," *Annals of the American Academy of Political and Social Science, The Future of Fact* 560 (1998): 17–27; Pablo Vila, "Appendix: Categories, Interpellations, Metaphors and Narratives. A Brief Theoretical Discussion," in *Crossing Borders. Reinforcing Borders. Social Categories, Metaphors and Narrative Identities on the U.S.-Mexico Frontier* (Austin: University of Texas Press, 2000): 227–249.

10. Bruner, "The Narrative Construction of Reality"; Bruner, "What Is Narrative Fact?"

11. Bruner, "What Is Narrative Fact?"

12. Bruner, "Life as Narrative."

13. Bruner, "The Narrative Construction of Reality," 4.

14. Bruner, "What Is Narrative Fact?"

15. Bruner, "What Is Narrative Fact?"; Peter L. Berger and Thomas Luckmann, *The Social Construction of Reality: A Treatise in the Sociology of Knowledge* (New York: Penguin Books, 1967).

16. Vila, "Appendix: Categories, Interpellations, Metaphors and Narratives. A Brief Theoretical Discussion."

17. Taylor, "A Critical Race Analysis of the Achievement Gap in the United States "; Marvin Lynn and Laurence Parker, "Critical Race Studies in Education: Examining a Decade of Research on US Schools," *Urban Review* 38, no. 4 (2006): 257–290.

18. Nicole King, "'You Think Like You White': Questioning Race and Racial Community Through the Lens of Middle-Class Desire(s)," *Novel* 35, no. 2/3 (2002): 211–230.

Acknowledgments

For they were all trying to make us afraid, saying, "Their hands will be weakened in the work, and it will not be done." Now therefore, O God, strengthen my hands.
—Nehemiah 6:9

While working on this research, I developed issues with my hands, neck, and shoulders. My swollen hands made it painful to type, and muscle issues made it hard for me to drive a car, let alone sit at my computer and work. I prayed this verse so many times, asking God to strengthen my hands to make me able to tell this story. I thank God for being the lifter of my head, my strengthener, my redeemer, and the finisher of my faith.

Thank you to the narrators who told me their stories. Without you, this work would not exist. You are owed so much more than what you have received. I hope this book honors you.

Thelma Osborne, my ninety-six-year-old Nana, told me early and often that I could be anything I wanted to if I put my mind to it. I decided in the sixth grade that I wanted to be a writer. In my twenties, when I told her I was writing a book (at the time, it was a novel), she was doubtful and wanted me to focus on my day job. I did that. And now, I've completed my first book, too.

Thank you to my parents, Gene and Cassandra L. Royal, who supported me even when they couldn't understand how, during my adjunct years, someone with a PhD was being paid pennies.

Thank you to my NCCU professors who saw something in me when I was 17 years old and have invested their time, interest, and energy in me since: Minnie Forte-Brown, Joyce Ellis, Floyd Ferebee, and Jarvis Hall.

Thank you to Gloria Ladson-Billings for being my favorite scholar out of West Philly, for mentoring me, for writing the foreword here, and for being my bridge builder and way maker.

Thank you to my Temple professors James Earl Davis, Bill Cutler, and with a special shout out to Christine Woyshner, who was never my professor but always tried to look out for me. I surely appreciate it!

Tarana Burke introduced me to Imani Perry in 2008. Imani told me I had to meet her mom, Theresa Perry, whose book *Young, Gifted, and Black: Promoting High Achievement Among African-American Students* I had fan-girled over. Ms. Theresa was the first person who told me the research I was doing on Black Philly educators and the politics of school reform would become a book. Thank you to these three brilliant sistas!

Boundless gratitude to my sister, Genyne, as well as to my crew—Vonda Brown, Melissa Lawson, Zakiya Sackor, Reshaun Carlton, Everette Thompson, and Vanessa Dodo Seriki—who listened to many stories about this work and pressed me to keep going.

Marc Lamont Hill read this work in many different iterations. His support has been immeasurable, and I will always be grateful.

Thank you to Rich Milner for introducing me to my Harvard Education Press editor, Jayne Fargnoli, whom I thank for not giving up on my work.

Thank you for reading drafts and giving feedback: Rema Reynolds Vassar, Akosua Lesesne, Stevona Elem Rogers, Sabriya Jubilee, Stephanie Black Dos Santos, Khalilah Harris, Jon Shelton, and Adell Cothorne.

Thank you for your insights: Keisha Allen, Ed Brockenbrough, Yaba Blay, Elizabeth Todd-Breland, Marcus Hunter, Jamila Singleton, Edwin Mayorga, Kevin Lawrence Henry, and Shannon Clark.

Thank you to these Philly folks: Charles Shirley, Thomassenia Amos, Helen Gym, Yaasiyn Muhammad, Shanee Garner Nelson, Ismael Jimenez, Kendra Brooks, Maisha Ongoza, Shakira King, Delores Robinson, and Tomika Anglin.

Thank you for the love and support: Yvonne Shepard, Toria Halstead, SaVonn Barnes, Destiny Stockton, Imani Stockton, Genise Richards, Kavia Saxton, Niambi Sampson, Eddie Grimsley, Hiewet Senghor, Lorraine Savage, Kelli Mickens, Mari Morales-Williams, Melinda Anderson, Kori Stoudemire, Sabrina Golphin, Candace Rogers, Kennietha Jones, Regina Bradley, Marcus Stafford, Kristen Bradley, and Nina Mauceri.

And thank you to twenty-three years of students. Thank you for letting me be your teacher.

About the Author

For more than 20 years, Camika Royal has been an educator, teaching middle and high school, coaching teachers, and supporting urban school leaders in Baltimore City, Maryland, Washington, DC, and her hometown, Philadelphia, Pennsylvania. Presently, she is an associate professor of urban education at Loyola University Maryland. Her research and teaching examine the racial, historical, and sociopolitical contexts of school reform ideologies, policies, and practices. She earned her bachelor of arts degree in English literature at North Carolina Central University, her master of arts in teaching degree at Johns Hopkins University, and her doctor of philosophy in urban education at Temple University. This is her first book.

Index